Wilson Harris

Twayne's World Authors Series

Robert McDowell, Editor of Caribbean Literature
University of Rhode Island

TWAS 663

WILSON HARRIS
Photograph by Anna Rutherford

Wilson Harris

By Hena Maes-Jelinek

University of Liège

Twayne Publishers • Boston

Wilson Harris

Hena Maes-Jelinek

Copyright © 1982 by G. K. Hall & Company
All Rights Reserved
Published by Twayne Publishers
A Division of G. K. Hall & Company
70 Lincoln Street
Boston, Massachusetts 02111

Book Production by John Amburg
Book Design by Barbara Anderson

Printed on permanent/durable acid-free
paper and bound in the United States of
America.

Library of Congress Cataloging in Publication Data

Maes-Jelinek, Hena.
    Wilson Harris.

    (Twayne's world authors series; TWAS 663)
    Bibliography: p. 179
    Includes index.
    1. Harris, Wilson—Criticism and
interpretation.
I. Title.   II. Series.
PR9320.9.H3Z77   1982   813   82-12082
ISBN 0-8057-6506-9

To the memory of my sister

Contents

About the Author

Hena Maes-Jelinek has a B.A. from Brigham Young University, a *"licence"* and a Ph.D. from the University of Liège, Belgium, where she lectures in English and Commonwealth literature. She has lectured and conducted seminars at the universities of Leeds, Aarhus, and Bremen and has been a visiting professor at the University of Abidjan. She is vice-president of the Société pour les Etudes du Commonwealth (France) and secretary of the European Association for Commonwealth Literary and Language Studies. She was a member of the Editorial Committee of the *Commonwealth Newsletter* and is now Editorial Advisor to *Kunapipi*.

Her publications include *Criticism of Society in the English Novel between the Wars* (Paris, 1970), *The Naked Design*, a reading of *Palace of the Peacock* (Aarhus, 1976), and a monograph on *Heart of Darkness* (London, 1982). She has edited *Commonwealth Literature and the Modern World* (Brussels, 1975) and *Explorations, A Selection of Talks and Articles, 1966–1981* by Wilson Harris (Aarhus, 1981). She has written the chapter on Wilson Harris for *West Indian Literature* (London, 1979). She is also the author of numerous articles on English and Commonwealth literature.

Preface

It is no exaggeration to say that Wilson Harris is one of the most original and significant writers of the second half of the twentieth century. He is also, as reviewers almost unfailingly point out, a difficult one, although extra difficulty sometimes arises from the reader's own incapacity to relinquish conventional expectations in art. Harris is a poet, critic, philosopher, and novelist. His major achievement is as a fiction writer and, mainly for this reason but also for lack of space, the present study concentrates on his novels. A similar vision informs his poetry and his fiction, but a more thorough analysis than was possible within the limits of this book would be necessary to show in what way Harris's many-layered poetry with its paradoxical language prefigures his fiction. It is to be hoped that some critic in the future will devote a full-length study to the imagery from poetry to fiction and to the development of specific images through successive novels. Whenever possible, I have given indications of such development.

Harris's criticism bears the stamp of his creative art. His essays were each written *after* the publication of a particular novel in an attempt to express theoretically the "vision and idea" arrived at intuitively in his fiction. Most essays written after *Tradition, the Writer and Society* were collected recently[1] and will help Harris's readers both to understand the novels and to trace the evolution of his thought. This thought or "philosophy," which will, I hope, emerge from my analysis, is naturally inseparable from the substance of the novels. This book pays little attention to Wilson Harris's life and contains no biography. Mr. Harris is uncommunicative about his private life and has given me as much personal information as both he and I deem necessary for an understanding of his work. I am very grateful to him for this information, which is inserted in the chronology.

In attempting to place Harris as a writer critics have compared him to Blake, Yeats, T. S. Eliot, Conrad, Melville, Joyce, and Faulkner. As a thinker, he has been linked with existentialism, with Buber, and with Jung. He clearly shares with the Romantics the belief that a spiritual reality is to be found within and beyond the phenomenal world. Like them, he wants to arouse a new sensibility among his contemporaries and regenerate their imagination. Some formal aspects of his work do connect him with the Symbolist tradition in English and American literature. On the other hand, though writing in English, he is very conscious of being a South American and has strong affinities with Latin-American writers. No comparison or label, however, can adequately define Harris's art, which, in both form and content, is uniquely his own. Though universal in its implications, its origin is specifically Caribbean, rooted in Guyana's landscape and history which, unlike other Caribbean writers, he views as a cause for neither despair nor protest. He does not deny its terrifying episodes, the polarization of Guyana's heterogeneous population (Amerindian, European, African , East Indian) into oppressors and victims, nor the psychological traumas that resulted from conquest, from the dismemberment of peoples, from exile and exploitation. They recur, obsessively, as individual and universal tragedies in all his novels, and throughout his fiction one feels his passionate concern for those he calls the "Uninitiate." But he rejects the finality of catastrophe, which, as he believes, when relived and "digested," offers an occasion for change and renewal.

Harris has been equally impressed by the extraordinary contrasts in the Guyanese landscape with which he became familiar as a surveyor. The jungle in particular with its contrary aspects of "season" and "eternity" is in most of his novels a metaphor for the Guyanese psyche, its conscious and unconscious components. Guyana's landscape has, like its history, contributed to his dualistic view of existence, but it is its essential mobility and instability that have convinced him that a similar mobility is necessary in the human psyche. Whether in content or form (characterization, narrative structure, *and* style) Harris's work is marked by a refusal to invest absolutely in one way of being or one mode of expression. He tends toward the reconciliation of contraries, not definitely, but in evanescent moments of vision within a constantly evolving pattern of separation and union. This partly explains the "unfinished" character of experience, as he presents it, and the lack of resolution in his narratives. His main concern is the creation of community. But despite the unity of being he sees in all life, he does not think it can ever be finally achieved. Wholeness is unfathomable, and his characters approach it only through a series of partial apprehensions.

In spite of their extreme variety in both form and subject-matter, Harris's novels can be viewed as one narrative canvas, at once spiritual autobiography and unrelenting quest for a new art of fiction inspired by a long-eclipsed native tradition. They are all "novels of expedition" exploring the multilevelled inner space of the human consciousness, upsetting given categories of being and modifying the characters' (and the participating reader's) mode of perception. We shall see that from the first Harris offers an alternative to the conventional English novel and that, through the re-creation of the history of Guyana and of the dispossessed, void-like condition of Caribbean man, he enlarges our view of existence and our conception of the human personality.

His opus to date can be divided into three phases. The first is made up of the Guiana Quartet, which contains Harris's first four novels: *Palace of the Peacock, The Far Journey of Oudin, The Whole Armour,* and *The Secret Ladder*. The Guiana Quartet offers a picture of Guyana's various landscapes and peoples and indirectly recalls important historical facts (like conquest and slavery) from early colonization to independence, though a major concern, in this as in Harris's later fiction, is with the growth of the individual consciousness. The Quartet was followed by *Heartland*, a significant transitional work between the first and the second cycle of novels, which ranges from *The Eye of the Scarecrow* to *Ascent to Omai*. This second phase is characterized by an increasing interiorization of experience and by a preoccupation with the creation of community and the kind of fiction the narrator-protagonist attempts to conceive. I have devoted the largest space to the discussion of these novels, not only because they are crucial to an understanding of Harris's thought and art (particularly *The Eye of the Scarecrow*) but because the complexity of their structure and imagery demands a more extensive analysis. What Harris calls "images in space" (both outer and inner) are the essential element in the unfolding of the narratives, whose logic often derives from the association and metamorphoses of such images rather than from plot, chronological or not. In the third fictional cycle, beginning with the Amerindian stories, the image, "painting" as a means of visualizaton in depth, an art of grasping the "inimitable," becomes the very instrument of exploration, though this development is already incipient in *Palace of the Peacock*.

Because of their dense, constantly renewed metaphorical texture, Wilson Harris's novels demand the same kind of detailed exploration as poetry does. My purpose has been to help the reader gain access to them, and for this reason I have devoted a whole chapter to each of the first nine novels, centering my comments on what I consider essential in each: plot, characterization, narrative structure, and, as much as was possible, language and imagery, without an understanding of which one cannot follow the development of the narrative. I found that the most suitable method was to keep close to the text and to explain it in its own terms. I have tried to avoid the kind of generalization that could not be verified by the reader until he had formed his own judgment of the novels. I have, however, traced the development of Harris's thought and of his major themes. I have delt more succinctly in one long chapter with the latest cycle of novels and the new elements it presents, trusting that the reader who has followed me so far will have acquired a sure enough grasp of Harris's art and its recurring features to be sufficiently helped by a more concise analysis. Because it was impossible to discuss all the Amerindian stories (a volume could be written on each), I have chosen to deal with "Yurokon," which fits in with "the novel as painting" characteristic of the third phase. The present study does not, of course, claim to be exhaustive. It only offers one possible reading of the novels among many, for, as is often pointed out, no one interpretation can fully account for the richness and the multiple facets of Harris's writing. I have tried, nevertheless, to deal with all major difficulties in both form and content and should like to add that there is no short way to reaching what is essential in the novels. They must be read with humility and patience.

I find no adequate words to express my deepest gratitude to Mr. Harris himself, first for the rewarding and enriching nature of his work, then for the warm generosity and patience with which he has always answered my questions. My warmest thanks to Eva Searl for the stimulating and helpful discussions we had when she was in Liège, and for reading several chapters of this book and making suggestions.

WILSON HARRIS

I am also deeply grateful to my friend Jeanne Delbaere for her encouragement and advice and for testing the clarity of some chapters.

Hena Maes-Jelinek

University of Liège

Acknowledgments

Thanks are due to Faber and Faber, Ltd. for permission to quote from Wilson Harris's novels: *Palace of the Peacock, The Far Journey of Oudin, The Whole Armour, The Secret Ladder, Heartland, The Eye of the Scarecrow, The Waiting Room, Tumatumari, Ascent to Omai, The Sleepers of Roraima, Black Marsden, Companions of the Day and Night, Da Silva da Silva's Cultivated Wilderness, Genesis of the Clowns*, and *The Tree of the Sun*. Reprinted by permission of Faber and Faber, Ltd.

Chronology

1921   Wilson Harris born March 24, in New Amsterdam, British Guiana.

1926–1939   Went to various schools of Catholic and Protestant persuasion in Georgetown before attending Queen's College from 1934–1939.

1939–1942   Studied land surveying (geomorphology, cadastral surveying, hydrography). Qualified to practice.

1942   Assistant Government Surveyor. Made first major survey expedition into the interior of British Guiana up the Cuyuni River (headwaters Venezuela) and catchment area. Landscape, crew, Amerindians on that expedition were to mutate into aspects of *Palace of the Peacock*, which was not written until 1959.

1944–1949   Government Surveyor. Led expeditions into the Cuyuni River, Essequibo River, Potaro River (Kaieteur Falls), and many other interior and coastal areas that affected vision of landscapes and peoples in the Guiana Quartet and succeeding novels up to Amerindian volumes, *The Sleepers of Roraima* and *The Age of the Rainmakers*.

1945   Married Cecily Carew. Divorced in late 1950s.

1950   Visited Europe, France, and England for the first time.

1951   *Fetish* (poems).

1953   Last major survey into interior.

1954   *Eternity to Season* (poems).

1955–1958   Senior Surveyor, Projects, Government of British Guiana.

1959   Emigrated to Britain. Married Margaret Burns, a lyricist and writer born in Edinburgh, Scotland. Lived in Holland Park area, London, which was to influence setting of the Da Silva novels published in 1977 and 1978.

1960–1963   The Guiana Quartet: *Palace of the Peacock*, 1960; *The Far Journey of Oudin*, 1961; *The Whole Armour*, 1962; *The Secret Ladder*, 1963.

1964   *Heartland*.

1965   *The Eye of the Scarecrow*.

1967   *The Waiting Room. Tradition, the Writer and Society* (essays).

1968   *Tumatumari*. Arts Council Award.

1970   *Ascent to Omai. The Sleepers of Roraima*. Arts Council Award. Writer-in-Residence, University of the West Indies and University of Toronto.

1971   *The Age of the Rainmakers*. Commonwealth Fellow, Leeds University, England.

1972   *Black Marsden*. Visiting Professor, University of Texas at Austin. Visited Mexico and began *Companions of the Day and Night*.

1973   Guggenheim Fellowship. Guest Lecturer, Aarhus University, Denmark, in April. In June attended special institute at University of Missouri, Kansas City, dealing with his novels and the novels of Chinua Achebe.

1974   Henfield Fellow, University of East Anglia.

1975   *Companions of the Day and Night*.

1976   Southern Arts Fellowship, Salisbury, England.

1977   *Da Silva da Silva's Cultivated Wilderness* and *Genesis of the Clowns*.

1978   *The Tree of the Sun*. Revised edition of *Eternity to Season*. Guest Lectureship, Mysore University, India.

1979   Visiting Lectureship, Yale University. Writer-in-Residence, Newcastle University, Australia, July and August.

1980   Visiting Professorship, University of Texas at Austin.

1981—1982   *Explorations* (essays). Visiting Professorship, University of Texas at Austin.

Chapter One

Voyage into Namelessness:
Palace of the Peacock

The first movement of the Guiana Quartet, *Palace of the Peacock,* is a prelude to the long narrative canvas in which, from one installment, or novel, to the next, Wilson Harris untiringly explores the West Indian consciousness while attempting to create a new art of fiction. Retrospectively, it is seen to contain the germ of most future developments in his novels as if, like the narrator in *The Eye of the Scarecrow,* the author "were a ghost returning to the same place (which was always different), shoring up different ruins (which were always the same)."[1] His subject-matter is indeed different and explored in new form in each novel, yet similar insofar as, in each, a central consciousness is involved in a process of disintegration followed by, or concomitant with (particularly in the later novels), a revisualization of what Harris calls the "architectonic self." His first experiment in fiction already evidences his wish to reject the conventional novel as inadequate to render the Caribbean experience. For he sees in the traditional novel an accumulation of selected elements meant to consolidate the world view of a dominating section of society and to persuade the reader that the plane on which the narrative develops has an inevitable and unquestionable existence. To the notion of consolidation, he opposes that of fulfillment, which implies a recognition of the self as "the latent ground of old and new personalities."[2] The modern history of Europe, where the traditional novel took shape, is marked by an accretion of power and the rise of the middle class, with which the novel mainly dealt. Over the same period, the West Indies were repeatedly invaded, their original inhabitants decimated, slaves and indentured laborers imported and exploited. Not the self-assertive individual but the "obscure human person" was, until fairly recently, the representative West Indian. However, though convinced that the West Indian was long confined to "a terrible void of unreality," Harris does not believe in the so-called "historylessness" of the Caribbean. The void in his novels is peopled with the victims of history. Each character seems to contain a capacity to accept, yet implicitly transform, the limits of Caribbean experience, and in each the soul is the equivalent of the phenomenal world into which successive generations of victims (Amerindians and runaway slaves) have disappeared. The West Indian soul is ridden with images of a terrifying past, of antagonisms between the conquerors and the conquered. Harris's narratives aim at freeing the individual from these polarizations

in a manner which fulfils *in the person* the most nebulous instinct for a vocation of being and independent spirit within a massive landscape of apparent lifelessness which yields nevertheless the essential denigration and erosion of historical perspectives.[3]

Erosion and *breakdown* are key words to grasp the dynamics of his novels. They apply at once to the basic pattern of extinction in West Indian and South American history and to the process in which the character who relives it is involved. For all the novels offer in part or in their entirety a revision of the past and an imaginative re-enactment of the dislocation imposed by circumstances on the psyche. This dislocation has inspired the form of Harris's art and the philosophy that underlies it, the search for a nameless eclipsed dimension that eludes all polarizations. The breakdown of the apparently static world of appearances in order to discover this eclipsed reality within and beyond them is basic to all the novels. It entails a disruption of traditional forms, plot, character, and narrative structure, and a reshaping of these elements according to an intuitive, visionary perception of the interrelatedness which, in Harris's eyes, is basic to all forms of being. Even the characters' mode of apprehension is being shattered and reshaped.

Palace of the Peacock initiates this movement of disruption followed by reconstruction or the promise of rebirth, which transforms catastrophe into a possible agent of release from an oppressive situation. The story line is simple and evokes the quintessence and repetitive pattern of Guyanese history: the invasion of the country by successive waves of conquerors in search of a legendary El Dorado, moved by the mixture of brutality and idealism that characterized all such expeditions, and the endless exploitation of land and people. Donne, a hard and ruthless colonizer, although also, as his name suggests, a man of imagination, is skipper of the boat in which he and his multiracial crew travel from the coastland savannahs to the inland mission of Mariella in the hope of enlisting cheap labor for his plantation. When they reach the mission, the Amerindians have fled, leaving behind an old Arawak woman whom Donne decides to use as a guide in his pursuit of the folk. From then on, the narrative centers on Donne's seven-day journey into the interior on dangerous nameless rapids between gigantic walls of forest and cliffs. One by one, members of the crew die, accidentally, from exhaustion, or murder when the underlying violence among them breaks out in a fit of frustration. They finally reach a huge waterfall, and with the two surviving members of the crew Donne begins to ascend the cliff until they fall and also meet their death. The story, however, does not end with the catastrophic ordeal toward which Donne has been travelling but with an illumination that grows out of his understanding of that very catastrophe.

The novel opens with a flashing vision of the imperialist conquest and the spirit of vengeance it aroused among its victims: Donne, the galloping conquistador, is shot by Mariella, the Amerindian woman he has abused and exploited. This is the content of a dream that seems to haunt the Guyanese consciousness and starts on his visionary quest the nameless I-narrator, who is Donne's inseparable double and his spiritual self. Together, they represent the contrary aspects, subjective and objective, of one being, who is both dead and alive. It seems indeed that Donne's death brings back to life the spiritual narrator who reintegrates his material prison, i.e., Donne himself, his "gaoler and ruler" (14). This is the starting point of the revival of the past, which strikes one as both an actual occurrence and an imaginative reconstruction of "Donne's first innocent voyage . . . into the interior country" (24). The opening of the narrative on the frontier between life and death suggests that the narrator's initial dream and his subsequent re-vision of the past take place in the timeless moment when man envisions his whole experience in a flash. This timeless moment merges with the conventional time frame, the three days' journey to Mariella followed by the seven days' progression toward the waterfall. In his later fiction Harris often uses this double time structure as a means of freeing experience from the single "inevitable" plane of existence to which it would otherwise be confined. In *Palace of the Peacock* the linear progress of the story tends to overshadow the timeless moment, although one is reminded of it whenever the narrator withdraws from the objective world around him and becomes lost in his apprehension of what he calls "the true substance of life" (59), actually the nameless dimension in which the Amerindian folk move. His mode of perception is also double and illustrates the contrasting possibilities inherent in each human being. At the beginning of the narrative Donne's "dead seeing material eye" evinces his own "living closed spiritual eye" (14). But his recurring intuitions punctuate the gradual transformation of the quest into a wholly spiritual one.

These intuitions are mostly stimulated by the landscape. It is sometimes a mirror for man's inner states and often a catalyst that modifies them. More important still, the glaring contrasts and uncertainties of the Guyanese nature are a phenomenal and spatial equivalent of the psyche, and the two blend in the narrative. Like the poet John Donne in *Hymn to God my God, in my Sickness,* the narrator identifies with the territory over which Donne, the explorer, rules. However, both "actual stage" and "symbolic map" (20) are more than they appear to be since both are pregnant with immaterial vestiges of the past and future possibilities, "hidden densities" which the narrator discovers in his progress toward self-knowledge. Throughout the narrative nature is alive with the unseen presence of the Amerindian folk who also live in the consciousness (and unconsciousness) of their pursuers, for they are part of the "complex womb" (41) out of which the modern Guyanese have sprung and are their spiritual ancestors. The correlation between landscape and self will appear from the following passage:

A brittle moss and carpet appeared underfoot, a dry pond and stream whose course and reflection and image had been stamped for ever like the breathless outline of a dreaming skeleton in the earth. . . . The forest rustled and rippled with a sigh and ubiquitous step. I stopped dead where I was, frightened for no reason whatever. The step near me stopped and stood still. I stared around me wildly, in surprise and terror, and my body grew faint and trembling as a woman's or a child's. I gave a loud ambushed cry which was no more than an echo of myself—a breaking and grotesque voice, man and boy, age and youth speaking together. (27−28)

"Outline" and "dreaming skeleton" are aspects of what Harris has called "eclipsed perspectives of place and community"[4] to which the narrator responds. He is overwhelmed by a powerful invisible presence in the forest ("ubiquitous step") and in his disorientation inner contrasting voices ("man and boy, age and youth") speak through him.

Another similar moment of revelation occurs in chapter 3 when the travellers detect on the river

a pale smooth patch that seemed hardly worth a thought. . . . Formidable lips breathed in the open running atmosphere to flatter it, many a wreathed countenance to conceal it . . . [the crew] bowed and steered in the nick of time away from the evasive, faintly discernible unconscious head whose meek moonpatch heralded corrugations and thorns and spears we dimly saw in a volcanic and turbulent bosom of water. We swept onward, every eye now peeled and crucified with Vigilance. The silent faces and lips raised out of the heart of the stream glanced at us. They presented no obvious danger and difficulty once we detected them beneath and above and in our own curious distraction and musing reflection in the water. (32−33)

This passage brings forth an image of the sacrifice ("corrugations and thorns and spears") that they will experience when two members of the crew, Carroll and Wishrop, die in the rapids. It evokes the buried existences ("silent faces and lips") in the stream of life and in themselves, for the obstacles encountered on the river are also inner obstructions ("ambush of the soul" [34]); they provide a good example of the way in which "images in space"[5] dramatize the characters' inner condition.

There is no apparent link between major events in Book I, the narrator's flashing vision of Donne's death, his disorientation in the forest, and his perception of ghostly antecedents in the river. However, through the unsettling effects of these disconnected experiences and of the partial revelations they elicit he begins to perceive the double nature of their journey. Whereas Donne is obsessed by his will to rule, the narrator senses in the crew and in himself "a desire and need" (25), "the longing need of the hunter" (30), which gradually takes the shape of Mariella and transforms the journey into an "immortal chase of love" (31). In her different guises Mariella has played a role in the individual lives of the crew and is a link between them as the inspiring muse through whom they hope to make a new start. She represents her people and identifies with the territory of the mission, also called Mariella. Like the crew, she is double-natured and contains such opposites as age and youth, innocence and guilt. Except when she appears as the old woman Donne makes prisoner and in the re-creation of her past relations with the crew, Mariella remains elusive and enigmatic to the end of the novel, at once an absence and a presence to be recognized in oneself since, as much as the crew, she is part of Donne's complex personality and of Guyana's heterogeneous population. The crew too inhabit Donne and the narrator's inner territory. Though flesh-and-blood people, they are "the crew every man mans and lives in his inmost ship and theatre and mind" (48). They are living embodiments of those instincts and passions that are deeply buried, unacknowledged, and therefore "undigested" sources of conflict. Unconsciously, they seem to enact the negative and positive potentialities contained in Donne and the narrator—possessive lust, cruelty, murder as well as the desire to be free from these self-imprisoning iniquities and to reach fulfillment.

It should be clear then that just as Harris presents a multiple reality which exceeds by far the limits of the perceptible world, so he enlarges our view of the human personality by conceiving the fictional character as a nucleus of selves, a "communtiy of being." In Book II, particularly, the crew seem to be living variations of the contrary states and motives contained in Donne and the narrator. They make "one spiritual family" (40) and are united by close or ambiguous relationships: the daSilva brothers are twins, old Schomburgh is afraid to recognize his son in the young negro boy Carroll. When not related, they seem to complement, or identify with, one another like

Donne and Wishrop, Jennings and Cameron, the narrator and Vigilance, who is also Carroll's stepbrother. Though this part of the novel takes place entirely at the mission of Mariella, it is prefaced with a line from Gerard Manley Hopkins's *The Wreck of the Deutschland*: ". . . the widow-making unchilding unfathering deeps." It is indeed while they stop at the mission that the hidden depths in the crew and their contrary impulses begin to manifest themselves in their present behavior and in the re-creation of their past. The narrator's feeling that he is "drawn two ways at once" (48), toward death and life, comes from his nightmarish re-enactment of Donne's death which ends with an intuition of Mariella's sorrow and is followed by a vision of perfection in an "eternal design" (47).

Later in the day the narrator becomes the medium of another visionary experience. When Donne arrests the old Arawak woman, the narrator is again obsessed by the undigested catastrophe that provoked the antagonism between conqueror and victim; he feels caught in a terrifying storm as Donne's ambition and hatred seek to envelop him and paralyze the crew in a deadly grip. The serial crimes committed by Wishrop are another example of the crew's affinity with death, for he has enacted "the desire they too felt in their vicarious day-dream, to kill whatever they had learnt to hate" (65). However, by purging himself of the desire to kill and later through his own death he frees the crew from their death-wish. Carroll, on the contrary, actualizes their birth-wish and need for harmony. When the crew quarrel over the necessity to pursue Mariella, his laughter strikes them "as the slyest music coming out of the stream" (63); it frees them from the tormenting passions that still root them in the soil of Mariella: "something had freed them and lifted them up out of the deeps . . . a reverberating clap of thunder and still music and song" (64). Music is "heard" in the narrative whenever Carroll comes to the fore; it is the expression of the deeper harmony the narrator intuits intermittently. Indeed, the light of vision floods his consciousness at intervals, then fades again, and until Book III when the crew begin to die, the narrative structure rests on this alternation between the narrator's moments of perception (his intimations of the roots of community in outer and inner territory) and the more matter-of-fact episodes in which significant fragments of the crew's lives are evoked.

Book III describes the crew's progression upriver until they reach
the falls above the mission of Mariella. The seven days allotted to
them for their journey are days of creation (171), which first implies a
process of breaking down: except for Vigilance, saved by his gift of
vision and his fruitful relation with the Arawak muse, the crew are
subject to a growing uncertainty while the "second death" decimates
their ranks. The source of their disorientation seems to be their
confrontation with namelessness, the third dimension, in which the
elusive folk move. The word *nameless* is repeatedly used to describe
an"otherness" that the crew fear in the world around them without
recognizing that they partake of it. It refers both to a primordial state
and to the fallen or eclipsed condition of victimized people.[6] Namelessness, as opposed to racial identity ("every material mask and label
and economic form and solipsism" [85]), is the source of genuine
community and is experienced as a preliminary to spiritual rebirth. It
is associated with the sacred or the divine, which in Harris's fiction is
not a transcendental ideal but suffering humanity (here the "unwritten lives"[7] of the folk) exiled beyond the pale of history. In the old
Arawak women the narrator discerns

the unfathomable patience of a god in whom all is changed into wisdom, all
experience and all life a handkerchief of wisdom when the grandiloquence of
history and civilization was past. (72)

The old woman's "otherness" exerts on the crew both fascination and
terror as she is briefly metamorphosed into the young Mariella who
seduces them once again and "embrace[s]" (73) them with the tumult
of the waters surrounding them. There seems to be on either side a
desire to engulf the other. When the crew symbolically rape the
Arawak woman, they are sustained by an "incestuous love" (73)
which is a denial of otherness and the cause of their own "self-
oppression" (75). On the other hand, by yielding to their irresistible
attraction for the "daemonic-flowing presence and youth" (74) of the
muse, they are in danger of complete self-surrender and annihilation.[8]
They are momentarily redeemed by Carroll's sacrificial death, just as
later Wishrop's drowning bears them "into the future on the wheel of
live" (102) and saves them for a further erosion.

As frightening as death itself is the ordeal through which they lose the support of the material world. When they reach the threshold of the unknown, they are both "on the threshold of the folk" (94) and of their own unconscious. Now the conventional limits between life and a deathlike state appear to melt away. Images of shattering and dismemberment abound in Book III, which express the crew's horrifying experience of their loss of identity and reduction to a "nakedness" similar to the folk's. From being the pursuers they have become pursued men longing for redemption by the folk, whose invisible presence is ascertained from such messengers as a flock of ducks, heraldic parrots, and the wounded tapir which prefigures the image of sheer energy Donne perceives later in the waterfall (134). By the second day the boat has "struck the bizarre rock and vessel of their second death" (100) yet continues upriver "driven by the naked spider of spirit" (102). Until the final extinction of the crew Harris seems to contrast the illusory strength of the material world they are so reluctant to relinquish ("the childish repetitive boat and prison of life" [104]) with a spiritual reality of which Vigilance alone is aware. Vigilance is the instrument of a vision "disruptive of all material conviction" (103). His "immateriality and mysterious substantiality" (103) recalls "the substance of the folk" (59) of which the narrator had an intuition earlier in the quest. This emphasis on the immaterial is not a denial of material reality. Rather, to relive catastrophe with understanding and the "eye of compassion" (108), as Vigilance does, brings about a visionary dislocation of the material world, which enables him to perceive beyond it the immaterial condition of the eclipsed folk. In this perception lies the mainspring of spiritual rebirth. There is now between Vigilance and the crew the same "spiritual distance" (104) as later between Donne and the carpenter in the waterfall (133). For the still-blind and confused crew must go through disintegration and fall into the void, as waves of victimized people have in the past, before the saving union with the "folk" can take place.

The final breakdown and breakthrough of Donne's personality occurs in Book IV, *Paling of Ancestors*, a title inspired by two lines from Gerard Manley Hopkins's *The Starlight Night*

> This piece-bright paling shuts the spouse
> Christ home, Christ and his mother and all his hallows.

These lines sum up the vision Donne perceives within the "paling" of the waterfall he has now reached and on the side of which he begins to climb with Jennings and daSilva. They have reached a primordial world in which opposites become reconciled: "before them the highest waterfall . . . *moved* and *still stood* . . . the immaculate bridal veil *falling motionlessly*" (128, italics mine). Donne now becomes conscious of an "invisible otherness" (141) around him and of existences that "contrast" with his domineering self. I have referred before to the spatial equivalence between the landscape and the Caribbean psyche. The escarpment of the waterfall seems to represent the great divide that tore the West Indian soul (particularly its Amerindian element) in the wake of conquest.[9] It is all the more significant then that, as he struggles up its face, Donne should visualize in it and, to use a Harrisian term, "re-sense" images of his Amerindian spiritual ancestry. The waterfall has a homogeneous surface and hammers with the inevitability of fate ("the hammer of the fall shook the earth with the misty blow of fate" [131]) yet is susceptible to breaking open and disclosing densities, "the subtle running depths of the sea, the depths of the green sky and the depths of the forest" (136). As earlier in the novel, the physical world opens onto a vision though it is now Donne who gains visionary insight. As he keeps ascending, moved by a longing to "understand and transform his beginnings" (130), he comes successively upon two windows in the misty veil of the waterfall and perceives first the image of a young carpenter or Arawak Christ, then a native virgin and child, not the glorified Virgin of the Christian church, though the two figures reconcile Christian with native elements. Since the beginning of Book IV the narrative has become wholly symbolical and, though described as concrete action, the quest does not issue in an actual meeting with Mariella or the folk but in a reshaping of Donne's imagination through what they represent. The rooms Donne envisions in the waterfall with their pictures of sacrifice and compassion seem to be projected from his (or the Guyanese and South Amercian) unconscious. As he comes to realize, they are the native element he has alway disregarded:

A singular thought always secured him to the scaffolding. It was the un-flinching clarity with which he looked into himself and saw that all his life he had loved no one but himself. He focused his blind eye with all penitent might on this pinpoint star and reflection as one looking into the void of oneself upon the far greater love and self-protection that have made the universe. (140)

The spiritual ancestors contained in the waterfall are bathed in a light that seems to flow from the very source of life.[10] The futility of erecting barriers of the senses and the mind in the material world is suggested by passages of an extraordinary metaphorical richness. I can only allude briefly here to the swift animal in the carpenter's room which, as already mentioned, seems to embody an energy or life impulse that assumes different shapes and defies the ordinary notions of space and time (134–135). It is the ceaseless movement of cre-ation, "the sculptured ballet of the leaves and the seasons" (135), that Donne visualizes. He is involved in a double process, being gradually reduced to utter nothingness and complete blindness (of the formerly "dead seeing material eye") while at the same time his true vision is being created: "He knew the chisel and the saw in the room had touched him and done something in the wind and the sun to make him anew. . . . He felt these implements of vision operating upon him" (132–133). The pictures in the waterfall of the sacrificial victims Donne used to ignore suggest that he himself now hangs in the terrifying void they have experienced before but this very void is the starting point of a reconstruction of the self: "the void of them-selves alone was real and structural" (141). Donne's conversion is due essentially to his apprehension of the native figures in "images in space." This spatialization of an otherwise ungraspable reality was to develop into Harris's conception of "the novel as painting" in which he attempts to retrieve through an accumulation of visualized "pic-tures" a deeply buried and "inimitable" reality (or light) that cannot be trapped or fixed in a single total representation. The folk in *Palace* move in this elusive dimension and, as already suggested, are never actually reached. When Donne falls from the cliff, he and the crew have "all come home at last to the *compassion* of the nameless unflinch-ing folk" (143, italics mine).

In the dawn of the seventh day Donne has disappeared or rather merged with the spiritual narrator, who again takes up the narrative in the first person and describes his and the crew's resurrection as well as the return to life of the formerly deserted savannahs. The narrator seems to have come to the very source of creation and to perceive together the material world and the reality that informs it: "a metaphysical outline dwelt everywhere filling in blocks where spaces stood" (144). More than that, it is his own vision, which he now shares with that of the muse ("the soul and mother of the universe" [146]), that seems to give life to the world he looks upon, suggesting that the vision of consciousness is the prime mover of life in man and nature

I felt it was the unique window through with I now looked that supported the life of nature . . . in the way I knew my hands and feet were formed and supported at this instant. (145)

Together with "the newborn wind of spirit" (the muse ?) the vision breathes life into dismembered creatures and transfigures the tree in the savannahs into the peacock:[11]

I saw the tree in the distance wave its arms and walk when I looked at it *through the spiritual eye of the soul*. First it shed its leaves sudden and swift as if the gust of the wind that blew had ripped it almost bare. The bark and wood turned to lightning flesh and the sun which had been suspended from its head rippled and broke into stars that stood where the shattered leaves had been in the living wake of the storm. The enormous starry dress it now wore spread itself all around into a full majestic gown from which emerged the intimate column of a musing neck, face and hands, and twinkling feet. The stars became peacocks' eyes, and the great tree of flesh and blood swirled into another stream that sparkled with divine feathers where the neck and the hands and the feet had been nailed. (146, italics mine)

Of all the metamorphoses of images in the novel, this is the most remarkable. It is worth pointing out that the sun, which at the beginning of the novel was a symbol of Donne's implacable rule, splinters into stars which become in turn the peacock's eyes: also that the palace of the peacock grows out of "the great tree of flesh and blood" and is therefore not a transcendental symbol but rather a metaphorical representation of community reconciling the human and the divine (the self and the "other") as its double vision shows: "This was the palace of the universe and the windows of the soul looked out and in" (146). Other members of the crew appear at the windows of the palace and Carroll's song is the "organ cry" of the peacock. As with painting when Donne was looking into the water-fall, so now with music which comes "from a far source within" (151) and is not so much an actual sound as an expression of harmony that defies all categories: light turns into "a muscial passage" (145) while "the echo of sound" is "outlined in space" (147). One is reminded here of Keats's line: "Pipe to the spirit ditties of no tone."

However significant the moment of fulfillment at the end of the quest, it is not a final achievement for this would once more paralyze the crew into a fixed and therefore oppressive attitude. Nature is seen as a vast canvas, "perfect" but still "unfinished" (144). Carroll's song "seem[s] to break and mend itself always" (147). And so the palace can only be an ephemeral construction, for life is a continuous ebb and flow, a repetitive pattern of dissolution and rebirth, whether in nature or in the individual human consciousness:

I felt the faces before me begin to fade and part company from me and from themselves as if our need of one another was now fulfilled, and our distance from each other was the distance of a sacrament, the sacrament and embrace we knew in one muse and one undying soul. (152)

The novel ends with the expression of a paradox that Harris was to develop in *The Eye of the Scarecrow*, the idea that the "other" is "near and yet far" (13). I would suggest, however, that the reality it conveys, that of a profound "unity of being" (59), is present, though as an underlying truth, in the body of the novel as much as at its climax, for the language creates throughout the interrelatedness that informs all life. Not only does Harris's language merge the sensuous and the abstract (see, in particular, Donne's ascent of the waterfall and the picture of the madonna and child) but also the animate and the inanimate. For example, the "outboard engine . . . flashed with mental silent horror" (21); the word "embroideries" refers at once to the waves on the river, the design of the Arawak woman's kerchief, and the "wrinkles on her brow" (73). As already suggested, consciousness and phenomenal world overlap. Now other categories or dimensions, like space and time also merge: "the animal light body . . . turned into an outline of time" (135). A word is sometimes used to describe opposites and convey their basic unity before this is realized; "nameless" and "volcanic" are cases in point. A single word or symbol will also cover a dual or even a multiple reality. The spider, for example, (recalling the West Indian trickster Anancy) is a symbol both of oppression and of creativeness. A single motif often leads to many variations and lends itself to metamorphosis. I have already drawn attention to the splintering of the sun into stars, then into the peacock's eyes. Another example is the house symbol and the "symbolic map" of Guyana (both referring to Donne's and the narrator's personality), which at the beginning of the novel appear in a spectrum of slightly differing images and are eventually transmuted into the palace of the peacock. The metamorphoses of images render the essential fluidity that Harris opposes to the fixity of human polarizations. Also contributing to the fluidity of the narrative is the presentation of opposties, first separately, then as a reconciled whole as in "He seemed to sense . . . its congealement and its ancient flow" (103). Harris's use of "and" is a distinctive feature of his style: it often links a series of varied images in an attempt to grasp an undefinable reality such as "a pearl and half-light and arrow, " which evokes the light that illuminates an "eternal design" (47); or creates a cumulative effect: "bottling and shaking every fear and inhibition and outcry" (73). These very brief remarks cannot, of course, do justice to the originality and richness of Harris's language. They can only call attention to features that require a detailed analysis if one is to appreciate the way in which his language disrupts the reader's conventional perception of reality while stimulating him to unravel the poetic associations and metamorphoses of images through which the characters' progress can be traced.

The creation of a native consciousness is not the outcome of a facile reunion of the crew with the folk but of an alteration of their opposition into an awareness of what they share. This is as far as the novel goes, and in this too it initiates an approach to the subject-matter to be found in all subsequent novels, since no final resolution ever takes place in Harris's fiction but only an erosion of the certainties and imperatives that imprison the protagonists within a one-sided and rigid sense of self. In later novels Harris warns against the danger of transforming the victim status into the instrument of a new tyranny and illustrates in his characters the need for an interplay of opposites. This freedom to move fluidly on both sides and so prevent new polarizations is, I think, conveyed in this first novel in the separation of those who have met in the palace ("I felt the faces before me . . . part company from me and from themselves"). The very moment of vision is apprehended in terms of a harmonious movement, and in this respect the dance of the peacock prefigures the liberating function of the "dance of the stone" in *Ascent to Omai*:

It was the dance of all fulfilment I now held and knew deeply, cancelling my forgotten fear of strangeness and catastrophe in a destitute world. (152)

Chapter Two

A Naked Particle of Freedom: *The Far Journey of Oudin*

The second of the Quartet's novels focuses on slavery as the most traumatizing West Indian experience and presents the attempt to enslave as the consequence of a possessive state of mind and as a contemporary as much as a historical reality. The old race of conquistadores has died out and their overseers' old mansions are put up for sale. But their spirit is alive in the acquisitive peasants who have just achieved economic freedom and are prompt to forget that their forefathers were exploited. Their sole ambition is to replace the old plutocracy. While they harbor the illusion that progress, or what stands for it in their narrow outlook, will bring about a new age, the antiquated pattern of master and slave reasserts itself in a different guise among the descendants of East Indian indentured laborers who live on the coastal savannahs.

The plot is based on the parable of the wicked husbandmen and raises the question of who shall inherit the earth and build a better future. The farmer Mohammed conspires with his brothers, Hassan and Kaiser, and his cousin, Rajah, to kill their illegitimate half-brother, to whom their father has left his property. By murdering the chosen heir, they sow the seeds of corruption and self-destruction and above all sin against the community, overthrowing "the secret participation and magic of ancient authority and kinship" (51). Shortly after the crime, the family begins to disintegrate as the brothers die one after another. Mohammed's downfall is precipitated by Ram, a money-lender and unscrupulous devil who represents the new ruthless power of capital and builds his empire on everyone else's ruin. Oudin, who closely resembles the murdered half-brother, appears out of nowhere and at first agrees to serve Ram and help him carry out his Machiavellian projects. But out of compassion for Beti, Rajah's daughter, whom he has been commissioned to abduct for Ram's benefit, he elopes with her and frustrates Ram's plans for the future. Thirteen years later Oudin convenants his unborn child to Ram (probably a reminder that the slave's offspring was the property of the master) and dies that very night. Beti swallows the paper of the covenant and deprives the devil of an heir.

The ordinary peasant world is so vividly re-created that it is easy to overlook the other dimension of reality that pervades the narrative and can be mainly perceived through Oudin's presence. He is a man of two worlds, in whom coalesce with equal credibility the historical and social role of the slave and that of the spiritual redeemer who sacrifices himself to free the community from their blind submission to fate. The two roles are interdependent; one mode of being does not prevail over the other but only makes sense in relation to it. Oudin's spiritual freedom is not attained by denying the material world but by recognizing and breaking through its apparently permanent or monolithic forms.

This release from a one-sided view of existence, the evidence of consciousness, grows out of Harris's mode of presentation and the novel's structure. At the beginning of Book I life is seen from a double perspective through the eye of the far-seeing Oudin, who has just died and whose vision unites the physical world with its immaterial counterpart. His hut is at first "drenched in dew . . . circled [by] the early light . . . with a vapour of spray" suggesting a "vague eternity and outline." When the mist lifts, the hut loses its mystery and appears as "a few planks nailed together and roofed by bald aluminium" (12). Oudin himself lies on the floor in "vague harvested bundles" but the early morning light, a "dim radiance of ancient pearl and milky rice . . . circulating within the room" (11), illuminates his "new freedom." As he recedes from the "match-box world" of the living, this world asserts itself as the concrete, familiar setting of human passions and fear. His united vision has split, leaving only the ordinary world of appearances, although his presence is felt "watching" over it throughout Book I.

Another way in which Harris conveys the duality of existence is through the juxtaposition of reality with memory and dream. The novel is shaped like a circle, a complete whole containing discontinuous time phases which correspond to different ways of apprehending life as the characters experience, remember, or foresee in dreams the coming of Oudin into their lives. In the center is the murder of the nameless half-brother (chronologically, the beginning of the plot) and the subsequent disintegration of the family, which benefits Ram but eventually leaves him dissatisfied, for he has spent all his energy in consolidating his empire and has become an impotent old man. The real end of the plot comes at the beginning of the novel with its promise of renewal and change. Its significance arises from the interaction of the many facets of time and the specific meaning attached to them since the quality of time varies with the nature of the characters' experience. The time to which Oudin awakes on the dawn of his death is a fruitful extension of his life on earth, "the dream of the heavenly cycle of the planting and reaping year he now stood within—as within a circle—for the first time" (11). Kaiser too awakes after death to time as a mysterious dimension harmonizing all its parts[1] but still longs to return to the world of appearances.

Liberation from objective time in dreams also gives the living access to knowledge that can either save or doom according to their willingness to trust what has been conveyed intuitively. Beti's dream at the beginning of Chapter 6 enables her to see in Oudin "the . . . image and author of freedom" (35), while Mohammed's, in the same chapter, only frightens him; he ignores its significance, preferring to "restore the time," that is "*his* image of time" (39, 40, italics mine). When he is threatened with bankruptcy, he begins to sense a quality in time that he cannot understand rationally and therefore calls a curse (91). In the novel as a whole the abrupt shifts from one period of time to another and from one mode of perception to another convey man's capacity to travel imaginatively between past, present, and future and so to grasp the significance of events or to envisage their remote consequences. As Beti's stand against Ram in Book I shows, this capacity can also stimulate action against the tyranny of particular circumstances.

Oudin and Beti embody respectively the reality and the potentiality of freedom. Oudin is a disinherited peasant who, when he first appears to Beti, seems to be chained to the earth yet to possess a freedom of movement that those attached to material wealth cannot enjoy:

Oudin's extremities . . . had turned to mud. He had crawled and crept far. He had risen to his feet to follow her, but he carried with him rings around his ankles, and islands off the foreshore. . . . (34)

He evokes the freed slave and liberator Toussaint l'Ouverture, not in his role as a black emperor, with whom Kaiser is proud to be identified (73), but as a man who, according to Harris, "may well have had peculiar doubts about the assumption of sovereign status and power." Oudin represents the alternative to that status, "the promise of fulfilment . . . in a profound and difficult vision of the person."[2] And it is in a specifically Caribbean role, that of the trickster who outwits the exploiters (Mohammed and Ram), that he frees Beti and helps Ram's debtors. Of unknown origin and indeterminate race, he represents all races that have been exploited at one time or another. He is throughout a catalyst who perturbs the established order and, for this reason, is called "a devil of freedom" (114). It may therefore seem paradoxical that, except when he abducts Beti, he should be a consenting tool in Ram's hands. This is because he is also part of Ram's world, the world of men, and cannot avoid being corrupted by it. He is no hero rescuing the community from without; his influence shows that revolution in Harris's terms is a slow process taking root in the *individual* amid the evils of ordinary life. When Oudin is moved by compassion, he risks his life to save Beti. In doing so, he relives the sacrifice of the nameless half-brother because he feels that to tie himself to an ignorant girl, so representative of the enslaved and unenlightened condition of women in the community, is equivalent to death.[3] Through his sacrifice he also begins to redeem the crime of his "brothers":

The basket-head on the ground was his own decapitated one, he realized, that the first of his ghostly executioners and pursuers had fished from the sea . . . . It was the first . . . offering of repentance and sacrifice he must accept in himself and must overcome, to be the forerunner of a new brilliancy and freedom. (105)[4]

However, Oudin's accomplishment remains limited by the circumstances in which he operates, and in the forest, where he escapes with Beti, he becomes physically and spiritually exhausted when he has filled his purpose. His depletion is in keeping with Harris's refusal to consolidate a particular state: a "heroic" Oudin would soon be locked up in a new "fate" and involved in a new kind of tyranny.

Beti is perhaps the best example in Harris's fiction of the way in which even the most ordinary person can dismantle the prison in which she (or he) is confined by the joint power of fate and unenlightened tradition. Illiterate as she is, she has saving intuitions. When her father dies, for instance, she senses that he only wanted to spare her the servitude and pain that had killed her mother, and she recognizes in Oudin the liberator who will light "the tall reflective fire . . . which was to illumine the constructive and relative meaning of the time" (54). Warmed by this fire, she becomes a figure of fertility and is able to take the lead in the forest when Oudin begins to falter. She is too ignorant of his motives to be capable of a detachment similar to his or to escape her condition altogether; she has "to keep one foot in a corner of the ruling past" (144) and cannot go further than her slender possibilities will allow. But she gains enough strength to defy the devil thirteen years later. When she swallows the paper of the covenant, an action typical of illiterate peasants who fear the power of the written word, she breaks the cycle of attempts to possess by dispossessing others in which Ram and her family were involved and so alters the order they wished to perpetuate. Limited as her achievement may seem, it unsettles Ram and brings to light his "insecure humanity" (18). When he eloped with her, Oudin wanted to "invent a human brain . . . and to ingrain it into the fibre of a race" (112). Ram sees that she is "a child [young but also newly created] and a daughter" (132), "the daughter of a race that was being fashioned anew" (136). Beti's pregnancies at the beginning (123) and the end (23) of her union with Oudin link together the two creative episodes in her life and contain the promise of the new age that, unknowingly, she is helping to build.

Mohammed and his brothers also want change but they can only conceive of renewal in terms of material wealth (see 52) and retain a primitive mentality. The brothers' behavior illustrates a major theme in Harris's fiction, namely, that in spite of his tremendous material achievements, modern man has not freed his mind from antiquated thought patterns. His insecurity and confusion are exemplified by

Mohammed ("half material hope, half spiritual despair" [59]), whose downfall is due to superstition and fear. The crime he has committed and the series of deaths that follow (these are accidental although he reads punishment into them) merely strengthen the hold of fate over him. Oudin offers him a possibility of release when he initiates a train of events that should urge Mohammed to pull back and re-examine his outlook. But, to the end, he remains afraid of self-knowledge. The forest, where he pursues Oudin and Beti, is like a hen ready to hatch him to real birth. When he resists, it shakes "its fluid feathers from him," and "he [cracks] the premature egg of his dying time" (130), i.e., dies prematurely because he has not learned to live. All he understands is that by blindly agreeing to be Ram's victim he has played into the devil's hands and strengthened his power.

Mohammed's meaningless death contrasts with the wish of his brothers to atone for their crime. The exploratory journey in *Palace of the Peacock* has already made it clear that physical death in Harris's fiction does not necessarily entail the death of the spirit. One must insist, however, that spiritual freedom is never a postmortem consolation; it is the fruit of a painful growth in consciousness and of a mature understanding of the antinomies of existence. In this respect, Oudin differs essentially from the fisherman and the woodcutter in whom Hassan and Kaiser are, as it were, "resurrected." For he embodies the sufferer in each man and in the community, the always resurging clown (he prefigures "Idiot Nameless" of *The Eye of the Scarecrow*), whereas Hassan and Kaiser seem to have returned to life to expiate their crime in much the same way as daSilva in *Heartland*.[5] At the moment of death, Hassan envisaged redemption as a withdrawal into emptiness (75), while Kaiser longed to return to, and consolidate, the world of appearances (121). After their "second birth" each makes a different use of his new opportunity. In the guise of the fisherman Hassan repents and allows Oudin to escape (105), after which he enters the stream (and is purified by this baptism of water?); "the black ball [of the sun]" and the "moonhead" appear to make one with his head on the surface of the water testifying to his inner reconciliation. The woodcutter, on the other hand, is a romantic idealist who would "enslave the world, with the best of mistaken intentions" (119). He remains indebted to Ram and wants Oudin to prolong his contract with the devil.[6]

The fluid life of the river with which Hassan eventually merges (an indication that he himself has at last begun to move and change) is but one example among many of the way in which the mobility of the phenomenal world contrasts with man's habitual resistance to change, an oppressive attitude that amounts to an attempt to arrest life. Throughout the novel, movement in nature conveys an intensity of livingness that men frequently deny. For instance, the circulation of the light in Oudin's hut (11) heralds the new fertile cycle into which he awakens. But Mohammed fails to grasp the significance of the circulating light in his room after his dream of Oudin (37), just as later in the forest he refuses to surrender to its dynamic and maturing influence (130). Ram too is afraid of the movement and change he foresees when "a blue window in the cloud [opens]" (135). He wants a son to perpetuate his power and "fill the widening blue crack in heaven" (135). That movement is linked with freedom and may stimulate consciousness appears from Oudin's "Far Journey" and Beti's shorter migration. Twice in thirteen years Oudin defeats Ram by starting on a journey which involves a progression in consciousness (the antidote to oppression). His first voyage frees Beti and possibly redeems the crimes of earlier exploiters in Caribbean history: "His first superstitious fears . . . were all the reflective faces of ancestral hate and killing turning weak and insubstantial in himself" (105). After his death his "journey" is toward "a new freedom," so that migration, a crucial factor in the formation of the Caribbean, is turned into an opportunity for spiritual emancipation. Unlike Mohammed, who feels threatened by the "conspiracy of time and history and migration" (38), Beti travels some way toward freedom ("it was as far as she had been able to . . . migrate" [127]). The words "far" and "great distance" are repeatedly used[7] to evoke an invisible plane of existence, the perception of which gives hope to some and disturbs others. So much so that Ram is defeated and shattered only when he can no longer ignore the duality of the living process nor the creative energy over which he is powerless.

A few words about the imagery will show that it carries some of the novel's important implications. Harris not only uses contrasting images that release a stimulating energy (such as the marriage between the sun and the moon): most natural elements have no fixed symbolic meaning and express now one thing, now its contrary, depending on the character with whom they are associated. Light and darkness alternate throughout the narrative. The sun symbolizes now life and consciousness, now death. The black sun is a recurring motif; it either corresponds to an eclipse of consciousness or foreshadows death as a necessary ordeal before rebirth.[8] The "spider-sun" seems to be Oudin in his Anancy role, and it is also Oudin who hides in "the gliding shadow of the sun" (15)[9] which Ram fears just before Oudin "dispossesses" him. The fertile conjunction between the light and the dark is perceived by Beti after Oudin's death: "It was as if noon . . . had become the stars of a universal night in which the fear of Ram had begun to vanish" (22). This prefigures her realization that Oudin has made her pregnant and that the emancipation she had dreamed of at the time of her marriage is now becoming real: "the smoothness of her skin was an intent and naked particle of freedom like one who had been stripped in truth at last" (23).

Images related to birth also have a dual significance. The seed is fertile for Oudin and Beti but is a source of self-destruction for the conspiring husbandmen who impregnate "the womb of subversion" (52). Mohammed's seed fails to give him the heir he wants, while his own rebirth is aborted in the forest. "Miscarriage and abortion" (85) have a literal and a figurative meaning as does the word *child*. If the male heir both Ram and Mohammed crave is intended to perpetuate their material power, it is Oudin's spiritual inheritance that Beti brings to life in her children and so transforms the "bargain" he signed with Ram into a "covenant." The umbilical cord (21,136) is another ambivalent symbol linking Oudin with the "child" Beti (born to new life after he has eloped with her) and her future offspring. For Ram it becomes a "twine of encirclement" foreshadowing his "possession" by Oudin (circle images abound, suggesting either imprisonment or cycles of fertility). I have pointed out that once he had accomplished his revolutionary feat, Oudin faded into a "faint servant." But, as usual in Harris's fiction, it is the faint, disregarded figure who carries the hope of rebirth and change. After Oudin's death the fearful Ram begins to fade in turn under Beti's contemptuous stare; the coiled twine stretches out and links the defeated master to his former slave, making Ram realize that he and Oudin are insepara-

ble and forcing him to acknowledge that their contract is other than
he thought:

The twine . . . would uncoil before him, so that stretched taut at last it drew
him forward as Oudin walked backward into the distance like a sleepwalker,
till their vision met in a way that shattered him to the core. (21)

Ram's disorientation is not a sure sign that he is finally defeated
and will change. There is a suggestion (and an implicit warning) that
the demon of possession will always try to reassert itself. Admittedly,
he recognizes the ascendancy of Oudin in a realm over which he is
powerless and realizes that he is dying to his former self. He appears to
be moving at last when he sees fragments of his own reflection in the
water "waving almost endlessly until the slices and fragments were
drawn together on a loose sailing thread" (25). Awareness of this
movement leads to an intuition of Oudin's presence within himself.
Soon, however, the "motion of the river" (26) is contrasted with the
fixity he has always maintained. There is a subtle shift to the past
when Ram first remembers Oudin's wedding, which he now sees as
"the launching and freedom of a release in time" (27); then he
recalls his coming "across an incredible divide of time and reality"
(29). The sense of someone at once near and remote reminds him of
his fear when he used the telephone for the first time: "He knew the
distance and the divide was there between himself and the other . . .
speaker, but his own reflection rose and deceived him until everything seemed nearer and narrower than it actually was" (29). In other
words, he gained new assurance by selfishly restricting the world to
himself.

By juxtaposing the expression of Ram's sense of insecurity with a
reminder of his self-assertiveness Harris shows that no victory is
ever final and emphasizes the need for a constant revision of the
premises of life. In this respect it is interesting to compare the
completed if shaky structure that symbolizes a desirable achievement
in V.S. Naipaul's *A House for Mr. Biswas* with Harris's house symbolism in *The Far Journey*. For Wilson Harris the finished house (the
"palace" Mohammed wants for himself) is only a symbol of material
welfare and dangerous consolidation of power (52), whereas the

never-ended construction evokes a pattern of life unceasingly making
and unmaking itself:

Sometimes it seemed [to Beti] that one cruel face emerged, sometimes
another . . . but containing all was a fascinating living house *whose windows
and walls crumbled and yet were able to erect themselves afresh in every corner*, so that
what dominated the phantasmagoria and cosmopolis of experimental life was
a shattering and contructive mystery, rather than an ultimate and dreadful
representation and end. (122, italics mine)

The necessity to allow all static frames of existence to crumble in order
to perceive the reality within or beyond and follow its movement has
been illustrated by the breaking up of time within a given sphere of
duration, by the "crash" which shatters Rajah's and Mohammed's
blindness (88, 132) when they die, and by the weakening of tyrannical
obsessions in individual characters.

The Far Journey owes its title to *The Secret of the Golden Flower*, a
treatise of Chinese philosophy which describes the birth of consciousness that stimulates progress toward spiritual freedom. The treatise
has also inspired some of the novel's imagery and a few cryptic
sentences like "The pot spoon flew from [Rajah's] hand, striking the
forehead of the sky [Oudin's] and burning a flashing place between
two stars and eyes" (87). It is written in *The Golden Flower* that "the
primal spirit is beyond the polar differences . . . [it] dwells in the
square inch [between the eyes]."[10] When Rajah sees Oudin, he is on
the point of selling his daughter to Ram, and he takes Oudin for the
murdered half-brother risen from the dead to warn him against
another evil action so that, instinctively, he tries to injure Oudin's
far-sightedness. Shortly afterwards a storm breaks out:

The heavens changed again, and grew lighter in the flowering incipient
reflection that one sees sometimes on a very dark night in the direction of
Georgetown . . . as one wanders over the savannahs, miles and miles away
from *nowhere*. The distance had *blossomed* into a spectacle far greater than this
. . . a kind of *crimson whiteness* and *spirit-fire* and blush. (88, italics mine)

Words like "blossom," "crimson whiteness," and "spirit-fire" clearly
evoke the fulfillment represented by the golden flower. This extract is

a good example of the way in which Harris uses a physical setting to convey a spiritual reality; it announces Rajah's journey to "a land that is nowhere" (89) described in *The Golden Flower* as man's "true home."[11] The "spirit-fire" is the light[12] whose "circulation" marks a first stage in the journey inwards. The expression seems to have served Harris as a model for the phrase "thought-sun" (100), which conveys at once the materiality and symbolical significance (consciousness) of the sun.

This esoteric language can be mystifying and has given rise to baffled criticism.[13] My objection to it is that, in spite of their poetic beauty, some passages are difficult to explain in their own terms. Harris, however, names his sources. The epigraph to Book I is quoted from *The Golden Flower*; it alludes to the marriage between heaven and earth (a metaphor for the fruitful marriage between Oudin and Beti) and the freedom from all entanglements achieved by Oudin. Other expressions of the liberating union of opposites described both in *The Golden Flower* and in *The Far Journey* are to be found in the marriage between the sun and the moon and between water and fire. As if in answer to the fisherman's question: " 'You believe fire and water ever mix?' " (104), they do mix on Hassan's funeral pyre; also when part of the blazing rum-shop, in which Kaiser burns, is flung into the river; and when the rain "grows" to meet the sky immediately after Rajah's "electrification" by lightning.[14] Though Rajah himself has feared this kind of retribution, he is at last released from his frustrating existence and self-enslavement:

The rain grew all around [Beti] and when she parted the grey curtain of the sky to approach him, she was conscious only of the gift and feast of freedom from travail and pain he had entertained for her, and of the fracture of a cruel bond within him. . . . (89)

There is a fundamental unity between the various religious and philosophical elements in the novel, which makes nonsense of religious prejudice and points to Harris's essential preoccupation with the spiritual in man. Like *The Golden Flower*, the parable of the husbandmen is concerned with the means of cultivating life. Through his symbolical decapitation Oudin identifies with John the Baptist,[15] then with Christ through his sacrifice and rebirth, as well as with Anancy, the African god. In the oppressed and saving Oudin Harris brings together the heterogeneous religious heritage of the Caribbean and even of mankind, for the Norse god Odin, "left . . . hanging from a tree" (62), like the dead half-brother whom Oudin resembles, also comes to mind. Harris unites several spiritual traditions but shows that as institutions upholding "fossil symbols"[16] religions can be instruments of oppression or self-oppression. Ram cynically advises Mohammed to take advantage of the mixture of Moslem and Hindu practice among East Indians to sell his cattle at a high price (actually, Ram has stolen and sold many of them himself), and Mohammed, who did not hesitate to kill his brother, is too superstitious to sell his cattle to the butcher. Clearly the characters' confusion is spiritual. The novel is a parable of modern times, in which man's basically weak, self-deceptive, or sentimental attitude makes him an easy prey to those who, like Ram, strive to enslave him materially the better to rule over his soul.[17] That his hold over the future should be frustrated by the slave and trickster of Caribbean history suggests that in Harris's view the truly revolutionary spirit that came to life in Toussaint l'Ouverture must be retrieved and inspire

a groping towards an alternative to conventional statehood, a conception of wider possibilities and relationships which still remains unfulfilled today in the Caribbean.[18]

Chapter Three

A Compassionate Alliance: *The Whole Armour*

The setting of *The Whole Armour*, a village on the Pomeroon River caught between the bush and the sea, is the only region in Guyana on which white imperialism and the large sugar estate have not left their mark. The inhabitants are nonetheless "capitalists . . . scraping together . . . every penny . . . without the ghost of a conception of what it means to belong to the grass-roots" (115). They have fertile land but don't know how to exploit it. The river brings down silt from the interior, and the crops are often carried away from the unstable soil into the sea. Yet the people ignore this instability (which reflects their own inner state) just as they remain unaware of their physical and spiritual confinement. Their life is saturated with tension and unsatiated passion that periodically explode into violence and murder.

In bare outline the novel evokes the symbolical birth of a people from the "womb" (61) of the exile Abram, their failure to assume responsibility for their development as a community, and their potential redemption through the sacrifice of Cristo. It opens with Abram's dream of his impending death and fall from the tree of community with its roots plunging not into the earth but into the sky (an allusion to the covenant between God and the biblical Abram, renewed by the birth of Christ). When he awakes, he leaves his hut in Jigsaw Bay to visit the whore Magda in the village. She, however, is obsessed with one thought: to save her son, Cristo, wanted by the police for the alleged murder of a rival. She wants Abram to hide him and argues that Cristo might be his son although this is in fact impossible. Her persuasiveness is inspired by her intense concern for Cristo, yet there is a sense in which what she says is true. For she and Abram represent the alien and unlawful element in the origins of the community, their dark truth and history [which the people deny], written in the violent mixture of races . . . as though their true mother was a wanton on the face of the earth and their true father a vagrant . . . from every continent. (49)

Neither Magda nor Abram is aware of this deeper truth. Nor do they believe in Cristo's innocence, although Abram has an intuition of it when he dies of a heart attack two months after taking in Cristo. When the frightened Cristo rushes back to his mother's house, she becomes convinced that he has killed Abram as well. They go back together to his hut and find that his corpse has been dragged to the foreshore and mutilated by a jaguar (called "tiger" by the Guyanese). Magda forces Cristo to dress Abram's corpse in his own clothes and so to exchange his identity with him. She is then able to tell the police that Cristo has been refused protection by Abram and been torn into shreds by the tiger. Supposedly dead, Cristo is free to escape into the jungle, where he spends forty days and nights, while Abram is said to have set out, full of remorse, in search of the "tiger of death."

Forty days after the alleged death of Cristo Magda holds a wake to which the Pomeroon people come, moved by the ambiguous desire to feed on Magda's generosity in vengeful compensation for their secret attraction to her:

Her mourning wake was a debt they must extract for the sovereignty she had exercised upon them in their weakness, men and women alike dominated by a furtive desire for unrestricted union with the goddess of identity, superior to a divided unsettled world. (50)

Paradoxically, the villagers, who refuse to recognize their true roots in Magda, their "true mother" (see above), are prepared to secretly worship in her, the "goddess of identity,"[1] a wholly illusory strength, the fruit of mere primitive self-assertion rather than self-knowledge or consciousness. Her self-assertiveness is most obvious in her fierce love for Cristo, whom she will not allow to be himself, insisting on acting through him, "the hiding mother in the son" (84). At the wake, however, several incidents occur which shatter the characters' fixed sense of identity (though not yet Magda's), forcing them to participate symbolically in an experience they would rather ignore. The people at the wake have chosen Peet as their "vessel of rehabilitation and defiance" (55), believing him to be equal to Magda, the "queen of fate," and hoping to experience their own "vicarious uplift" (54) through him. When Peet reaches Magda's room, she is so repulsed by him and by the vulgar spirit in which he offers her money that she fights him and wounds him in the head. The stunned Peet first experiences Abram's death in an hallucination, feeling that, like Abram, he is carried away by the tiger. Then he sees Cristo reborn out of his (Peet's) wound unclothing him as he had unclothed Abram. The new Cristo he sees bears the tiger's mark, a long scratch from eye to lips, the stamp of his forty days' ordeal in the forest and of his victory over the tiger of death. When Peet comes to himself, Magda urges him to put on a shirt of Critso's (as she had forced Cristo to clothe Abram in his shirt) so that Peet *is* a medium, though of an unexpected kind, having undergone the death of the father and envisioned the rebirth of the son.

His vision of truth shatters him and he is now figuratively the only dead person or "corpse" (55,71) at the wake, but he becomes filled with a perverse need for release for he has only exacerbated the crowd's and his own sense of frustration. He finds a scapegoat in Mattias, his daughter's new fiancé (her first fiancé was Cristo's alleged victim); he identifies Mattias with Cristo seeing in both of them the tiger that long ago provoked his wife's death and now, so he says, has raped Sharon, his daughter. Mattias is killed accidentally, though there is a sense in which Peet's and the crowd's drunken excitement has been leading to this murderous climax. Meanwhile, Sharon has been called upstairs by Magda, who gives her a letter from the runaway Cristo. She is still a virgin, convinced that she is "innocent" although several men have died failing to possess her. Throughout her confrontation with Magda, the older, jealous woman is like a tiger to her as she had been to Peet. Her countenance is a "mirror" in which Sharon is invited to recognize her own guilt for the violence she has provoked. She tries to reject all responsibility although she cannot help feeling "seduced, refracted and distorted and nearly shattered" (80) by Magda's tigerish countenance. When she offers with equivocal innocence to show Cristo's letter to Mattias, Magda shows her Peet's dollar bills torn and plastered with his vomit, the evidence of "her own true roots" (84) and relatedness to guilt. Sharon can no longer repulse

Magda's "mirror of seduction"; she is "raped" by "living nature," the tigerish Magda. And as Sharon is forced by her to share in a guilt which at that very instant surfaces again in the killing of Mattias, her former self is symbolically annihilated and her cry fuses with Mattias's death-cry. At this moment of climax she experiences at once Mattias's death ("dying on the scaffold . . . [his] murdered cry in her own virgin throat" [84]) and her imminent union with Cristo.

In the next scene Sharon is making love with Cristo in the jungle and reliving "the terrifying process of enveloping seduction" (84) his mother had exercised over her. An important change has taken place, however. In her union with Magda she was brought into contact with the "incestuous tiger" (84) or "hermaphrodite of the species" (80). This is the mask of uniformity—the negation of all individuality—that Magda (the goddess of identity) has been wearing, matching in this Peet's "incestuous *persona*" (49) (he represents a collectivity that denies its heterogeneous makeup). When the white Sharon unites with the black Cristo three weeks after the wake, they shatter the mask of uniformity, and "the gross burden [of the community's unacknowledged origins and of their nature] flowered and moved" (85). This is also the moment of fulfillment and completeness, an encounter with "death and life" (84), followed by a revival in nature which mirrors the lovers' rebirth. Animated with a new sense of responsibility, they have decided together that Cristo will give himself up.

It appears that after the wake Peet has committed suicide. Magda, no longer a powerful enigmatic idol, has become a frightened and childlike woman. Cristo is now free of her influence but she still lives only for him. When he abandons his earthly life, she has no inner resource left, an indication that her strength was rooted in her obsessive "incestuous" identification with Cristo:[2]

Something had drained out of him, blood or sap, and in passing out of him it had also served to reduce all her fantastic compelling ardour and frustration into powerlessness and petulance. (131–132)

When her mask falls (131), she is but a desperate and impotent mother who, for the last time, urges Cristo to escape. However, to flee like

the Caribs, or the runaway slave he saw in himself in the heartland
(123), would amount to assuming again the burden of guilt he and
Sharon have managed to lift, and repeating a historical pattern that
may have been inevitable at one time but must now be left behind.
Cristo chooses to sacrifice himself so that a new conception of life may
prevail. The pietà-like scene at the end of the novel shows him sitting
with his head on Sharon's lap, listening to their child crowing at the
moment of his execution a year hence. The police surround the house
but Cristo now feels that "No one could intervene and trap the
essential spirit" (130).

The achievement of a sense of responsibility and of spiritual freedom is a central issue in the novel and is inseparable from a mature
understanding by the young, educated generation of "the meaning of
individual innocence and guilt" (70). The development of these major
themes brings out the possibilities of building up a real community
(the genuine sharing of life and death experienced by the young)
which contrasts with the surface homogeneity[3] that the collectivity (as
distinct from community) is trying to preserve at all costs. Their
herd-like unanimity on crucial occasions (the wake and the ensuing
inquest) clashes with the genuine interrelatedness illustrated in the
structure of the narrative, which progresses through the experience
(real or symbolical) by some characters of what others have undergone, such as Cristo's, then Peet's identification with Abram's death
in Books I and II. In Book III the first section juxtaposes Mattias's
death with Sharon's symbolical annihilation by Magda, while in the
second section Sharon relives her own experience and Mattias's,
grasping their meaning and giving it further depth when she unites
with Cristo.

As so often in Harris's fiction, the unacknowledged elements in the
characters' personality or environment have an unreal and dreamlike
quality until they become assimilated into their growing consciousness. Moreover, individual characters seem to form one whole in
which the center of experience shifts from one to another though not
all are aware of its significance. There is a chain-like recognition by
the young of shared responsibility, stimulated by Magda and Peet,
who force guilt on them though they themselves are incapable of
facing it. Yet it is through the acceptance of guilt that real commu-

nity is shown to exist potentially. Cristo, who knows he is innocent of the murders Magda imputes to him, first accepts "the fabulous injustice of guilt" (29) only in order to escape, but his very flight makes him see the truth of Abram's assertion: "Nobody innocent" (23). Mattias, who throughout the wake has grown aware of his former isolation and passivity, also accepts the guilt thrust on him by Peet in order "to redeem the relics of crippled perspective" (77) and free the crowd of self-deception. They, however, deny their vision of truth, i.e., the proof given by Mattias's death that Cristo is innocent. They must have a medium and a scapegoat because they reject all genuine participation in life or death.

An essential feature of Harris's organic concept of community is, as already suggested, the absence of a fixed boundary between the dead and the living as well as the necessity for the living to revive and digest in their own consciousness the experience of the dead. During the wake the dead and the living merge in Peet; Mattias perceives the "serial features"[4] of the dead in himself (69,72), while the "serial fused moment" (84) or "serial vision" (87) of Sharon's encounter with Magda links her with a violent past she has always denied. Their growing need to grasp the nature of the legacy of the dead in themselves ("all the restless spirits are returning to roost in our blood" [115]) links together Mattias's experinece at the wake with Cristo's in the bush. Mattias's "waking eye"[5] perceives the head of the "walking tree and family of mankind" (74). Cristo, who at Jigsaw Bay had lost his self-control when he sensed the presence of "long-dead ghosts" (23), identifies with the dead of the heartland. For the two young men the "monsters" of the past become agents of transformation. Their retrieval by Cristo together with what Harris calls "the compassionate alliance of the dead with the living" (42) demand a reinterpretation of history that must help to create a new vision of the future.

Awareness that real community embraces the dead and the living is cognate with a perception of the double-faced view of reality and of the relativity of truth. The all-embracing symbol of the tiger brings together the many faces of truth and serves as a counterpoint to the numerous images of splitting and dismemberment. Harris hints at the tiger's "symmetry" by juxtaposing in the epigraph to Book III (*Time of the Tiger*) the first two lines of Blake's poem, *The Tiger*, with two lines from St. John of the Cross's *Cántico espiritual*. The tigerish violence and passion of the participants in the wake reaches a climax in this part of the novel, and Mattias's sacrificial death prefigures Cristo's metamorphosis into "Christ the tiger." But the symbol extends beyond a rigid duality. Its function in the narrative is a good example of Harris's associative method, for the main themes of the novel (innocence and guilt rooted in violence, identification of the characters with the spirit of the place, and birth of a community from individual self-knowledge and retrieval of the past) develop from the tiger imagery. The different features of the tiger can be apprehended at some stage in all the characters and in many forms of the phenomenal world. The whole region seems to reflect this tigerish capacity and offers contrasts of darkness and light. Taken as a whole, the tiger's attributes reveal a community of being in the living creation and even between the living and the dead.

When Magda and Cristo approach the forshore of Jigsaw Bay at the beginning of the novel,

the subdued subterranean *roar* of the vital repression of the surf began to invade their stranded senses . . . the bay would grow violent and treacherous with the new erosive impact of the sullen seas . . . Magda . . . was looking down . . . at a foul mixture of universal *foaming* soap. The water *hissed* and swirled hungrily and evilly around her powerful limbs." (34, italics mine)

The bay evokes the destructiveness of the tiger, which Magda and Cristo are on the point of discovering, and foreshadows the suppressed instincts of the crowd gradually rising to the surface and breaking loose at the wake. When Peet relives Abram's death, the sea and the tiger make one in his hallucination and merge with the sound of the wake, which is in fact destroying him through Magda:

[The sound] assailed him, full of pounding threatening *sibilance*, a striding breath of grandeur, whispering and overlapping and rising notes in a hushed vagrant *roar* that suddenly grew and became so deafening he was transported to see the flecks of *tigerish foam* on a dark fluid body, *striped by the animal light of the moon*, flying across the room towards him. The glistening dim fangs sank into the bellying sail of his chest. (57–58, italics mine)

At this stage the tiger becomes the symbol of Peet's annihilation ("the void held him now in its frightful jaws" [58]) before carrying him through the landscape of his and the crowd's spiritual confinement: "[the shadows] ran between a dim wave of crested sea and a dark forest of cultivated night, the sensational corpse of the medium of man borne swiftly by the living tiger of death" (58).

Throughout the scene the tiger symbol conveys the aggressive impulses of both Magda and Peet: he has been attacked by her but has also tried to spring at her so that he is assailant and victim like the tiger later killed by Cristo. Peet and the crowd see and fear the tiger in others yet are unaware of it in themselves.[6] Magda is a superb incarnation of its attributes, now "soft and feline" (39), now menacing or ferocious and pitiless, as in her conversation with Sharon when she (Magda) truly becomes a universal symbol of the wilderness in mankind. We have seen that as the "incestuous tiger of the jungle" (84) Magda is the possessive mother, keen on shaping her son's life and acting through him: she is also the embodiment of the crowd's narrow and gregarious sense of identity, equally represented by the tiger Peet had hunted and failed to catch years before.

Peet's failure to catch the tiger in the jungle was clearly due to his fear of facing the truth about his and the population's origins, the "monster's head" (90) of their dismembered body, which was nevertheless a "vision of buried fertility" (91) since, however distasteful their early history, to come to terms with it would be a first mature move toward renewal. Keeping in mind that the jungle in Harris's fiction also represents the characters' inner self, it becomes obvious that the tiger is also the "free spirit" that the population have hounded more deeply into themselves (88); it is "the lost soul of all generations, the tiger roaming through the trackless paths" (88). So that the tiger of death represents not only the crowd's "incestuous self-destructiveness" but also the unacknowledged soul of their heterogeneous ancestry.[7] When Cristo kills the first, he resurrects the second and identifies with it. He has evoked a tiger from the beginning[8] and is clearly the naked (42,70), harmless (68) tiger that left no tracks in the courtyard at Sharon's cousins' (71). He tells Sharon that, having fallen in the muck, he was yellow and black (122) like the Caribs with whom he was running deep into the forest. He did not shrink, like Peet, from the dismemberment suffered by his historical ancestors. On the contrary, he submitted to it, and this symbolical "splitting" emptied him of all that he was prior to his rebirth. He was made whole again by the Caribs' Shaman, who gave him the tiger skin he (Cristo) is wearing as a reward for his moral victory. This visionary version of his ordeal complements the more prosaic one in which he simply killed the female tiger that ripped his cheek; it is a good example of the way in which vision frees the trials of the past from their merely destructive effect and discovers in them a spiritual asset.

Cristo's reappearance in the region coincides with the end of a period of drought. He is now the "universal bridegroom of love" (85), and his earthly and "divine" roles coalesce in the poetic image of the tiger. This image also symbolizes the marriage between the earth and the moon and the illumination or coming to consciousness heralded in the phenomenal world:

The moon stood high overhead. Its full radiance had been intercepted by the forest so that the light which still fell and painted stripes and bars under the trees was purplish and vague and blue.
   A branch in the air suddenly cracked like a pistol-shot, broke and descended, ripping open a shaft and a window, along which the thwarted flower of the moon now bloomed in a mysterious bulb of fulfilment in a dark confused room. (85)

Like the peacock in the Quartet's first novel, the tiger is a dynamic symbol of harmony evoking the never-ending process of life and death: "Dark and light, light and dark: all stripes" (124); the tiger's skin is a symbol of wholeness, the concrete form of the "whole armour of God" that Cristo deserves when he overcomes his self-division and fear of death.

The moon imagery is closely linked with the tiger symbol since, in conjunction with the sea and the earth, the moon expresses the tigerishness of the phenomenal world and its own light partakes of the animal's nature. Cristo first appears to the hallucinated Peet "with an incandescent flame and eye . . . the colour of the skin was blue as one of the shadows of the moon" (59). From then on and as long as he remains hidden in the forest Cristo is to Peet at once the tiger and "the man in the moon" whom Peet fears as a reminder of his weakness

(91,93). Any particular exegesis of the poetic image of "the man in the moon" will perhaps seem irrelevant. Still, it seems to me that (though rooted in the concrete universe) it conveys the subjective and "other-worldly" experience undergone by Cristo in the jungle. During those forty days while he was thought to be dead he discovered the reverse side of reality, the death his ancestors went through in their dismemberment, and he also saw in those ancestors the unreclaimed part of the community. Significantly, Sharon too is said to be in the moon (89,101) after she has heard "the brooding voices of the past mingling with apprehensions of the future" (102) and has joined Cristo in the forest. When she is able to see her father in a new spirit of compassion, she perceives him "in the moon's blue effulgent eye" (85), free from his sense of guilt and at last appeased. The association between the moon and a "living" death finds some support in traditional religious symbolism.[9] The moon, which dies itself and is reborn after three days, is an obvious symbol of resurrection, transformation, and growth such as Cristo experiences. That it is linked with his rebirth becomes obvious when he envisions his coming execution and sees the trapdoor opening on the "Dawn on the moon" (126).

I have suggested that Cristo's symbolical dismemberment in the forest and Sharon's annihilation bring them back to their origins by compelling them to recognize their ancestry. Characteristically, it is their physical environment that unites them with their forebears. Several times in the narrative real community has been represented by a tree (see, among others, 65,72,74), and as Sharon and Cristo make their way back to the house, "the smell of a mingling of roots and leaves and branches [was] all turning into a web of cognition that entered their blood" (98). This identification with the land and its historical inhabitants enables Cristo to tell Sharon: "we've begun to see ourselves in the earlier grass-roots . . . We're reborn into the oldest native and into our oldest nature while [our parents] are still Guyana's first aliens and arrivals" (114). And further:

There's a whole world of branches and sensation we've missed, and we've got to start again from the roots up even if they look like nothing. Blood, sap, flesh, veins, arteries, lungs, heart, the heartland, Sharon. *We're the first potential parents who can contain the ancestral house.* (115 – 116, Harris's italics)

The young people's maturity and their identification with the land and its early inhabitants replace the surface strength and cohesiveness of their elders. When Magda reappears, the roles are reversed: "The magical identity and heredity had departed" (132); the potential community is now in Sharon and Cristo.

Since the first visitation of the tiger on the foreshore of Jigsaw Bay the action, whether lived or imagined by one character, seems to have followed the movement of the sea, gathering momentum, then subsiding momentarily to return with greater energy. In Book IV the conversation between Sharon and Cristo provides a long pause when time itself seems to have stopped to give him some respite. However convincing Cristo's analysis of his own conversion in that conversation, its didacticism is perhaps too obvious. This is the only place in the Quartet in which the author appears to speak through the mouth of his protagonist. Cristo's new outlook is a further development of the gradual psychological change first noticed in Mattias: it is more articulate and significant, but his own rendering of it compares unfavorably with Mattias's intuitive discovery of unsuspected resources in himself under the pressure of the wake. It is probably this didactic section that elicited from one critic the comment that *The Whole Armour* is "Harris's most obviously political novel to date."[10] Harris suggests, however, that no political solution will redeem the community. When Cristo says "Nobody *need* carry a self-righteous political chip when the only slave-driver we've had is ourselves" (115), his plea is to the effect that politics cannot redeem history or be a substitute for the self-knowledge that must precede regeneration. His faith is in the individual: "*Now* is the time to make a new-born stand, Sharon, you and me" (116), and his behavior confirms Harris's unashamedly spiritual alternative: "[the burden] of a total perceptive responsibility belonged only to the shadow of atonement in the Saviour of Mankind" (110).

The conclusion is not, I think, that Harris subscribes to the recurring pattern of sacrifice imposed on innocent men by their insensitive fellow beings. Sacrifice too is a double-edged action in his fiction. It can be performed and even accepted by the victim as an inexorable ritual meant to placate whatever gods one believes in. But genuine sacrifice involves a surrender of all the trappings of personality in a spirit of compassion and humility. In order to be creative it entails a voluntary reduction to what is vulnerable and frail. Cristo is clearly a victim of "the lust of the law" (101), of the people's still-vivid hunter's instinct (focused now in the police), and of their need to punish someone for the violence they are unable to eradicate from themselves. He is also a victim of their inhumanity: Mattias's father is heartbroken after his son's death, yet he still exacts the death of another young man. But Cristo's attitude modifies the meaning of the sentence passed on him. By submitting to the law instead of escaping, he makes a free, responsible choice. He does not reject the ordinary world of men, because it is in and through that world alone that he can perceive the "immaterial and elusive" (130) reality of which the legacy of the past is so essential a part. Admittedly, he cannot be sure that his and Sharon's changed outlook will be much more perceptible than the "miraculous dawning frailty" (99) in nature to which the people of the region have not yet awakened. While waiting, between life and death, for his arrest and inevitable execution, "his mind was so empty it had become a frame for the future" (129). So the "future" lies in the individual human mind and its always-renewable capacity to create. Cristo is now utterly free of the trammels of his earthly life and has reached the utmost stage of consciousness accessible to man, the double vision by which he transforms the sanction of human law even before its "implacable strokes" have fallen on him. The immediate future will bring the reassertion of an inescapable division—the birth of his son in time and the timeless progress of his spirit toward making "its declaration to all the other spirits of light" (111). Spiritual freedom and consciousness are once again presented as man's main purpose, a prerequisite to the forming of authentic community. In this intrusion of the spiritual upon the social Harris clearly sees the redeeming feature of the sacrifice men are always prepared to impose on whatever Christ is among them.

Chapter Four

The Immaterial Constitution:
The Secret Ladder

The Secret Ladder centers on the confrontation between Russell Fenwick, a government surveyor, and Poseidon, and old farmer and fisherman who rules over the few survivors of a tribe of runaway slaves. Fenwick and his multiracial crew, an unruly body of men, have come to measure the average flow of the Canje River prior to the construction of a reservoir that will irrigate the East Indian coastal plantations but will also drown Poseidon's poor land. An unusual spell of drought delays the completion of their task, and Fenwick is faced with the problem of keeping in hand his increasingly troublesome men while coming to terms with Poseidon, who tries to sabotage his work. Things come to a head when Poseidon is accidentally killed by Bryant, an African like him and the only member of the crew who worships the old man, seeing in him his spiritual grandfather. Embittered by the death of their ruler, the villagers decide to bring Bryant and Catalena, his mistress, to trial. As the night wears on and their despair increases, they even make up their minds to kill their two prisoners. Bryant and Catalena are saved *in extremis* by the return of the two messengers who had been sent to fetch the instruments of the law. They believe they have killed one of the crew, and the villagers, thinking the jungle police will turn up, take to flight without even burying their dead leader.

While bringing together the themes of the earlier novels (the unity of mankind, possession and dispossession, the nature of freedom and responsibility, of innocence and guilt) *The Secret Ladder* explores the meaning of authority, another value that Harris deems essential to the creation of a new community. This novel counterpoints in many ways the voyage of self-discovery described in *Palace of the Peacock,* in which the ancient folk move further and further into the heartland. Poseidon's tribe, on the contrary, have become fixed physically on their barren land and psychologically in their condition of victim and must be retrieved on both levels from their underground world. In the first novel Donne and the crew reach fulfillment by *ascending* the waterfall toward heaven and the folk. In the later one the confined world of the Canje, in which Fenwick moves toward Poseidon, is repeatedly described as "hell"; each surveying trip entails a *descent* into unstable ground and shakes Fenwick's former convictions.

The complementariness of the two novels is further exemplified in the self-realization specific to each protagonist. Once he begins to ascend the waterfall Donne's visionary task is a reconstruction of the "structure" supporting the material world; Fenwick's much more tentative vision is made possible by a stripping of veils which enables him to catch a glimpse of that structure. The world he lives in is more dense, not reduced to its essential elements as in *Palace of the Peacock,* and he is himself a more fully conceived character than Donne, an ordinary man concerned as much with the physical comfort of his men as with the motives behind their behavior. They too are solid characters but also personae in his consciousness. He must struggle with their various attitudes as with so many forms of deception to be discarded. Once again the narrative develops on several planes. Fenwick's thoughts and emotions as well as the crew's seem to radiate from one many-levelled consciousness that Fenwick charts as he charts the headwaters of the Canje. His encounter with Poseidon in the course of his surveying work confronts him with a tangible evidence of the most deeply buried element of Guyanese history, slavery, which, he realizes, is a monster he and the men of his generation must still learn to face.

The usual correspondence in Harris's narrative between landscape and man is illustrated in a masterly way through variations on a few basic images. One of them, the river, links Fenwick's task with earlier explorations of Guyana in the Quartet:

He liked to think of all the rivers of Guiana as the curious rungs in a ladder on which one sets one's musing foot again and again, to climb into both the past and the future of the continent of mystery. . . . The Canje was one of the lowest rungs in the ladder of ascending purgatorial rivers, the blackest river one could imagine. (152)

Unlike the nameless river in *Palace of the Peacock,* the Canje seems hardly to move, yet is no less threatening since its apparent immobility not only covers unseen dangers but is a sign of arrested life such as Jordan, Fenwick's cook, embodies:

He pointed to the river which scarcely appeared to flow in the late afternoon light like a snake whose motion had been reined into graver stillness than ever and embalmed for good. (159)

The barely moving river reflects a deep-seated conservatism in the crew (manifested in Jordan's stark opposition to hope and progress) and in Poseidon, who rejects integration in modern society. The old leader has lived for so long in the jungle that he is hardly distinguishable from its elements. At their first meeting Fenwick observes him with wonder "as if he saw down a bottomless gauge and river of reflection" (155). "Bottomless gauge" and "river of reflection" suggest that Poseidon is a static mirror concealing nevertheless unknown depths to be surveyed by Fenwick. This meeting seems to have been long delayed ("He could no longer escape a reality that had always escaped him" [155]); though it is followed by a shower of rain, the apparent forerunner of fertile change, dryness soon prevails again. Like his Greek namesake, Poseidon can be a source of both fertility and drought and it is mainly this latter capacity that he shares with the crew.

The crew are divided into day readers and night readers of the gauge installed by Fenwick to measure the heights and depths of the river. Throughout Book I (*The Day Readers*) the prevailing drought, as much an inner as an outer phenomenon, coincides with the manifestation among the crew of their worst impulses and prejudices. The malaise that oppresses Fenwick is enhanced by his inability to point to its source with any accuracy and by the restlessness and suppressed violence he discerns in the crew. Jordan contributes more than a little to the stifling atmosphere of the camp. Equally merciless toward the crew and Poseidon, whom he would expel from his long-tenanted territory by calling in the jungle police, he advocates the letter of the law and does not hesitate, under its cover or in the name of order, to recommend oppression. Jordan (alias Gorgon) is the head cut off from the body and the heart of the community and a stubborn obstacle to their reunification. Fenwick has for some time found it convenient to shelter beind Jordan's "mask of stone" and his authoritarian manners instead of attempting to create a genuinely human bond with the crew. As a result the men "camouflage" their complaint, and the general distrust increases. Similarly, the meaning of Poseidon's complaint is withheld from Fenwick although he is greatly disturbed by the old man. As a government agent, Fenwick is naturally bound to be looked upon as an oppressor by the villagers, and it makes him uneasy to realize that he is a tool of oppression, just as he is perturbed by Weng's assertion that he (Weng) has modelled his severity with the crew on Fenwick's own. It confirms the surveyor in his suspicion that Weng, the merciless hunter, has so far acted as his own doppelgänger, a fact he had perceived intuitively and with great alarm just before their conversation started. Weng had come upon him suddenly and for a moment a trick of the light gave Fenwick the illusion that Weng's reflection on the river was actually his own (175).

Exposure, erosion, and dismemberment offer other examples of analogy between natural phenomena and psychological truths. All three are a source of frustration but offer a possibility of change and renewal through Fenwick's attempted dialogue with the "sacred" reality they bring to light. Whether accidental and resented or accepted as necessary (see Fenwick's "loss of face" [193, 231]), exposure runs counter to man's obsessive need for shelter from the often frightening business of living which makes Fenwick use Jordan and his interpretation of the law as a shield. At the beginning of the novel, just after he has heard the complaining voices of his men die away, Fenwick sees them approaching in the clearing:

The sun shone through dark flesh to illuminated skeleton, the greenest garment to the whitest bone.

It was this sensation of exposure and defeat, amounting to confusion, one experienced standing in the clearing. . . . (143)

The crew's fear of exposure (of revealing their inner self) is mainly a fear of being taken advantage of, as Jordan makes clear to Fenwick when he tells him "They [the crew] see naked sentiment on you brow and they get afraid at once you might be exposing them. . . . "(215). Final exposure is experienced by Catalena, stripped naked and made vulnerable by Poseidon's followers (see 255), and it is through her, the "muse of community," that Fenwick symbolically reaches a painful state of bareness, the ultimate and necessary stage in his shedding of the biased attitudes in himself that are also embodied in the crew. For Poseidon too exposure (or, as Fenwick says, the "resurrection of the buried community" he represents) involves the erosion of a diehard self-protective posture. Erosion is characteristic of the Canje area; even the higher land near the riverhead is "uncertain ground . . . continuously threatened by an erosive design eating slowly across the river's catchment"(152). Once more Harris makes remarkable use of a region's topography to convey a psychological reality. Fenwick first discovers that "Every tributary had buried its grassy head in a grave of wilderness"(152); then he realizes that owing to a "misconception" based on deceptive air photographs the head of the Canje's main tributary, the Kaboyary, appears to be cut off from its body:

In the savannahs, he had discovered, the Kaboyary had lost its original banks, and its watershed, too, had been swamped and eroded. . . . No wonder an empirical hiatus or gulf existed, to a bird's-eye view, severing the river's head from its trunk and feet. . . . The mysterious foundation of intelligence, the unity of head and heart had become for him, Fenwick knew, an inescapable obsession. (173−174)

The geographical and psychological dismemberment Fenwick reads in the river is the objective equivalent of a subjective vision conveyed by his dream of a decapitated white mare (see 164−165). The two images evoke the dismemberment of the Guyanese community, whose original founders (the former slaves now living at the riverhead) are ignored and cut off from the main body. But this dismemberment also prefigures the decapitation of the Gorgon, a sign that a petrified situation is being modified by qualities of the heart (Perseus'?[1]).

From the first, Fenwick senses in Poseidon a catalyst, the "new divine promise" (164) that will counteract Jordan's "Medusalike" influence on the crew. Through Fenwick's discovery of the divine in Poseidon Harris makes it clearer than ever before that the divine is, in his eyes, a hidden, mysterious dimension in the human and that he associates it with the frail but undying victims suppressed from, or buried in, one's consciousness. Characteristically, Fenwick sees a god in Poseidon when he is most sensitive to the vulnerable man in him:

"I confess I owe allegiance to him because of his condition, allegiance of an important kind, that of conscience, of the rebirth of humanity. . . . It is the kind a man gives to a god." (183)

When he reaches Poseidon's house after his trying climb over the Gorgon's neck, a fallen tree "wreathed by creepers and snakes of vine" (197) recalling "an old Gorgon's head" (206), he is struck by its contrasting features (solid though disintegrating, foreign and native, ideal and primitive) and perceives in the *crumbling* human abode a "depth more lasting than time . . . the stamp of a multiple tradition" (200). "Tradition" is at once the expression of the endurance that links Poseidon with the gods and a stumbling block in Fenwick's attempt to create a dialogue with him. For Fenwick is not blind to Poseidon's ambivalence. The old leader's continued and voluntary burial in the Canje region and the static order of life it has engendered have made him into "an old monster of deception" (164) for the crew, who either deny him and his followers and are taken by surprise when accumulated feelings of resentment erupt and strike back at them, or turn him into an idol as Bryant does, thereby confirming him unwittingly in his state of self-oppression. In both cases deception leads to what Fenwick calls a "misconception" of the African. Poseidon, however, protests in the name of an illusory freedom since it has only served him to withdraw into a primitive condition from which he refuses to move, perpetuating the effects of "catastrophe and fate" (184) that had sent his ancestors to the Canje two hundred years before. This is where Poseidon and his followers differ from the folk in *Palace of the Peacock*. Harris shows here that the victim status can become a tool of oppression of both self and others (as Poseidon's followers oppress Bryant and Catalena) in the same way as the victor exploits both his victim and himself.

Analyzing Poseidon's condition in a letter to his mother, Fenwick explains that at the time of the abolition of slavery something went wrong and no real freedom was attained. Like Cristo in *The Whole Armour*, Fenwick is in fact proposing an alternative to what was then a *political* failure when he says "the issue for me is *fundamental and psychological*"(171, italics mine). It is an alternative that involves the individual rather than the state; hence the impact of his personal sense of guilt. His emphasis on *"misconceive"* (171) when he points to the danger of misconceiving the African also throws light on the nature of his approach, for conception as a corrective to misconception rests on imagination, consciousness, and intelligence whose "mysterious foundation," Fenwick says, is "the unity of head and heart" (173). Poseidon is still "the emotional dynamic of liberation" (171) his forebears had been, not, however, through the "blind emotional tide of excess" (184) he had first aroused in Fenwick through Bryant, but because reduced as he is to a state of human nakedness and deprived of the apparel that usually hides man's essential being, he has moved Fenwick to recognize in him this fundamental reality. There are frequent references in the novel to what Fenwick sees as the "parody[2] of a universal and uncapturable essence" (246) which the various forms of exposure, erosion, and dismemberment in Book I have enabled him to glimpse. By the end of Book I, facing Poseidon's house, he is able to interpret the visionary dismantlement in which he is now fully engaged and which complements the creation in *Palace of the Peacock:*

The seven beads of the original creation had been material days of efflorescence and bloom to distinguish their true material character. But now the very opposite realities of freedom were being chosen (not phenomena of efflorescence but shells and skeletons) to distinguish an immaterial constitution (which after all was the essential legitimacy of all creation). (206)

The "naked design" he has discovered earlier and the "immaterial constitution" partake of the spiritual tradition within and beyond all material existence that Fenwick has recognized in Poseidon's house, and it is from this tradition that he wants to develop his new conception of authority.

In Book II (*The Night Readers*) it appears that the kind of authority Fenwick now wants to wield cannot be the tool of a rigid institution but grows out of his awareness of "the spirit of the law" (258). When Jordan tries to persuade him not to fire Perez, who has gambled away Catalena, his wife, Fenwick is firm for the first time ("I've got an intuition now—the kind I can't withstand" [212]) and draws his strength from his intuitive perception of what is sacred in human beings and cannot be gambled with by individuals or the power they represent. The first effect of his insight into what Poseidon stands for is a change in his attitude toward the crew with whom he now deals directly and treats with more discrimination. If he is more strict with Perez, he is also more generous and humane toward Chiung, to whom he gives his own coat and helmet, an act that will unexpectedly force him through a new frightening though fruitful disorientation. The day readers' work in Book I has exposed their self-deception and led to Fenwick's confrontation with Poseidon, giving him an intuition of the old man's double nature. The night readers, Chiung particularly, bring to the surface their own (and Fenwick's) darker impulses and teach him to "read" his own personality.

Fenwick's cosmic reverie at the beginning of chapter 6 extends his discovery of the "immaterial constitution," making him feel that he too is one of the elements in space linked to all others by invisible threads and stamped with the "loftiest tradition" (224) discernible in Poseidon's house. However, after he has experienced "the poetic frenzy and delirium of a god"(223), his elation suddenly shrivels up when he discovers Chiung apparently dead at his feet. Fenwick is now unsettled by reactions he would not have thought himself capable of, which shows that he can be deluded in the same way as Poseidon and can combine, like him, the essence of a godlike nature with the most primitive instinct for sheer physical survival. The hidden energy— both active and passive—associated earlier with Poseidon and the landscape over which he rules now rises in Fenwick and shakes him:

the black Canje foamed and bristled and encircled a revolving purpose and propeller somewhere *in the vague region under his feet*.(152, italics mine)

it signified the resurrection of Poseidon . . . whose flight from slavery had ended right here, in the ground, *under one's feet*. (175, italics mine)
Fenwick was filled by a dark wave of uncontrollable panic which rose out of the black river *under his feet*. (224, italics mine)

The first two sentences are quoted from Book I and suggest respectively the existence of an unknown threatening force under Fenwick's feet in the river (which is also the river of his unconscious) and the trapped condition Poseidon wishes to perpetuate. In the third sentence the panic rising from under Fenwick's feet confronts him with the specter of his own unfreedom. He sees immediately that Chiung has been mistaken for himself since he was wearing Fenwick's coat:

His mind had turned into a sieve out of which everything fled save the mystique of selfish relief. The sensation of involuntary freedom was as automatic as the reflexes of panic and the springs which had moved his feet. (225)

By equating "the mystique of selfish relief" (the only sensation Fenwick experiences) with "involuntary freedom" (as opposed to freedom consciously and painfully achieved) Harris draws attention to the limitations of the sense of freedom experienced by those who are spared the torments imposed on the oppressed. When his spell of blind self-preoccupation is over, Fenwick becomes engaged in an uncompromising confrontation with himself. Much as he would like to move and run from the scene of his humiliation, he cannot; his feet "[grow] cold as stone," and this fixity seems to exteriorize his instinct for self-preservation, which, he now discovers, is as strong in himself as in the Canje "primitives." It is also this instinct that he must fight in the crew, who have responded to his call and who would go to war against Chiung's assailants in the name of their own will to survive. The whole scene is a dramatization of the inner struggle that eventually frees Fenwick from the prejudices represented by the crew. In his precarious and vulnerable position on the stelling platform just above the water, he feels threatened as Poseidon must have felt, though unlike him, Fenwick agrees to the dissolution of his earlier convictions and accepts the painful uncertainty it arouses in him. As he struggles toward a deeper consciousness, his inner state is reflected in the light his torch throws on Chiung (his unconscious?) at his feet: "the temperamental switch [of the torch]" (224), "the cowardly torch" (225), and "a disordered nervous beam" (225). Release comes when Chiung (who was merely stunned), pressed by Fenwick, gets rid of "the plaster of hypocrisy."

The alternation, in the scene, between Fenwick's conscious intro-spection and Chiung's barely articulate and hesitant account of what happened shows that their two contrasting approaches to the discov-ery of truth are complementary and necessary. The story told by Chiung (who admits he is guilty of the theft that provoked the wrath of Poseidon's followers) is like a re-enactment of the conflict that has set the surveying team in opposition to Poseidon. The question here is not one of right or wrong since both parties are wrong in some way and they could be drawn into an endless chain of vengeful acts; it is primarily one of self-knowledge, as Chiung's difficult self-revelation shows. Like Weng, he is one of Fenwick's alter egos and his con-fession, the deeper meaning of which escapes him but not Fenwick, gives the surveyor a glimpse of the depths registered on the bottom-less gauge of his consciousness.

Book III, *The Reading*, develops out of the juxtaposition of *The Day Readers* with *The Night Readers* and confirms Jordan's inability to be of further use to Fenwick. The latter now turns to the "insubstantial models or witnesses" (239) he had summoned from his deeper self when he cried out in panic after discovering Chiung unconscious on the stelling. The suggestion is that his inner being is peopled with these "hallucinated ghosts" (the ghosts of his and Guyana's past) whom he saw "when he flashed the light of his thought" (240). He now questions them, as it were, through the agency first of Van Brock, delirious with malaria, then of Bryant and Catalena, who have just returned after her own delirious torment at the hands of Poseidon's followers.

The reading takes the form of an inquiry which yields not so much definite answers as a method of interpreting experience and therefore is a conclusion to the Quartet as a whole. On first meeting Poseidon, Fenwick had been unable to read a meaning in the movements of his lips, but after his final rejection of Jordan (the storekeeper of a rigid past) he finds he has grown better "at reading the constitution of another man's lips" (241). The rain has begun to fall, erasing the marks of drought and leaving "a clean but cracked slate" (239), an indication that the past is not wiped out but has been "displaced" because revived and given new significance by the living. This is the point of the apparently irrelevant story told by Van Brock, who has involuntarily killed his grandmother (as Bryant kills his "grandfather" in Poseidon) though the old woman really dies of the death ("decapitation") of memory. Her golden ring, lost by her grandson — a dual symbol of love and possession which recalls the theme of *Palace* — is her only link with a vanished past. By recovering it from the swamp in which she is to be buried and restoring it to her finger, Van Brock turns her grave into a womb, for his act of love brings her back to life in his consciousness.

For Bryant, on the contrary, killing Poseidon signifies the death of his hopes of recognition by his ancestor. He does not understand any more than Poseidon's followers that the old god was a catalyst to a new age and could, as Fenwick sensed, lead to "a threshold of consciousness" that is equally "the ground of self-contempt and idolatry" (193). In these words Harris expresses a concept that is fundamental to his whole work, namely, that any experience (such as meeting Poseidon) can either deceive or be a source of vision and that the material world is the only door to a consciousness of the reality that informs it or to a "reading" of the "immaterial constitution." The reading can never be final nor wholly reliable since, as Fenwick suggests, "every material image" as well as "the conception of a supporting canvas" (man's understanding of what informs appearances, see 239) are basically untrustworthy. Put differently:

The pure paint of love scarcely dries on a human canvas without a modicum of foreign dust entering and altering every subtle colour and emotional tone, which affects the painter as well as the painted property of life. . . . (247)

I have already suggested that Harris associates the sacred or the divine with the suppressed and unacknowledged victims of men's ambitions. When Poseidon dies (having completed his inspiring mission) his role is taken over by Catalena, despoiled by Poseidon's followers turned oppressors. Like Poseidon, she is now "weak" yet "indestructible," "a naked spirit," and the same "expiring breath" runs over her lips as ran over Poseidon's when he fell (254—55). Her weakness, however, is, as with Van Brock's grandmother, a channel for rebirth. The manner of her release (the unexpected chain of events set up by Fenwick's generosity to Chiung) implies that the basest motives (the twins' cupidity and wrath) can save, whereas the loftiest (such as Bryant's unbounded love for Poseidon) can kill or destroy. More important still, it shows that an unpredictable element can always release a frozen situation (see the "crash" in Harris's later novels). Poseidon's disciples intended "to execute a picture of the void" (257), i.e., to bury Bryant and Catalena together with Poseidon and the instruments of the law, thus obliterating the actors of an attempted dialogue (for Bryant had been sent to Poseidon on a mission of conciliation). Instead of burying their own past and its unrecognized inheritors (Bryant and Catalena who are phantoms to them as they themselves are phantoms to Fenwick), they decide to flee and are set in motion again, vanishing once more into the heartland:

The law could not be buried, nor given to the dust. There were always copies and current records (since mankind began) of the covenant time would have stopped to imprison. No one could force a void in the spirit of the law even with an act of humility or the surrender of one's land and property. Least of all by damming the ghost of responsibility. (258)

We know that by his sheer survival Poseidon has challenged Fenwick to the recognition of the moving reality behind static appearances and that Fenwick has derived his new conception of authority from that moving and *free* reality. This is the "spirit of the law" (of the covenant between god and man and therefore between man and man) in which, he says, no void can be forced because this spiritual essence can never be completely eradicated:

The instant the prison of the void was self-created, a breath of spirit knew how to open a single unconditional link in a chain of circumstance. (258)

In other words, the self-created "prison of the void" or annihilation by man of what is most essential in himself, i.e., the consciousness of his relatedness to past and future generations, cannot stop this dynamic spiritual reality from breaking through and revealing itself.

This philosophical conclusion is directly relevant to the concern with West Indian history implied in the passage from T.S. Eliot's "Little Gidding" used as an epigraph to Book III. Harris is saying that the so-called void of West Indian history is self-created, and he has shown that the crew and the descendants of runaway slaves alike were prepared to create their own "historylessness." The conflict between Fenwick and Poseidon's followers is not resolved since their fear puts them to flight and remains an obstacle to change. The very fact that these survivors of Guyana's early history disappear again into a landscape that Fenwick sees as the necessary ground of exploration (a theme further developed in *Heartland*) shows that they remain an elusive element of Guyana's population with whom those who seek to define themselves as Guyanese must still come to terms. To such a quest there can be no final conclusion. From Poseidon, "the grand old man of [Guyanese] history" (170), have risen "the silent accents of an ageless dumb spirit" (156). The distress of obscure men spoken in those silent accents, rather than the grand feats of recorded history, is for Harris the inheritance of a people and must be investigated. His quest reaches further than Guyana. Doesn't Poseidon's name link him with the origins of another civilization and even with primitive humanity as a whole? Allowing imagination to qualify the technologist's task, Fenwick has gone through a disintegration of established habits of thought and experienced the insecurity of that primitive condition. The only certainty that the Quartet offers—that of the existence of the invisible folk among the crew—has been reached at the end of *Palace of the Peacock.* The last paragraph of the Quartet, brings together the ascent toward the folk described in the first novel and the "immortal descent" (Poseidon's?) that has enabled Fenwick to enquire into Poseidon's role in his own consciousness. This paragraph looks backward to the creation of the Guyanese soul in *Palace* and forward to the unending quest for that soul described in the following novels. In this respect too—and not merely in the dawn of Fenwick's more fluid consciousness—the beginning is in the end.

Chapter Five

Between Two Worlds: *Heartland*

Heartland has received little critical attention although it is an essential fragment of the "infinite canvas"[1] of Harris's opus. It can be seen as a novel of transition which unexpectedly revives characters from the Quartet. Also the main character, Stevenson, stands midway between Fenwick and the narrator in *The Eye of the Scarecrow* in that his "drama of consciousness" is stimulated by events and characters outside himself, while (like characters in the later novels) he becomes a vessel in which the past is re-enacted and modified as "vision" increases; in which also the tension between life and death plays itself out continually in different shapes.

After a reversal of fortune Stevenson has come to the heartland to work as a watchman for the government. He was working for a company headed by his father when the accountant ran off with a large sum of money. The accountant's young wife, Maria, was Stevenson's mistress and she too disappeared suddenly. Although Stevenson was innocent (or thought he was), he was saved from a charge of conspiracy by the sacrifice of his father, who repaid the stolen money, then died in an accident that looked very much like a disguised suicide.

After the "crash" Stevenson began to lose his self-assurance. But not until his terror at being thought guilty mingles with his terror at being alone in the jungle, does he start on the introspective adventure that turns his watch over the jungle into self-examination and self-judgment. Under the impact of his terror Stevenson's eyes open to the greatness of his father's sacrifice, and only then does he experience the reality of his father's death as if it were his own. At the same time he sees that the flight of his mistress is genuine only when he loses his inner certainty, for she is not only "the muse of the soul" (27) but the soul itself. That he should be able to experience and "re-sense" her flight and his father's death shows these two individuals to be part of the "community of being" each man carries within and belongs to outside himself. The quest they generate is for the meaning of death and its relation to life or for the reverse side of life and its mystery.

At the beginning of the novel Stevenson's growing insecurity takes him to Kaiser, the caretaker of the heartland depot. Significantly, Stevenson's three encounters in the jungle are with characters who either died or vanished in Harris's first two novels: Kaiser, daSilva and the Amerindian woman Petra. Their reappearance illustrates Harris's conception of death as a passage into an "ever-living present." Kaiser, who was burned to death and "resurrected" as a woodcutter in *The Far Journey*, combines the frailty with the endurance of humanity. His survival and the peace of mind he has achieved testify to the persistence and the gradual transformation of the substance of suffering and anxiety into understanding. While the earlier novels expressed the need to bring to light and redeem the errors of the past, *Heartland* shows the process of atonement taking place. DaSilva has survived the trials of the crew in *Palace of the Peacock* to expiate the murder of Cameron. In *Palace* he was clearly his brother's shadow or doppelgänger, "a reporter who has returned from the grave."[2] Now he tells Stevenson: .

"I turning into the ghost of the reporter of the *one* court of conscience after all—comprising nobody else but the mystery of me (or you) . . . DaSilva. DaSilva . . . Stevenson. Stevenson." (44)

Through the repetition of their names daSilva suggests that each man has two selves, one of which might be the disturbing, invisible presence in the heartland. Their conversation (38−44) contains hints to the effect that Stevenson is exploring an inner world (in Harris's words "a climate of the mind") as well as moving toward a purgatory in which daSilva, like Virgil for Dante, serves him as a guide. It may be objected that this is an unlikely role for a poor, shadowy porkknocker[3] to assume, although pork-knockers are apparently known for their speculative turn-of-mind. But daSilva is precisely one of the humble who are ignored in ordinary life and, for this very reason, whom Harris associates with the neglected inner self or with the dead. Both daSilva and Kaiser offer Stevenson the wisdom of the folk, which the old Arawak woman represented in the eyes of the crew in *Palace*. In *Heartland* the legendary names of this original crew "were becoming their own shadowy essence at last" (43) as if daSilva's trial and "self-judgement" ("I was condemn to remain back . . . like if I was jury and judge over myself all rolled in one" [43]) were transforming the tensions of history into wisdom.

That the refinement of digested experience into spiritual fulfillment adds to the mysterious content of the heartland depot will appear when Stevenson's own trial takes place. When he decides to face his ordeal, however, he feels like a gambler "with visionary resources" (21). The key to Kaiser's depot is "the paradoxical key of all substance" (21), and Stevenson fears that "there might be nothing at all within the storehouse of the heartland" (28). In other words, his fear, partly due at first to a selfish concern for his reputation, becomes a metaphysical angst arising from the possibility that he might be gambling his future on a nonexistent reward. To find an answer to the fundamental question "Is there anyone or anything in the heartland?" is the real purpose of Stevenson's watch. As might be expected, the jungle is also a symbolic heartland. But rather than develop simultaneously on two planes, the narrative shifts from the material to the spiritual and sometimes shows Stevenson struggling between the two. He and Kaiser are the "watched" of Book II. However, both watchers and watched play either role. Stevenson is constantly aware of another unseen presence watching him. Petra, who has obviously been watching Stevenson, feels watched and threatened by unseen pursuers. DaSilva, on the other hand, does not doubt there is an unseen potential interlocutor[4] in the jungle and anticipates Stevenson's inquiry by asking who or what the other might be.

In response to that unseen presence Stevenson feels urged to explore roads previously unknown to him. The first time this happens he is on the point of opening the depot when he hears a branch crack underfoot and is led into a gloomy corridor in search of a possible trespasser. This dark portage is a ground of invasion and flight, for he follows in the wake of ancient tribes who have successively penetrated the heartland and been torn by the same doubts as modern prospectors:

"The golden age they wished to find—the Palace of the Peacock— may never have existed for all anyone knew" (31). Stevenson loses his way and is trapped in the undergrowth of his own emotions and fears. His struggle to free himself from the rock-like "hand of death" (32) is a struggle between "form and being, matter and spirit" (32), con- trasts which, perceptible in the phenomenal world itself, betoken the existential enigma he must unravel. His penetration of the heartland is toward a frontier of existence where life and death meet. This becomes clearer when he follows the "ancient line" toward the depot after his boat has disappeared, and the necessity to venture again "into an interior where one saw oneself turned inside out" (48) makes him conscious of the purpose of his march and the obstacles he must overcome:

It was the selfish fear of experiencing fear, the selfish love of the possession of love one was being summoned to . . . see through by abiding to a . . . refusal to shrink from . . . the demoralizing contact and content of death. (48)

On this second occasion Stevenson is involved in a "primitive ordeal of initiation" (51) and although he walks against the "harden- ing . . . arteries of the bush," "a fluid passage" (a sign of movement and life) remains which makes "new communication, even communi- ty" (51) possible. Significantly, his own physical reactions to his sense of another presence bring forth a response to the steps he has taken toward "the *contact* of death"; it is a response from

the intimate forest of *relations* like an army on the march branching to enlist him after their aeons of stubborn withdrawal from *human contact*. (52, italics mine)

As he advances further toward the lower station following daSilva, whose rations have been stolen from the depot, Stevenson's eyes "grow sharper than a needle" and "his emotions [fall] into step within him upon a meaningful thread of being" (56). When Stevenson faces death in daSilva, who has fallen into a giant chasm between two boulders, he reads the potentiality of "being" in the fusion between life and death incurred by daSilva (58).

From his first to his second experience of death (his father's and daSilva's), Stevenson has progressed between two worlds epitomized by "the light and the shadow" (13), or meeting in "the everlasting green vault [as] half-night, half-day" (29) until after daSilva's death the creation of the watch begins "between the death of morning and the birth of afternoon, between individual darkness and light" (62). There is also a corresponding meeting of contrasting elements in nature ("half-air, half-earth" [12]) or states ("half-monkey, half-man" [58]) which show the constant interplay of opposites within man's inner and outer world. The mysterious source at the root of these contrasts stimulates the gamble Stevenson feels he takes whenever he is faced with a fundamental choice:

Would he be confronted finally by an impossibility of escaping from himself, living or dead, or would he discover an identity of abandonment which would inform him and sometimes lead him like his own shadow into the subtlest realization of time? (21)

"Identity of abandonment" is a key phrase in the passage (and in Harris's fiction generally) for it describes the self-surrender Stevenson must achieve, not to one of two things but to a fluid state that allows for the free play of the two. At the end of Book II he has made some progress toward the renunciation of one-sided assertions when he recognizes the contrasting possibilities inherent in each situation:

He was beginning to look into the obscurity he had once turned away from as if he now knew . . . that every climate of terror and essential clearing of security were actually the same umbrella, capable of providing spiritual cover or becoming equally another inhospitable material pole. (55–56)

As in *The Secret Ladder*, the juxtaposition of contrasting states (*The Watchers* and *The Watched*) gives rise to a dynamic process issuing from the two. When Stevenson reaches Kaiser's depot, Petra, the Amerindian woman, appears. She is presented as the muse of *Palace of the Peacock*, who has now changed her name and is on the point of giving birth to a child conceived by Donne or daSilva. Her new name evokes the strength but also the fixity of rock. And indeed from the moment of her arrival she feels symbolically *pinned* to the caretaker's house as daSilva was supported within the order of place and both had become the host of a besieged mankind, needing to draw into each new flesh and blood from the helpful herd and pack. (65, italics mine)

This sentence introduces one of several motifs adumbrated in Books I and II, which now fuse to answer the question first asked by daSilva: Who and what is there to discover or "read" in the heartland (see 40)? The question itself recurs in different forms and generally implies reciprocity which is the prime mover to the "creation of the watch."

The belief that, in Kaiser's words, "man need man" (20—21) runs through the novel and is illustrated by the many instances of physical and spiritual hunger felt by Stevenson, daSilva, and Petra.[5] Although Kaiser is the official supplier and keeper of the material heartland depot, there is clearly a storehouse of spiritual resources to which the other three contribute and on which they feed. DaSilva is aware of it and tells Stevenson: "We got to nurse all our nonexistent resources to the last bitter farthing" (41). It becomes clear in Book III that this store of resources, maintained by the give and take (and the sufferings) of human intercourse is the "what" daSilva and Stevenson have tried to elucidate. At the beginning of the "creation" Petra (the muse and soul), who in *Palace* had met the need of the crew, is, as suggested above, in need of being reinvigorated for she and daSilva have long been struggling "across a faint landscape":

A faint landscape it was because of the eclipse of time, the end of a long hazardous phase of discovery and conquest. . . . This faintness was akin to a constellation of renewal and rebirth appearing, for this age and time, in the underworld sky of the jungle, and upon a horizon which coincided with the end of empires when the darkness of rule becomes the absolute light of consciousness. (66-67)

It seems therefore that a long phase of "discovery and conquest," during which the store of the heartland depot has both accrued and been eroded, is at last on the point of bearing fruit. As the crimes of the past are in process of being redeemed and daSilva is allowed to die, the heartland depot can be opened to enable Petra to give birth to the child conceived long ago. It matters little whether the crew in *Palace* was a historical or a modern one (it obviously stands for both), but it is certainly important that Stevenson, a modern Guyanese, should help bring to life the offspring born of the meeting between conqueror and conquered.[6]

The "creation of the watch" (the birth of vision or consciousness) begins to take place when Stevenson moves toward Petra (64–65). This enables her to move too and to relive her journey from the time she was sent away by the tribe, because pregnant by Donne, to the moment of her delivery. She then offers herself to be "consumed," "devoured alive," and this complete self-surrender clearly entails the birth of her child (see 70). In the same way Stevenson's self-surrender, overcoming his fear of "abandonment," must entail his own spiritual rebirth. While helping Petra give life to her child, he identifies her with Maria, his vanished mistress, so that her delivery appears as the denouement of both a historical and a personal tragedy. *"Like a numinous boulder informed by legs and arms as well as by the universal heart of man,"* Petra, no longer a static rock, is free to *"resume the journey of the past"* (71), i.e., to be on the move again as a dynamic source of inspiration fed by the experiences and sufferings of men and feeding them in return. Mutual self-surrender (hers and Stevenson's) is the answer to the "who" and "what." For they themselves (and "the other" within each of them) are the mysterious watchers (and watched) in the heartland. The "what" is what each is willing to give of himself or herself to the other. This "what," the "process of relations" (42) created by a genuine opening to "the other," gives substance to "the law," which, as we saw in *The Secret Ladder*, evokes the covenant between men. Another word for it is El Dorado as Stevenson's first impression of daSilva makes clear: "On his lips had been written such need it was almost as if the black cup were the transubstantiation of gold" (38). However, it later appears that the self-surrender implied is not as complete in Stevenson as he thinks.

Stevenson's meeting with Petra takes place on an "extreme frontier" (71), the frontier between life and death toward which he has been progressing. On his way to the depot he imagines the construction of a road that would lead to the meeting point between the two:

It was touch-and-go like fish to bait, flame to match, the essential inner and outer realities of construction, life-in-death, death-in-life. (53)

When he approaches Petra, "the banquet of reality they shared, life-in-death, death-in-life, was now finished and indivisible" (65). Death (in daSilva) seems to serve as a gateway to life: "[Stevenson] was in a position to observe daSilva as if he saw through him into [Petra's] mounting agony" (65). The birth of Stevenson's vision of consciousness described in chapter 7 stems from the juxtaposition of Petra's travail in chapter 5 with the description of daSilva's death in chapter 6, while in these two chapters their ordeals (Petra's and daSilva's) are shown to be indissociable. Before describing Stevenson's own trial, however, a few words must be said about the implications of daSilva's death.

As already mentioned, physical death in Harris's fiction does not necessarily entail the death of the spirit but rather offers it the opportunity to develop toward a maturity it was incapable of in life. After receiving a mortal blow daSilva recalls that his dog had died that he himself might be cured of a bout of fever:

This was an involuntary function death would be totally incapable of achieving if one were allowed to lock oneself away in the absolute prison of oneself. (78)

This incident gives daSilva a clue to the double question: "Who . . . did *one* happen to be, ruling whom and ruled by whom?" (78), and the episode shows that it is in the individual person that an answer must be found both to the question of identity and to the mystery of conquest or "rule." The sacrifice of daSilva's dog illustrates Harris's conception of the person as including innumerable agents or "substitutes," capable of states of being that range from the highest spiritual consciousness to an animal-like existence of subjection and suffering. In the muse too coalesce such extremes "from animal servitude to bearing the burden of the world's need for love" (64). The substitutes or creatures within oneself are the actors of a drama of conquest one exploits and feeds on. Self-discovery amounts to a recognition of those creatures within one's heart (or the heartland of the country) and of the community one shares with them. That is why the death of daSilva after his atonement for past crimes and the understanding it gives him of the "process of relations" within himself means "the extinction of empire" (58, 67):

[it] made one see how intolerable it was to succumb to the brittle wiles of servant or master one had acquired (or contracted oneself to) from birth into death. (78)

For Stevenson the "process of relations" has involved experiencing death (his father's and daSilva's) and facing again his mistress in Petra. Through other people's predicaments he has once more felt the shock of the crash (80), which made him aware that he shares with others "the vivid moment of accident or disaster . . . wherever it occur[s]" (80). He has thus reached the "ground of loss" on which he must surrender his instincts for selfishness and possession. But when he goes in search of food for Petra and finds on his return that she has disappeared with her child, he is as shocked as when his mistress ran away at the thought of having been plundered (psychologically) and humiliated. Now "the greatest and subtlest trial of himself" (85) begins with the need for self-judgment that he situation demands. If there is a "law" of the heartland, it is according to that law of reciprocal self-surrender that he must judge himself. He is forced to confess that after their "memorable embrace . . . she had seen through his duplication of sentiment to the core of his necessity to mount a guard over himself" (85). In other words, she has seen through his unconscious motives, his pride[7] and refusal to give up the "possession of love," and has thus exposed the self-concern inherent in his act of goodness:

Would one ever learn to submit gently to the invisible chain of being [Stevenson wonders] without attempting to break loose and run after something or someone one knew as inadequately and helplessly as one knew one's own hand upon one's own heart? (85)

Stevenson's relapse (largely motivated by his need for security) and his question show his awareness that freedom from solipsism, and vision, can be neither complete nor final. Indeed, Stevenson's terror and need for "spiritual cover" (56) suggest that man might not be able to face a full revelation of the mystery at the heart of the universe. Throughout the novel he has progressed through the contrasts of the phenomenal world and experienced the tension between, and release from, opposite states of being, which finally teaches him "to bridge [his] awareness of dual proportion" (89). Now, like the muse, he must be on the move again and follow "the living stream" informed by this duality. The stream is like a "crack in the floor or prison of the landscape" (89)[8] and will take him along the endlessly disintegrating and resurging road toward self-release. That he is also moving toward his own death is implied in the postscript.[9]

The novel as such ends with the uncertainty that has informed the whole narrative. This uncertainty is an admission of the mystery of life and death and their inseparable manifestations (whether light and darkness, love and hate, the gift of oneself and the negation of the other); it is also an incentive to explore their "alliance." Man's irresistible attraction and repulsion for each accounts for the jigsaw pattern of Stevenson's progress in the wake of those he has discovered in both outer and inner heartland and who, like him, have added to its substance:

And so the longest *crumbling* black road Stevenson followed in the scorched or drowned footsteps of every witness, accuser and accused, judge and muse, in the fiery submersion and trials of dreams, was but an endless wary flood broken into *retiring* trenches or *advancing* columns, *all moving still* towards fashioning a genuine medium of conquest, capable of linking and penetrating the self-created prison-houses of subsistence, these being the confusing measure of vicarious hollow and original substance.

Stevenson did not know where the road led. He only knew it was there. (90, italics mine)

Chapter Six

The Heart of Inarticulate Protest: *The Eye of the Scarecrow*

In both form and content *The Eye of the Scarecrow* and the three following novels make up a new phase in Harris's fiction. Their subject-matter is, even more specifically than in *Palace of the Peacock*, the subjective imagination, its working on memory, and its transformation of the raw material of life. Experience in these novels is wholly internalized. The protagonist is not the author but he too is engaged in creating fiction insofar as he is an "agent" in whose consciousness the reconstruction of the past takes place. His quest is for a new way both of apprehending life and of rendering it. The main character's disorientation in the earlier fiction culminates in *Heartland* in the equation of his consciousness with a "vicarious hollow." This is now the protagonist's initial state of emptiness or breakdown, a state that results from catastrophe but goes together with a freedom from the tyranny of conventional reality, the tyranny of facts as opposed to their inner truth. We recognize here the creative possibilities Harris discerns in catastrophe, which does not merely bring about a change of outlook in the protagonist. The "crash" which shatters his safe, known world reveals the livingness of the subterranean reality it (the crash) brings to the surface. One has the impression of a dialogue between the perceiving consciousness and the material it perceives, "the flood of animated wreckage" (15) that runs to meet it and on which the protagonist refuses "to impose a false coherency."[1] All concessions to a linear progression in the plot are now rejected. The characters' failure to apprehend their past experience as a whole and the disruption of time as a rigid frame of existence make for a fragmented narrative structure. But this surface fragmentation is counterpointed by what the narrator in *The Eye* calls "phenomenal associations" (13), subtle links conveyed by a complex network of related images. Harris's following comment seems to apply to this novel in particular:

The peculiar reality of language provides a medium to *see* in consciousness the "free" motion and to hear with consciousness the "silent" flood of sound by a continuous inward revisionary and momentous logic of potent explosive images evoked in the mind.[2]

The "drama of consciousness" recreated by N. (the nameless narrator) in his diary covers a nine-month period (the time of gestation) beginning on Christmas Eve 1963 and ending on 25 September 1964. N.'s declaration of intention as he makes his first entry shows him to be a more advanced and more highly conscious character than either Fenwick or Stevenson, who both had to free themselves from rigid assumptions and constrictive habits of thought in their relations with others and their understanding of the past:

I am hoping it may prove the first reasonable attempt (my Journals in the past were subject to the close tyranny and prejudice of circumstance) at an open dialogue within which a free construction of events will emerge in the medium of phenomenal associations all expanding into a mental distinction and life of their own. (13)

N. is already sufficiently aware of the limitations of any given "realistic" version of the past to refrain from imposing on events the one-sided logic of a chronological time sequence and outer perspective. By trusting past events to speak for themselves and associate according to an intrinsic, not an imposed, significance, he recognizes that the past may have a distinctive, dynamic quality, "the stranger animation one senses within the cycle of time" (14). This explains his willingness to surrender from the start to a "visionary organization of memory" (16) rather than "succumb to the dead tide of self-indulgent realism" (15). N. is confronted anew with undigested experience and to modify his understanding of it is the purpose of his recollection. His consciousness is a vessel flooded by contrasting images of the past, whose juxtaposition and consecutive alterations as they arise from increasingly deeper levels of reminiscence and imaginative grasp give the novel its structure. The three books of the novel deal with the same material in a different form, incidents in which N. and his friend L. (Location engineer) were involved in 1948 and farther back in time between 1929 and 1932. Books I and II, *The Visionary Company* and *Genesis*, evoke these two periods in reverse order, though the creative reconstruction also covers the years between 1932 and 1964 ("twice sixteen years of 'ebb and flow' " [34]), not a time span of memorable events but years during which N. grew attached to the surface reality of life, an attitude he is now trying to break down.

The pivot of N.'s reconstruction is the year 1948, when he went into the jungle with L. in search of gold deposits and was "invalided out" (100) after a crash that "created a void in conventional memory" (15). The state of inner disruption he experienced then corresponds to the shattered, stunned condition of the victims of historical catastrophe that the evocation of 1948 brings to mind, particularly the strike and riots in Guyana. As N. resumes this condition in imagination, he recalls seeing the "scarecrow" face of L., a sudden and transient shattering of his features, which gave N. such a shock that it provoked in him a "a void of conventional everyday feeling" (15). Thus vacancy in *conventional* memory and feeling is the initial state of his recollection.

As a result of N.'s attempt to free himself from given versions of the past, images emerge into his consciousness in an apparently haphazard way. Time itself is dislocated, and some reminiscences that come under the heading 1948 actually refer back to 1929. The images are aroused through phenomenal associations of place, smell, or sound. Sometimes also, like the narrator's memories in *Palace*, they seem to "spring from nowhere." Each memory epitomizes the essential meaning of N.'s search for "the visionary company," the eclipsed lives that peopled his childhood and early manhood, and all are connected by subtle links that form intricate compositions of many-layered significance. In Book I alone the scarecrow, a unifying metaphor, sends out numerous ramifications. As an image of disruption it first appears in "the cracked surface of a depression after a naked spell of drought" (14) that N. glimpses on L.'s face; it becomes the "dislocated image"

(16) of the Georgetown foreshore, then the scarecrow figure of the dying governor of Guiana, "a shirt cast over branches of rib and bone" (29), himself a symbol of the moribund British Empire; and finally it assumes the shape of the crumbling tenements of Waterloo Street, an image of disintegration that contains, nevertheless, the seed of rebirth: "the golden centre of inspiration, the most subjective scarecrow earth of all" (32).

L. is totally unaware of his metamorphosis into a scarecrow, not realizing that his surface composure can be broken down and yield an unknown view of himself; through most of the "drama of consciousness" he plays the role of a passive and unconscious participant. This links him with all the figures of the past who seem to have been equally unconscious—the Guiana strikers, whose action "bore such a close, almost virtuous resemblance to the unprejudiced reality of freedom" (18−19), the Water Street beggars crippled by "self-deception" (17), the "unfeeling and unseeing" hearse-riders, and Anthrop, anonymous man suffering the depression of 1929. The unconscious "scarecrow of shadow" (19) also links together the funeral procession of the strikers with that of "the nameless paupers of charity," who also perpetuate a "self-sufficient life of doom, the seal upon all eyes, on all the senses of the world" (20). Connected with the scarecrow figure is the image of the ghost of a runaway slave whom, as a child, N. thought he saw hanging from a tree over the "sliced surface of the canal" (another image of disruption) on what used to be plantation ground. The runaway slave evoked a spirit of freedom which even as a child N. was hoping to attain (35). In his failure to achieve it, however, the ghost may equally represent the figures of the past enslaved by others or by their own failure to achieve consciousness, and it suggests as well the immobility in which the figures have remained confined, trapped for so long in N.'s consciousness. Other associations grow from the basic metaphors. The ghost of the dying governor, for instance, reminds N. of the dying soldiers on a painting of the battle of Waterloo, who like the strikers form a funeral procession—of figures of conquest this time— and, like them, were consumed by their "rage for an ideal" (21).

These overlapping associations suggest that out of the initial image of the scarecrow and its many variations there grows an underlying network of relationships that illustrate the victor-victim syndrome and point to the helplessness of those who were twice lost: the beggars, strikers, nameless paupers, Anthrop, all leading a buried existence in a time of depression, then eclipsed again in the folds of memory. N.'s reconstruction is punctuated with intuitions of the void in which the figures of the past used to live, the invisible dimension to which the unprivileged were relegated. The unconscious protest of the derelict Water Street beggars was born "of a kind of *hollow* silence" (17); the strikers were blocked by "the devil's *abyss* . . . nihilism of spirit" (18); the poor man's hearse, unlike that of the rich dead, lacked sides of glass through which the coffin could be glimpsed and aroused in N. the suspicion that it might be empty, and when he visited his grandfather's tenements, N. could perceive the "*hollow* darkness" (30, all italics mine) at the tenants' back. On reaching Anthrop's hovel during that visit, N. was subject to a fit of sickness during which the stable image he beheld was suddenly reversed. He experienced a "sensation of upheaval, the stigmata of the void" (33), i.e., he suffered briefly the sense of anguish, the impression of living in a bottomless world, which is the normal condition of the inarticulate poor. In the moment of sickness, while his vision of Anthrop's room was reversed, N. perceived in it "a half-naked woman, his wife, with twins at her breast" (33), whom, in the light of what he knew of Anthrop's existence, he associated not with the "new-born" but with the "new-dead" (33).

To sum up the double significance of this incident, the "stigmata of the void" are scars of the living death or deadness expressed by the metaphors of the scarecrow, ghost, and funeral procession; and N.'s perception of this gives him, if not a clear understanding, at least an intuition of the "dual proportion" that now serves him as a starting point in his quest, what he calls "the self-reversing game of reality of the banquet of life on death" (35). Each image of the past is an incentive to N.'s perception of this process of self-reversal and offers, however elusively, a clue to the discovery of an opposite reality. The very structure of Book I is based on a juxtaposition of images of life and death and the duality that each evokes. So the funeral processions that N. remembers as he begins his diary are counterpointed by images of life—for example, of N. "riding out of the womb" (23) (resurrecting from unconsciousness) after a serious operation. At that time, however, he awakened to a restrictive existence, for he became "a slave to the futility of hardness" (35), i.e., to a one-sided, apparently static reality. Indeed, there is no example, in Book I, of the deeper, third dimension of being which it is the purpose of N.'s quest to discover; there are only intuitions that the "hollowness of spirit" (27) he re-experiences with humility and compassion can be the source of a regenerated vision. He once dreamed that he found himself in a large secret room where he visualized his first source of inspiration:

the sleep of an immaterial unsupported element: the armour of the poor, and I knew then how dread and necessary it was to dream to enter the striking innermost chemistry of love, transcending every proud chamber in the inexorable balloon of time. (23)

Just as he finds in that room the "revolutionary goal" (22) he pursues, so he glimpses in the Waterloo Street tenements "the subterranean anatomy of revolution" (31)[3], an incentive to discard the "primitive manifesto" (32) by which men live and to reach "an immaterial element" (32) through his imaginative identification with the scarecrow. Precisely because it was disintegrating, the world of 1948 was laying bare its own fountainhead of change. But as N.'s present inner reconstruction implies, the mutation toward "a new unspectacular conception of life" (99) must first be realized in the individual psyche.

The very types of behavior which in Book I elicit a sense of "misconceived beginning" (35), such as N.'s false start in life in 1932 and the strikers' premature demonstration in 1948, are shown in Book II, *Genesis*, to be prime movers in N.'s development of a new vision. The contrasts evoked in Book I are now being transmuted into personal confrontations both in the outer world and in N.'s consciousness. *Genesis* is presented as a dateless diary in which incidents of 1932 and 1948 echo each other and foreshadow a future (2048) still shaped by man's "familiar obsession [the desire to possess]" (47). In Book I the past was freed from a static historical perspective by the a-chronological reconstruction of events and the juxtaposition of remote time sequences. In the dateless diary the shifts from past to future intimate timelessness and stimulate the process of transformation that is beginning to take place in N.'s consciousness.

The initial image in Book II is of the mud figures N. and L. fashioned shortly after N.'s return from hospital in 1932. N. was keenly disappointed because his friend appeared "wooden and unable to enter into the spirit of the game of beginning to make everything new" (39). But looking at the figures again after L. had left, N. suddenly saw "all the sap of life rise anew" (40) in one of the figures on the ground. The metamorphosis of the lifeless lump into an animated figure occurs through N.'s insight into the concealed sorrow, the subjective element, that has gone into its making. This creative act is born out of the conjunction of contrasting elements, L.'s passive participation and N.'s realization that he has inflicted pain; it re-enacts the original genesis, whose description prefaces Book II:

> There went up a mist from the earth, and
> watered the whole face of the ground.
> And the Lord God formed man of the dust
> of the ground. . . .

The missing words are "and breathed into his nostrils the breath of life; and man became a living soul" (Gen. 2:7). By breathing life into L.'s figure, N.'s vision provides the missing element, just as later in the "jungle of conception" (48) N. turns up, a "living soul" (77), to save L. from death. Further still in their exploration, he reaches the meeting point between "breathlessness" (deadness) and "*breath—*mist" (93), the mist that fertilized the earth.

L.'s "translated figure" (40) contains "the heart of inarticulate protest" (41) and becomes a metaphor for the exploited muse and the people she represents. It is first associated with mother earth, then with N.'s own mother, who appears as both a "victim" of love and intent on "devouring" someone else in the name of love. This in turn calls up the naked woman inside Anthrop's room, then L.'s dead mother, whom, as he dreams of her, N. pushed into the role rumor had given her while she was alive, that of the mistress of Anthrop, rich civil engineer and twin brother of the poor hearse-rider, who was also N.'s stepfather. Even while he is pushing her, N. realizes that she "lives and moves" (45), i.e., that she is not a senseless being to be manipulated at will. Finally, the mud figure is associated with Hebra, the prostitute N. and L. send for in the jungle in 1948. She is also called Raven's Head like the lost town the men try to locate. N. is struck by the insensitiveness with which L. takes her. As a matter of fact, he too takes her with "blind lust" (52); though he at first shrank from touching her, he awakes by her side having unconsciously possessed her after all. Hebra is a deceptively lifeless mud figure again in Book III, in which Scarecrow succumbs to the "habit of trying to fashion her into his own image" (87).

This development of the mud-figure image throws light on the characters' instinctive and often unconscious attempts to exploit others. Even L. (himself repeatedly pushed by N.), who never suspects evil either in his own or in other people's motives, does so. Yet because he does not challenge the existing order of things, he helps to perpetuate it by taking advantage either of Hebra or of the "creatures of little weight and substance" (59) who transport his gigantic dredge into the interior. N. realizes that even Hebra, their victim, is intent on possessing them. The two friends now appear as the twins Anthrop's wife was feeding, though by nursing them, Hebra is also determined to assert her own existence. N.'s perception of this makes him discover

a force of obsession in things I had only dimly dreamt before . . . to question . . . Things and persons whose life of obsession lay *less within themselves and more within myself*, within *my* lack of a universal conception, of *their* conception (the unborn folk). (53, italics mine)

"*My* lack . . . of *their* conception," N.'s acknowledgment that he has so far failed to conceive or see others into existence, parallels his recognition of life in L.'s mud figures at the beginning of Book II: "the thing *I* created with my own eyes out of one of the pieces *he* had made" (40). The two passages show that vision is what resurrects the "unborn folk," the seemingly dead, buried in memory ("the nameless forgotten dead"[4]), and THE UNINITIATE (103) ("the nameless sleeping living"), i.e., the apparently nonexistent multitudes excluded from the rituals of privileged societies.

The metamorphoses of the mud-figure image give N. to understand that, even when consenting to their own plight, the victims have feelings and a life of their own which he must revive. The second discovery he makes is that the nameless dimension "animates" the retrenched territory they inhabit. When he travels to the jungle with L., he is in search of his father's innocence while L. is solely interested in what relates to the outer expedition. He is impressed by the technical merits of a bridge built by N.'s stepfather, while N. sees in that bridge "both a trapdoor [for those who stop at its outer reality] and a poem [giving insight, through its very materiality, into the unknown beyond]" (50). While both stand on the bridge, N. becomes aware of the "dazzling sleeper of spirit" (49), a sudden awakening and subsiding of an inner reality taking visible shape under his eyes. In this evanescent phenomenon he recognizes a manifestation of the nameless dimension: "*it*, the trespass of feeling rising anew out of the stumbling labour and melting pot of history" (49). While still on the bridge, he feels, rising within himself, a "daemon" or "muse of place" (51), Hebra, whose "black mask" (56) is associated with "*it*—the accumulative ironies of the past, the virtuous rubbish-heap and self-parody of ancestors in death" (56). N.'s intuitions of the meaning of *it* imply that the territory they are exploring (which is both outer and inner space) is a repository for the sufferings of the past, in which, as N. realized through his childhood dream, "every dumb fact" (47) became converted into apparent nothingness. Out of this converted experience, *it* now "ris[es] anew," indicating that the mute sufferings of victimized people subsist as pent-up energy, "a ceaseless ferment of unwritten lives,"[5] capable of exploding as it now does in N.'s memory. The appearance and disappearance of *it*, whether as "dazzling sleeper of spirit" perceptible in nature or as an inner intuition, coincides with a similar dual movement characteristic of Raven's Head, the mining "ghost town" the two men are trying to discover:

For centuries . . . mysterious locations had been plumbed to disappear and return once more into the undisclosed astronomical wealth of the jungle. *Raven's Head* . . . was one of these relative establishments whose life of eternity sprang from a pinpoint conception of poetic loyalty to the idea of everlasting justice: they (such relative establishments) belonged to those who voluntarily began to relinquish the right they deserved to a place in them—whose recovery of them lay therefore within the heart of an acceptance of great distance from them. But such a decision to relinquish what one desperately wanted to find tore at the roots of all possession and conventionality. (54—55)

N. had already been warned in a childhood dream of the need to be distant from (while recognizing the otherness of) what he is after, when he sensed the presence of creatures who, he hoped, would "consent to be shaped by [his] command and tongue" (43) but who vanished as soon as he struck them. They too follow in his consciousness the ebb and flow N. has discerned in the "dazzling sleeper of spirit" and in Raven's Head since they are "sometimes capable of recall, sometimes elusive and sealed and forgotten" (43). Moreover, they are linked with Raven's Head or Hebra through what N. calls "the phenomenon of dust" (39), for in Hebra's town he perceives "distantly . . . the almost breathless fall of the condemned blossom of earth—the freedom of promise in dust" (55). The image of the "dusty insects" (55) is a recurring one (see also 17,63), which expresses the insubstantiality of both the neglected creatures in everyday life and the spiritual region toward which N. moves, "one's immortal undiscovered realm, a land of creatures living freely everywhere and nowhere" (35). Like the mud figure, this image links together the two sections of Book II and its major discoveries: one, that creation in this context means *seeing* "persons and things" that are usually invisible because taken for granted; two, this perception of life in "the other" is parallel with his (or its) autonomous emergence into life.

In Harris's earlier fiction recognition of the "folk" or "ghosts," both living and dead, was largely a one-way movement dependent on the main character's willingness to explore. In this novel the encounter and incipient relationship between one and "the other" is due to a double movement: eyes opening to the existence of that "other," who is also susceptible of travelling toward oneself across the frontier behind which he (she or it) normally lives retrenched. In *Heartland* Stevenson had moved toward an "extreme frontier" and envisioned, but not experienced, what lay on the other side. Now for the first time since *Palace of the Peacock* the main character is shown travelling beyond the frontier of the known world. As N.'s eyes open to the unborn folk's "life of obsession" in the jungle, he understands that this life lies

Less in the open question of their [the unborn folk's] apparently submissive being and more in my ultimatum of fixed instincts, beyond which . . . I hesitated to go (even dared not go) since it would mean crossing a "dead" masked frontier as if this were a living disguise and territory in fact. . . . (53)

Actually, the "fixed instincts" erect the " 'dead' masked frontier." When N. and L. progress toward Raven's Head, the obstacles they meet are "a magnetic *instinctual* load of rock" (54, italics mine), stifling habits of "jealous proprietorship and conviction" and N.'s "rage for self-justification" (55). In spite of his many insights N. is not yet prepared to dismantle his self-erected defenses, although he now knows that it depends on his self-surrender whether or not he will reach Raven's Head. He still refuses to "confess . . . to . . . his unlicensed censor of space" (56) (to the scarecrow within him) as he does in Book III when he loses his identity.

Book III, *Raven's Head*,[6] describes, as it were, from the inside N. and L.'s approach to the lost town or territory, which is clearly a metaphor for the buried past, for the state of deadness to which the uninitiate are confined, and for that innermost region of the individual psyche that Harris sees as both the storehouse of undigested experience and the vessel of its transformation. N. has now disappeared as identifiable narrator since he has travelled beyond "a frontier of existence" (69) where personality gives way to the emerging "other" (first L., then Hebra). The first two sections of the reconstruction of the journey (covering chapter 6 and the beginning of chapter 7) are still part of the dateless diary. They describe the various approaches to Raven's Head and give the first dramatized version of the encounter between the exploring consciousness and "the other," whom in *Genesis* N. had perceived only intuitively or in dreams.

of the crash recorded in the once-more-dated diary. The explorers are seen again as N. and L., though the overlapping of their personalities [disclosed in the earlier version] still prevails, making it impossible to discern which of the two saved the other from execution after their violent quarrel with each other and with Hebra. N. is now reconstructing his *"Fall into Ancient Passage"* (76) and writing from that dark room of memory. The images that return to him are both L.'s snapshots of Raven's Head and his own memories of a dream in which now one, now the other ("I"/"he") is seen "digesting" catastrophe (79−80). They have reached the innermost depths made accessible by the shattering of appearances recorded in the first version, a "stunned, breathless, post-mortem" (77) condition (that of the "visionary company" in Book I), and in the "visionary room" (82) into which they descend (the room N. had envisioned as a child ? [22]) they fulfill their need of each other. It is here that the "transubstantiation" of one into "the other" takes place after the customer (N./L.) of the visionary room has recognized "his own blurred spirit of seasonal image" (82) in the Water Street beggar. However, no sooner has the transformation taken place than the new scarecrow issued from it is faced with his new role, that of "the innocent unborn 'soul' who was destined to be charged with an account for murder" (83).

If my reading of the novel is correct, what is then realized might be described as follows: In *Genesis* the "unborn folk" are apparently nonexistent as a result of N.'s failure to see them into existence. What is now disclosed is the sacrifice the "unborn" are continuously called upon to make. Sacrifice seems to be of two different kinds. There is the uninitiate's acceptance of their own death (through meaningless trials provoked by men or nature), which L. explains to his friend: "Someone had died for us . . . THE UNINITIATE. ACCEPTANCE OF BLIND MURDER" (103). This is the kind of sacrifice L. (men in general) never stop(s) taking for granted, an attitude which, as already pointed out, links him with the unconscious victims. Equally devouring is the sacrifice made or imposed out of love. Hebra represents the "unborn folk" but as soon as the scarecrow born of the conjunction of victor and victim comes into the "living death" which is her normal state, he runs the danger of being fascinated by her. At one stage in the exploration there seemed to be a correspondence between N.'s desire to discover the source of a spiritual tradition and Hebra's wish to restore "her spiritual bridge and sacred mining town" (53) though even then he suspected that she wanted to possess him and L. Now that he has reached that source, he is becoming intoxicated with it and anxious to possess it, so that *it* is now "a priceless jewel whose rarity bred every astonished witness of jealousy of love" (88). The relationsip that develops between Scarecrow and Hebra contains, I believe, a warning against a form of spiritual cannibalism and insatiate hunger for love. Scarecrow has toward Hebra the same attitude as formerly (in what one might call the outer world) since he is "trying to fashion her into his own image" (87)—denying her intrinsic being—only to discover that he is becoming enslaved by his desire to possess her and the increasingly higher price he must pay to "execute" her (deny her otherness). It is this urge to enslave that makes the genius or muse of a spiritual tradition into a whore.

The "murder" described in chapter 8 has both a literal and a figurative meaning, though I feel the figurative carries more weight since at this stage, in spite of the physical movements of the characters, the inner dimension prevails. At first, Scarecrow denies Hebra's existence and in doing so denies his own, projected into hers, much as in the first version of the crash hitting the cow had crumbled his own will. And just as in the earlier memory of his intercourse with Hebra he had discovered in her "a life of obsession," so he now discovers "her living currency" (88). In the outer-world encounter recorded in Book II, N. and L. could not accept the fact that "a price was about to be placed upon [their] heads" (53), that *they* could be the object of a transaction too. Now Scarecrow "[gives] himself up to be sold to the highest bidder" (89), i.e., agrees to change places with the whore, and this self-denial brings about the second "conversion." Scarecrow's acceptance of his own death makes possible the birth of Idiot Nameless.[11] The nine months of conception have been months of successive conversions and self-surrenders, and the exploring consciousness is now seen to break through from within Scarecrow, riding out of the womb, not like young N. "safe and established in his own private being" (36), but after surrendering the last shred of identity and greedy will. For this to be possible, however, Hebra too confesses to solipsism. After Scarecrow has invested himself with her garment, *her* "transubstantiation" takes place, and the explorer feels at last he is at the end of his quest, uniting in his resurrection "long lost father [whose trial in the jungle he has relived] and newfound son [the nameless spirit-child]" (91).

N.'s understanding of "the art of murder" (90) is his ultimate discovery and is cognate with his perception of the "enigma of life" (90), the coexistence of opposites, "the twins of breath and breathlessness" (90). To break the balance between the two is to "murder" one for the sake of the other. They are not alternatives but *together* form "the apprehensive soul and image of an unknown capacity" (90). The paradox lies in that either can "murder" or "be murdered" ("the surprising or surprised life-blood" [90]) and that even an apparently harmless desire for "the other"[12] can engulf him (her or it). Hence the mutual self-surrender of Scarecrow and Hebra, which at last makes possible the birth or resurrection of Idiot Nameless. The confession the narrator sends to L. sums up one transformation (of N. and L. into Scarecrow) and foreshadows the other (Scarecrow's and Hebra's self-denial). The confession itself is called *The Eye of the Scarecrow*, suggesting that to confess is to create the Scarecrow's double vision. It starts with a reference to Scarecrow's confession of "murder" but ends with Nameless's own confession and is signed "IDIOT NAMELESS," as if the very act of confession or self-surrender were itself the doorway to namelessness. Nameless has developed from N.'s continuous shedding of the layers of personality paralleled by increasingly deeper insights into "the other," whose fascination he must also resist. When Nameless writes "It is the *consciousness* of the continuous erosion of self-made fortifications that is the 'material' of my confession" (86), he is not merely summing up his achievement but describing a process that can have no end.

The state of Namelessness or "negative identity"[13] (101) reached by N. is the ultimate development of that "identity of abandonment" Stevenson was hoping to achieve in *Heartland*. The void entered by N. as he began his diary, unquestionably accepted or else fought with the blindness of despair by the victims of history, has become a creative dimension. Nameless's last perception before he reaches complete freedom is of the "CAPACITY and DENSITY" (88) of the apparent void. The womb he has re-entered ceases to exist as void, and the "*unimaginably frail and indistinct*" (94) essence (soul, spirit, *it*) he has discovered through the density of the reconstructed past and the lives of the uninitiate, convinces him of the reality of "inner space" (94), which is at once a vessel for past experiences and for future possibilities. Indeed as an ever-to-be-recreated state, Namelessness, a "transparent vehicle of age and youth" (88), implies a dynamic rapport between past and future. There are many expressions of it in the novel as of the "haphazard penetration and shifting movement" (77) across the barrier of opposites that N. feared in his youth (45). N. had glimpsed this movement in the "dazzling sleeper of spirit" and in Raven's Head. The latter remains the "ghost of . . . arousal" (83) of Nameless's growing sensibility and consciousness. To resist the temptation of pinning her down is the very essence of his art:

The continuous birth of poetry needs to be more . . . than an imitation of a preservative fluid: it is the life-blood of *seeing* and responding without succumbing—in the very transparent mobility of consciousness—to what is apparently seen and heard. (97)

The identification of Raven's Head with the elusive and fluctuating ground of art is the climax of the transformation of N. from diarist into artist. In *The Eye* Harris's intense concern for a genuine, realized community of men coalesces with the elaboration of a new "authentic" art of fiction; or, more accurately, this concern appears as the source of his art in the structure and narrative texture of the novel. The evocation of concrete, outer-world incidents runs through an intermediate approach to them which combines outer with inner perspectives and leads to a wholly inner, abstract, or structural reconstruction of experience. These changes in the mode of perception go together with an increasingly deeper commitment on N.'s part to the "person of obscurity" (101) whose trial he is reliving. His "double vision," as we have seen, is there from the start but as an intuition to be realized, and this realization and the interiorization of experience are accompanied by a gradual change in narrative method. N.'s rejection of "self-indulgent realism" (15) in Book I is immediately followed by a breaking up of the narrative continuity, which expresses a crumbling of the surface reality of existence and offers a glimpse of the "fluid logic of image" (95) that underlies the apparent "confusion of [outer] forms" (57). This discontinuity goes together in Book II with a juxtapostion of styles[14] matching N.'s descriptive recreation of his relationship with L. and his intuitive or visionary perceptions of the nameless dimension. There are frequent shifts from the comparatively straightforward re-creation of an outer reality to a reconstruction of symbolical actions or manifestations that refer back to that outer reality. This second manner is further developed in Book III. The characters have by then become symbolical figures in the explorer's consciousness (the dreamer/the driver, "rich man or poor man, customer, artist or engineer" [83]) or they are reduced to "I" and "he," "one" and "the other," the essential agents in any human relationship, and duality is then expressed through a shift in the point of view. The action is wholly symbolical too, "refined" into a mere outline of significant movements. At this stage N. has become the "medium of capacity" (14) he set out to discover, the vehicle of a mobile consciousness and imagination sharing (or aiming at) the unborn state of eclipsed existences.

From the static void of the figures of his youth to the "living" void of namelessness[15] the narrator has been probing the very source of creativeness and the possiblities of language. The MANIFESTO OF THE UNBORN STATE OF EXILE that concludes his quest is an epitome of this exploration and recapitulates its main discoveries. It describes language as the other expression of the "medium of capacity," the organ of the nameless imagination:

language alone can express (in a way which goes beyond any physical or vocal attempt) the sheer—the ultimate "silent" and "immaterial" complexity of arousal. . . . It is the sheer mystery—the impossibility of trapping its own grain—on which poetry lives and thrives. And this is the stuff of one's essential understanding of the reality of the original Word, the Well of Silence.[16] (95)

In his description of the role of language Nameless insists on its fluidity ("the impossibility of trapping its own grain") and its transforming power. We have witnessed the gradual metamorphosis of the scarecrow from a "dead" into a "living" image expressing a dynamic relationship. Nameless also emphasizes the capacity of language to transform what is, ironically, unconscious and blind into an illuminating "scale." At several points in the novel either L. or Raven's Head illumines N.'s consciousness in a flash,[17] and the flash itself is "living distinctive otherness" (101). At the end of the Manifesto "the other" (again L. and Raven's Head linked together) emerges once more and immediately subsides in Nameless's consciousness. The groping for "the other" starts all over again through The Black Rooms of VISIONARY COMPANY and GENESIS and ends with the POST-SCRIPT OF FAITH IN DARK ROOM OF IDENTITY, offered as an answer to the nihilism and despair that prevailed at the beginning of the quest. There is no end to that quest, however. Raven's Head represents a condition "into which we are still to be born" (107), which perhaps, as N.'s terror of the conversion into namelessness shows, can never be fully or finally entered, though it can be glimpsed and responded to in a way that alters the fundamental polarizations of existence. What is open to a man is the midway course made accessible by his normally partial vision:

The drama of consciousness in which we were involved, part-knowing, part-unknowing, dim and voluntary, illuminating and involuntary, was infinite and concrete, simple and complex at the same time. (81)

Chapter Seven
A Primordial Species of Fiction: *The Waiting Room*

The story of Susan Forrestal, which serves as a starting point to the adventure in consciousness that plays itself out in *The Waiting Room,* is told by the author in an introductory note. Susan is a woman in her early forties who became totally blind after three eye operations. Some twelve to twenty years before this (the timespan is left deliberately vague) she was the mistress of a man whom she deeply loved and who left her after a violent quarrel. He disappeared into the heartland and was never heard of again. Susan married another man when she was already blind but, in spite of his attentive care and over-solicitousness, she continued to be haunted by the memory of her lover. With both men she kept an antique shop, which was destroyed with most of their belongings by an explosion that killed Susan and her husband. Only their diary or logbook survived, though partly obliterated. The novel is a reconstruction of the substance of this diary. It is easy enough to piece together the known facts of Susan's existence and to trace her growing awareness that through most of her adult life she has self-deceptively posed as a victim and ignored her own possessiveness. But to be content with this would be to reduce the novel to "the self-sufficient story line"[1] of conventional fiction that Harris rejects.

Joyce Adler in her pioneer review of *The Waiting Room* and Michael Gilkes have both drawn attention to the community of thought between this novel and Harris's critical essays on fiction in *Tradition, the Writer and Society*. I shall refer the reader mainly to the essay "The Writer and Society" and draw his attention to two sentences in the first paragraph, which can be read as a summing up of Harris's purpose in *The Waiting Room*:

I shall try to trace what I perceive to be the outlines of a drama of
consciousness in which the writer is involved as both a passive and a creative
agent. It is as if within his work he sets out again and again across a certain
territory of *primordial* but broken recollection in search of *a community or species
of fiction* whose existence he begins to discern.[2]

"Community or species of fiction" indicates that Harris abolishes all
distinction between the reality he evokes (community) and the evocation itself (species of fiction). Fiction does not merely "represent"
reality; it *is* reality conveyed by a self-effaced writer who, as the
"Author's Note" in *The Waiting Room* shows, sees himself as a mere
agent through which the characters' experience re-enacts itself. While
in the passage just quoted Harris emphasizes the role of the novelist
"in search of a . . . species of fiction," in the "Author's Note" he
insists rather on the independent existence of that fiction. Just as the
narrator in *The Eye* hopes that "a free construction of events will
emerge" from his recollection, so the author or "editor" of the
Forrestals' diary sees in the material it records "a natural medium of
invocation in its own right" (10). There is thus a reciprocal movement
of the writer and his material (whether characters or the content of
their consciousness) toward each other, which corresponds to a similar
movement between the characters and the ghosts who people their
inner being. There is no identification between the author and the
central consciousness in the novel. Rather, as all characters live
through him, they become in turn "agents of [his] personality"[3] and
thereby help abolish its limitations.

The serial enlargement of the author's and his characters' personality through the retrieval of buried existences is partly what Harris
means when he equates the re-creation of community with fiction.
Seen from another angle, this equation is linked with Harris's attempt
to avoid "consolidation," i.e., sharply defined, self-sufficient characters, as well as the formalization into one given view of reality of one
possibility of narrative development to the exclusion of all others.
One finds instead in Harris's fiction, particularly in *The Waiting Room*,
a fluid reality constantly metamorphosing itself, and characters described in their attempt to break down the contours of personality in
order to realize (i.e., conceive *and* achieve) their participation in

a common being and consciousness. In *The Eye* the narrator sheds his identity in order to reach namelessness and he does this by reconstructing the same events at increasingly deeper levels of his psyche. He discovers a series of alter egos in the form of animal substitutes, an old man, and a young boy, and finally the archetypal dreamer and driver. At that stage he has become "primordial character [or] species of fiction."[4] In other words he has reached, temporarily and with one part of himself only, a state in which to the extent that he relinquishes his identity, to that extent he partakes of a pre-individualized, pre-historical consciousness common to all men.

The Waiting Room begins and largely takes place where *The Eye* ends, on the threshold of "primordial fiction," on the threshold only because, as the endings of Harris's novels show, man cannot and should not surrender finally to namelessness, and therefore genuine community can never be completed. The novel concentrates on the borderline between basic opposites: Life/death, identity/nonidentity, consciousness/unconsciousness, as well as between the manifold expressions of male and female being. It is important to remember that the word *primordial* is used, both in Harris's essays on fiction and in this novel, with the double meaning of *primeval* and *fundamental* and that these inseparable connotations refer to the form and content of the narrative. With respect to both, the novel is stripped of all inessentials. It is pure, quintessential fiction in which, to use Wallace Stevens's words, "reality changes from substance to subtlety."[5] Through the exploration of basic human relationships it lays bare the most fundamental instincts and feelings (such as possessiveness, love, and hate) tracing them to compulsions, now unconscious, among the residua or archaic existence in every man's psyche. It is naked, elemental existence that Harris conveys here, though in the light of earlier novels it clearly corresponds to what has so far been presented as either alien, apparently nonexistent, or "dead" within man and outside him.

This novel also fulfils Paul Valéry's never-achieved aim of writing "un roman cérébral et sensuel."[6] There is not only fusion between thought and feeling but, as will be shown, the expression of thought (particularly the concept of community) through sensuous imagery. The characters assume various forms of being as they re-enact the crucial phases of their relationship. Harris writes in the "Author's Note":

By *fiction* I do not mean to deny certain literal foundations but rather to affirm these absolutely as a mutual bank or living construction of events. (9)

Susan Forrestal is physically present throughout, although her presence is rendered more concretely in the second part of the novel. She is obsessed with the memory of her relationship with her lover. The sexual act and the gestures of love make up the best part of what Harris calls "literal foundations." The manner of their rendering, however, changes with the symbolical metamorphoses of the characters in Susan's consciousness. Susan and her lover are woman and man making love but their embrace is rendered through a multitude of natural forms. To give only a few examples, he is day and she is night (25). In one passage she is at first the sea "foaming white far under him around each black penis of rock," then "a flowering plant lying crushed beneath him," and finally a "wave of land beneath him" (29 – 30). Later she is seen on a cosmic scale as a *teardrop"* (46), which is actually the earth for Susan's consciousness is also "skull of the world" or "universal waiting-room" (22), and in the drama she enacts with her lover, they are the *"dramatis personae* of the universe" (50). Not only do these images reveal the nature of Susan's relationship with her lover, they suggest as well that there is a sexuality of the elements in the cosmos and illustrate Harris's view of a universe in which there is no sharp division between forms of life and their function. Another aspect of community, this time between animate and inanimate being, is conveyed through one of the basic images in the novel, that of Susan as sail and deck of her lover's vessel (19). At the climax of their intercourse each "embrace [s] and [is] held in turn by a 'deaf' mast" (47). This is both Susan and her lover holding and held by her/his partner, who as " 'deaf' mast" or flesh is an unconscious but saving "other."

The Waiting Room has two parts, *The Void* and *The Vortex*. In a sense the characters move in the void from beginning to end. Since Susan is blind, even the room in which she sits, the material locale of her life with her husband, must give her a sensation of void. Geographically, it is placeless, its location in memory street (seen in the reconstruction as "void of memory") having a primarily symbolical significance. The void is also Susan's condition of disorientation after her lover's departure and after her eye operations; and at a further remove it is the state from which the "dead" characters are revived by the author. Finally, the void is to be linked with the "positive fiction of nothingness" (10) Susan sees in her lover. The paradoxical juxtaposition of "positive" with "nothingness" points to the transformation of a sterile condition into a "living one." This takes place in the waiting room, i.e., Susan's room on the literal level and a metaphor for her consciousness and even for the universe, the three (actual room, consciousness, universe) representing the three overlapping planes on which the "drama" occurs. This vessel of transformation is itself a protean symbol all through, whose many metamorphoses must be traced in order to follow the movements of consciousness it harbors. At the beginning of the novel, for instance, Susan indicts her lover in the "convertible void of the waiting room" (20) (her consciousness), while at the end the waiting room is a cavern and a womb (still Susan's consciousness) in which her lover achieves vision. While tracing its metamorphoses, one soon realizes that the waiting room is both the seat of a specific function and the function itself, the two sometimes presented together as in "late room, early capacity" (25), "unpredictable room, unearthly function" (45), "curious vessel—mnemonic device" (52), or conversely "Dream and capacity. WAITING ROOM" (76). This reminds us that the object of exploration in Harris's fiction is always its own instrument. Moreover, the waiting room is the symbol in which time and space merge: "the 'waiting room'—part-present, part-past, part-future—was falling through the dust of space" (54).

The association of Susan's consciousness with the waiting room needs to be qualified. Susan is the muse who initiates the process of memory, but the characters she brings to life in her "drama of consciousness" have an existence of their own. Her first gesture is one of self-effacement:

Susan Forrestal was blind. She drew the palm of her hand slowly across her face as if to darken her own image, and to discover therein another sun of personality. (15)

As soon as she has brought her nameless lover (the other "sun of personality") into being, the consciousness becomes his, then shifts from one to the other, and in the second chapter lies with an impersonal "one," which is neither Susan nor her lover though it partakes of both. This shift in consciousness repeats itself throughout Book I (Susan's husband does not appear in the narrative until Book II). The point I am driving at, one that is consistent with Harris's view of his characters as "agents" of consciousness, is that the waiting room does not represent the consciousness of one character only; it is Susan's but it is also her lover's. Furthermore, it is the nameless condition out of which Susan's memory retrieves her lover, "A room one shared with the thief of all ages" (21). As a disembodied memory or "sheer phenomenon of sensibility" (11), the lover is referred to as "he" throughout the novel. However, the evocation of his memory or of the essence of his personality inevitably revives the real man as well: "the growing shelter . . . he began to suffer turned . . . into a total presence he regained and knew. Like a garment—necessary and binding and absurd—'he' had forgotten he still carried or wore" (16). As already mentioned, the novel takes place on the borderline between opposites, among which are the actual and the "quintessential" personalities of Susan and her lover. The waiting room is a two-dimensional reality which contains these and all other opposites:

The waiting room was saturated with warm blood and chill: the dim senses of birth, the remote senses of death, the cold and hungry senses of love. (21)

The content of Book I is the gradual transformation of the liaison and its rupture from the source of frustration it was before and after the lover's departure into a life-giving relationship. Book II counterpoints Book I and shows that the lover was as ill-treated by Susan as she was by him. It also deals with the lovers' conscious apprehension of the transformation that took place in Book I. Although the first four chapters of the novel recall their alienating quarrels, each contains a moment of illumination and gives evidence of the community of being which it is the purpose of the process of memory to realize. There are moments of repulsion and attraction, of antagonism and coming together within the larger serial illumination and the ever-deepening spiral of Susan's memory. In both its positive and negative aspects the relationship is reciprocal: each is the other's "shadow" (16, 19), but the lover still fears Susan's possessiveness, while she feels he still arouses in her contradictory feelings of hate and love. They are locked in mutual accusation although Susan is the most vindictive, working herself up to a climax of indignation and *"indict{ing} him out of her sightless eyes"* (20). Yet at the height of her wrath her cry "Thief. Thief"[7] summons a "third nameless person [the impersonal consciousness already mentioned] . . . whose abstract *presence* now encircled one in the ruin of all atmospheres" (21). This anonymous existence (collective unconscious or primordial being?) confronts Susan and her lover (the pronoun "one" applies to both) with their own senselessness—the lover is deaf as Susan is blind. As a result they are faced with the very means of their fulfillment, their catastrophic blindness and deafness, though they are still skeptical of the unity it will help them to achieve.

Chapter 3 shows Susan and her lover still trying to establish their respective responsibility for their present crippled condition. Nevertheless, in her state of extremity Susan finds herself on the threshold of vision ("ledge of night, edge of dawn," [23]) and we see indeed that she wants "to conceive . . . an extreme but true vision of him"[8] (24). Her former pregnancy is now symbolical of her new incipient conception of her lover. She realizes that he raped her out of an excessive love for her, "the apple of his eye." He, on the other hand, becomes aware of his self-deception and sees that she was but a "daily ornament" or "morning woman"[9] in "his" room, a view of herself she accepted like "a self-created fetish" (23). Through their common partial discovery they are "translated, in an instant of arousal" (26) yet still fear the disorientation that must accompany the obliteration of their personality. Each is still a "reflection" rather than an object of true vision for the other. But through their coming together on the brink of vision "with his eyes of morning as well as hers of night" (25) and in a sexual climax ("orgasm" [26]) the reflection is momentarily broken and the understanding reached that each is the instrument through which the other will reach self-knowledge by being recognized both in his/her nakedness ("stripped") and as the idol ("fetish of the void" [26]) each has been and must cease to be for the other.

Chapter 4 further illustrates the lovers' contradictory impulses of disinterested love and possessiveness. The contradiction is contained in the title "Silence Please," Susan's command expressing at once a desire to possess the other by silencing him and the unselfish longing to reach the silence and fulfillment allied to namelessness. The command soon turns into a reconstruction of her lover's former assault on her. He is so furious that she imposes this role on him still that he is determined to act it out in revenge. Each is again seen taking advantage of the other. He at first tries to ignore her, then is made to realize that he has indeed crushed her. On the other hand, when he tries to approach her in tenderness, she reacts like a "trigger of fury" (32), yielding to an "assumption of being" (33)—an assertion of selfhood—similar to his own (27). Each is now a naked elemental force incomprehensible and frightening to the other and in this role each seems to be a manifestation of the "master thief of love." Susan is by turns the exploited one and an "ancient and devouring" figure moved by "the daemon of all possession" (32, 33), while he bursts upon her with the forcefulness of an "ancient storm" (37). Nevertheless, this clash of contrary forces issues into a moment of creation. A first step is made toward it when Susan, aware of the eclipse she has imposed on her lover, attempts to retrieve "him" beyond the "mould of appearances" (34), but becomes so intoxicated with the gesture of self-surrender this involves on her part that "she overemphasize[s] the role of domination" (36) she has played in the past. The real moment of creation occurs when Susan relinquishes all one-sided attitudes and former self-deceptions and agrees to "the loss of individual elements and powers" (37). The dark glasses she dons then in order to cover her spiritual nakedness become paradoxically their joint instrument of vision. Both have by then reached the crucial stage of helplessness and weakness at which they can be translated into "species of fiction and freedom" (38) and are indeed shown sharing the free movements of the elements.[10] All opposites are momentarily joined and apprehended together, and the silence they longed for can be "heard" at the heart of the storm.

This instant of togetherness and creation, when "the lightning of breath" (39) is released, is followed by the need to understand the mystery of their mutual exploitation. Distrust has not wholly disap-

peared and each fears the effect on himself/herself of the other's need
for reassurance and power. As a result, each is caught in a cycle of
conflicting reactions of self-contempt and hostility toward the other.
The way out of this deadlock is, as already suggested, the dissolution
of the rigid mold of personality ("mould of cruel refinement," [41]) in
order to discover that each biased assumption contains its saving
opposite. So, her lover's awareness of his former lack of control
transforms his assault (storm) upon Susan into "THE VERY RECK-
LESS SPECIES OF GRACE" (40), and he is astonished to see that the
brutal energy unleashed upon her can reveal itself as "the beauty of
freedom . . . at the very heart of the storm" (40). Though in essence
this chapter presents the characters' jigsaw progress from tyrannical
assumptions to a confession of them, it describes mainly the lover's
change of attitude, just as Chapter 5, which counterpoints it, describes Susan's. The last section contains a series of images of disruption that must first be re-enacted and digested in order to be creative.
Before this happens, however, Susan recalls the feud she had with her
lover before he left her, and this shows them once more hardened and
locked in struggle, he, "doctor and lover rolled into one"(43), appearing now as an essentially threatening figure.

The moment of creation and liberation in Chapter 4 expands as the
drama reaches its climax in the two central chapters (5 and 6). The
operation that made Susan blind has turned her inwards and will now
at last cure her inner blindness. The effect of the operation merges in
her consciousness with that of the two events for which she indicted
her lover, his "rape" of her and his departure. Hence her keen pain
when "*buried* past and *revival* in the present" (44) are confronted.
Hence also the paradoxical association of penetration with separation
and excision, of "arousal" with "extinction," and of convergence with
flight, a paradox which expresses Harris's concept of community
through what he calls "convolutions of image."[11] These involve in an
extraordinary orchestration the basic images (or variations of them) of
the four previous and the four subsequent chapters: the knife (axe,
razor, sword); the sun alternately associated with the lover and Susan
in their destructive roles; the cavern or womb; the natural elements;
and, most important of all, the vessel with its animate and inanimate

features: captain, member (both sexual organ and member of the crew), mast or pole, sail and deck.

Immediately after the operation Susan's vision still appears to be blocked by irreconcilable extremes, "ancient of suns . . . winter landscape" (45), as her lover's is by fire and ice in the last chapter (78). She is *"stricken blind"* but soon awakes to a healing darkness, and what had been a source of frustration becomes a source of rebirth. The actual pain of the operation is followed by the realization that her (and the world's) sorrow, "tear . . . body of feeling" (47), so far eclipsed by resentment and reproach, has "survived like indestructible evanescence" (47), so that suffering, physical and moral, stimulates her awareness of her earlier self-deception. Her "waking 'dying' pain" (45)—she awakes from unconsciousness and dies to her old self—has brought her to the threshold of the "cavern of reality" (45), her own formerly obscure self, in which at the end of the novel her lover achieves vision (77). There is indeed a sense in which each "dies" into the other's darkness, for his/her deeper self overlaps with the other's. Though it seemed to Susan, as he operated upon her, that her lover was "the stone of the sun" (44) assaulting her, after the operation she sees that

. . . *The blazing abstract scar of instrumental day now slowly faded into darkness, thief of night or creation, whom she loved and hated in turn with all the violence of separate convictions. . . .* (45)[12]

Her lover is now becoming a dark inner sun (the antithesis of the "ancient seal" [15] she had first summoned) who shares with her the "abstract blaze of solid darkness" of the "cavern of reality." "Blaze" and "darkness" express the reconciliation of opposites that is taking place. For Susan the night is now becoming *"light"* through a "dying wound of illumination" (46). The origin of this mutation is to be found in the "frailty of convertible properties like a healing thread" (46) that has subsisted all those years in the apparent void of the waiting room: residues of feeling, as already suggested, and above all the lovers' true motives as Susan finally admits when she "unravel[s]" (71) the thread. She had told her lover to go when she wanted him to stay, and he had taken her at her word, dismissing her while he secretly wanted her to follow him (71−72).

The "dying illumination" that eventually enables Susan to come to terms with her past and achieve a symbolic union with her lover is one form among many of a paradoxical and dynamic duality, process rather than fact, i.e., passage from darkness into light rather than final attainment of light. In this mobility of consciousness a series of poetic metamorphoses occur which transform the "healing thread" into "a scale of 'dying' colors," "existential of the rainbow" (a symbol of heterogeneous totality), which becomes *"teardrop* . . . held upon the fixed coil and station of the whirlpool" (46), thus at once still and moving. Because in this conjunction the lovers no longer attempt to tyrannize over each other, they are again as free as the natural elements. At this point the tear (Susan's consciousness, filled now with the lovers' embrace) turns into a cosmic vessel, no longer the vessel in which they were joined in vindictiveness in Chapter 1 but a metaphor in which the sexual act coalesces with Harris's original version of the "myth of the flight of Ulysses from Circe."[13]

In his critical interpretation of the myth Harris sees a saving union between contraries in the cooperation between Ulysses and his crew, who have tied him to the mast of his vessel, then made themselves deaf. Ulysses is a conscious artist who can listen to the otherworldly song of the muse without succumbing to it, thanks to the crew who steer the dancing vessel with which he makes one, though they are as senseless as its inanimate mast. The crew become "a dramatic agent of subconsciousness,"[14] exteriorizing in space through the dance of the vessel a reality too obscure for them to articulate. An important aspect of Harris's rendering of the myth in *The Waiting Room* is the utter reciprocity of the lovers' roles:

One embraced and was held in turn by this "deaf" mast to which one was truly bound and secured within the elements of distraction, paradoxical structure of liberation, and within a certain undefinable radius of which—acute coherence and conversion of the soul—lay the choirs of vision—sheer tenacity (even profane curiosity) of the "awakened" eye within the latent *crash* and operation of darkness, sheer relative *beam,* heavy and light, gravity as well as ironic weightlessness. . . . (47)

In their embrace each lover is Ulysses "nailed" to the other as to "negative anthropomorphic crew (eclipse of sight—or was it sound?)" (48). The flight from Circe and the Sirens, inspiring though dangerously fascinating goddesses, is a flight from a tempting but terrifying absolute which drives men to destroy others and themselves in their attempt to reach it. That is why it is also a flight from what in oneself can succumb to temptation: the weakness that turns man into an animal and the "self-regard" (47) that makes him deny others and kill. Ulysses can listen to the voice of the goddesses—and to that extent participate in their infinity—because the crew agree to make themselves deaf to a temptation they could not resist and sacrifice themselves to make Ulysses' flight possible. They are thus paradoxically a source of weakness (temporarily neutralized) in oneself *and* a means of liberation. Each lover has been the victim of the other's lust and of the self-regard that made him/her want to pursue and possess him/her as an absolute. Susan was raped (even if symbolically) but, in Book II, she pursued her lover like a hunted animal, pinned him to the wall, and "punctured" him as he had punctured her, giving him "holes for eyes" (57). Each is the other's insensitive mast and sacrificial crew reduced to blindness and dumbness (because deaf) by the other's senselessness or "brute soul of solipsis" (50). But their embrace becomes "life-giving" when self-knowledge enables each to recognize that the other is not a mere *"tool and plaything"* (51) but a saving instrument. Susan becomes both Penelope (the patient, serving wife) and Circe, just as in Book II her lover identifies with her husband, who has given her all that she lacked before, "security, marriage, a home" (69) even though he is unaware of the deeper needs the lover satisfies. In their dual role each lover presents the two faces of the rationale of man's existence: choice and fate. Though these may seem identical at the instant of reconciliation (49), the similarity is deceptive, for choice can only take place *through* fate, i.e., thanks to the sacrificial fate of the dumb within and without oneself:

Cloud or seal, blocking of ears, blinding of sight which rendered one and all immune and faithful guides or servants of each other through the unenviable passage of the underworld. Vessel of reality. Bond of translation. (78)

This sums up the many instances in the novel when Susan and/or her lover are seen reaching understanding or vision through the other.[15]

The "conversion of the soul" (47) occurs through an awakening of the senses arising from a full recognition of, and participation in, the other when each understands that what used to be a source of tyranny in their eyes is indeed a source of liberation, and their "very state of brutal relation" begins to usher "in the fantastic irony of a *common flesh*" (53). The rebirth achieved through this union is of two kinds, for the revival of the senses leads to a renewal of sensibility, i.e., an awareness of what threw the other into the void and of the livingness of what seemed dead. First, their *"common flesh"* is heard "singing in one's ears," then the "MOUTH OF THE VOID [seat of darkness but also of an *'immaterial conviction'*47] SANG for the first pointed incredible time" (54). The contrast between "common flesh" and "void" is contained, I believe, in the title of Chapter 6, "Thing," which describes both the concrete reality of the lovers and the nameless energy at the heart of the void.[16] This ambivalence involves Susan in constant shifts from consciousness to unconsciousness and from a perception of "abstract" reality to its concretization. It determines the structure of Book I, which is not a one-way but a two-way spiral, until at the moment of climax Susan perceives the two movements together as "Thing. . . . It was the only thread of ascent and descent into the hold of creation" (52). Significantly, the moment of vision does not cancel this ambivalence. It is a perception of community as illustrated by the myth of Ulysses, a moment of poise when contraries are perceived in their complementarity and the exploring consciousness is aware of both without identifying with either:

he dared to lean as never before (without actually falling) upon the abyss of invention and confront the technical blast and hollow within which she stood. (52)
She knew she stood on the threshold of resigning herself . . . to . . . a third seeing vessel and party . . . lying between "him" on one hand, and "herself" on the other. (60)

The implication is that one surrenders to one's own and the other's darkness and namelessness (the "third seeing vessel") without staying there finally.

The rebirth that occurs as the void turns into living vortex is only complete when Susan's husband is part of it. At the end of Book I Susan and her lover are *"drawn by the skin of the vortex into the other's rent and beauty of consciousness"* (54), becoming reconciled to the ambivalence of the waiting room, its terrors (arising from the disorientation due to a broken state or loss of a stable self), and its visionary capacity. At the beginning of Book II "the vessel of the room was almost pitch black save for the spiralling light of the horns" (57), i.e., the light of understanding issuing from the darkness of the vortex. At first, it seems to Susan that her husband is an obstacle to her newly achieved fluidity and freedom of consciousness, for she does not realize that the "unpretentious obscurity" (61) into which he fades as a result of her preoccupation with her lover can be part of a healing darkness. Admittedly, her husband's solicitous guard over her is not devoid of an unconscious wish to possess her by his generous attitude, and her accusing cry "WATCHMAN. WATCHMAN" counterpoints her earlier "Thief. Thief." The two, however, merge in Susan's consciousness, for her husband's sense of impotence when she tells him on the phone that she wants *"nothing"* makes him as helpless, and therefore as spiritually naked, as she and her lover were when deprived of their senses. Her husband too is in the void, and she cannot visualize him (she met him when she was already blind) any more than she can now visualize "him," the "abstract" lover: *"Blank. Black"* (62). The two words refer to both men and in their context link her two pregnancies, the fruit of her union with what each man represents, phenomena of sensibility and material comfort. Husband and lover make one when the telephone conversation is cut off and *"nothing,"* the other's (husband and lover) shadow, begins to move as if " 'nothing' were 'something' " (65). It is only now that Susan's operation is utterly successful (as opposed to "technically" successful in Book I) and she grasps the full significance of her lover's departure in the *"Theatre of darkness"* (70), formerly "operating theatre" (43).

The counterpart of this "theatre" for the lover is the nameless cavern he is exploring in search of a spiritual El Dorado in the heartland. There has been a shift of scene, and the last chapter re-creates the lover's achievement of consciousness in terms that parallel Susan's. It is entitled "Blast" (a variant of the operation) and evokes a series of explosions that may shatter a man's world or his perception of it and nevertheless open the way to a new life. There is the explosion of the seal of the sun,[17] of memory, and of the Forrestals' house with the shattering of their logbook. In the wife of his Amerindian guide the lover sees Susan returned to him. When the guide is struck by a bushmaster, he identifies with him, thus acting out Susan's identification of lover with husband and suffering the impact of catastrophe experienced by another. The "holes in his skin" (76) become "puncture of memory" (77) through which "he" sees Susan in a new light. Vision is achieved in the darkness of the cavern, an image that prevails in the rest of the narrative. Apart from the literal cavern the lover explores, immersing himself in the river that runs through it, it is a cavern of death, an underworld in which the lover recovers his senses. It is also the "cavern of reality" and more specifically the "subterranean cave of Susan" (77) (linked with the sexual imagery in Book I), in which he sees that "the faint stunned eyes [Susan's] . . . grew bright . . . stars of consciousness blown by the very fist of night" (77). In other words, the lover sees now, thanks to the regenerated eyes of the muse.

Finally, the cavern is the underworld of the "middle passage" (78) and the lover is "medium of history" (59). Through the mutation of the lover's relationship with Susan, Harris explores the possibilities of genuine community or participation in the "other." The wife-husband-lover triangle, which appears in one form or another in most of his novels, can symbolize, among other things, men's rivalry for the possession of the earth. The middle passage, one of the most catastrophic historical facts resulting from this rivalry, gave birth to a so-called "New World." The dramatization in this novel of the regeneration of the "raped" muse offers, through the metamorphosis of basic human relations, a view of possible change on a wider scale and of the possible creation of a really "new" world. In the cavern the lover hears "a new distant faint blast":

He *knew* . . . that the blast he now heard had actually occurred ages ago: and that, at long last, it was able to reach him in an echo long muffled and nurtured and preserved (like the sound of the sea in a shell). (79)

This delayed blast is that of historical catastrophe and "he" (phenomenon of a renewed sensibility) relives "with new awareness—his descent through the door of the middle passage" (79). The change this implies is not in himself only but in the past he relives, and the lover could ask with Susan "Was it ten years or twenty or ages ago one relationship had died and another begun? In our end is our beginning" (70). In both form and content *The Waiting Room* substantiates this answer. The discontinuity of the narrative, each chapter presenting a new layer of spiritual experience and the potentiality of renewal, corresponds to the disjointed diary or shattered logbook in which the three characters have participated, the substance of their broken lives. The "punctures" they suffered ("holes for eyes" for the blind Susan and her hunted lover, "holes in his skin" for her husband) turned into passages toward a new beginning, and it can be said that their outdated outlook crumbled with the explosion of their antique shop. Through the mutation of their personality (the gist of their recreated lives), each was seen to be the other's guide, unconsciously in Book I, consciously in Book II. The union of these contrary capacities was rendered symbolically by Ulysses' and his crew's "participation" in one another. The crew can also be said to represent the deaf and dumb of the middle passage, who were unable to communicate owing to their lack of a common language. There is thus a suggestion that Ulysses, the imaginative artist, is sustained by the dumb victims of history to whom he can give voice. Indeed, when the lover tells Susan *"art is the phenomenon of freedom"* (66), "The 'deaf' within her stirred and listened. The 'dumb' she cherished began to speak" (66). Clearly, Harris's rendering of the myth harmonizes the divided personality of modern man and revises his "misconception of god . . . man . . . beast" (50) while intimating that he is a composite of all three.

Chapter Eight

An Epic of Ancestors: *Tumatumari*

The "treaty of sensibility" in which Susan Forrestal and her lover participate in The *Waiting Room* lies at the very center of the characters' preoccupations and is given a wider significance in *Tumatumari*. Formerly a community of feeling between individuals, it now involves the recognition of a community of existence between peoples, man and nature as well as society and nature if Guyana (any country or civilization) is to survive. *Tumatumari* concentrates on the effects of the traumas of history on the soul of individuals and peoples. It covers not only the history of one family and of Guyana from the end of World War I to the late 1960s; symbolically, it also embraces the trials and growth of a people over centuries as well as its potential future. Like Harris's earlier fiction, this novel establishes a correlation between the exploration of the past and an art that grows out of the individual's modified perception of its generally accepted meaning. Here too form and the metamorphoses of psychic content are interdependent and linked with the capacity of a young woman called Prudence to contain and transfigure the experience of her family. Her imaginative reconstruction suggests that catastrophe need not be an imprisoning ordeal but that the very losses incurred in the past can give birth to a liberation of consciousness.

At the beginning of the novel Prudence suffers a nervous breakdown due to her child's death at birth, closely followed by the death of her husband, Roi, decapitated on a rock in the rapids of Tumatumari. Her father, the historian Henry Tenby, died several years before and it is his together with Roi's history that is re-enacted through Prudence. However, Harris's use of a central consciousness as a medium of reconstruction is more complex than in the earlier novels. For Prudence is a medium within a medium: her memory is both independent and fused with Roi's consciousness as he descends into the waterfall and looks back on life "as in a dream unravelling itself" (19) (in much the same way as Oudin in *The Far Journey* looks back upon the "match-box world" when he dies). Prudence, then, participates in Roi's descent and sees "her own guillotined sun of reflection" (17) in the water. Not only is the reconstruction seen from both Prudence's and Roi's point of view (as the rocks press against one another in the blinding water), but Roi is both dead and "dying" (see, for example, 84,102). He "dies" through the narrative, and the timeless moment of his death is counterpointed by Prudence's at the end of the novel. Though a catastrophe, his fall releases images of the past, "inner spaces," that restructure themselves in Prudence's consciousness:

FROM WITHIN THE ROCK OF HISTORY—dark room of TUMATU-MARI—Prudence now looked out with Roi's drowned eyes as if the landscape of memory had been assembling itself unobtrusively over the years into a number of technological signposts. (72)

The instant of the fall and Roi's beheading are thus the imaginative nucleus of the novel, from which the major and many-faceted theme grows and the images proliferate. The central metaphor of decapitation, reproduced in innumerable variants, is nevertheless the gateway to a perception of wholeness and "the deepest alien unity of mankind" (67). The very first image is that of a "head" Prudence discerns in the river below the waterfall, in one sense a mere "object" or "thing," in another a symbol of her dead child or of her husband rising again from the bottom of the whirlpool. This duality, reminiscent of the double function of "IT" in the earlier novels, prefigures the significance eventually glimpsed by Prudence in her husband's decapitation. In Book I the "head" is subject to several transfigurations pointing to a different reality. Prudence sees in it a "mask" and "a reflection of her own features" (14). There are forms of it in living nature, in the "revolving glance of the 'black' head of sun in the water" (15). The face of Rakka, Roi's Amerindian mistress, is like "the mask of the sun" (16) while in her mother's death, due to malnutrition, Prudence discerns the "death mask of the sun" (22). Rakka and her mother represent the "vanquished Indians of the sun" (33), the original inhabitants of Guyana who have lost their primal vision of a sun-god, "rock of the sun" (32), and, insofar as they have been deprived of this natural sovereign, have been decapitated as a people. From the start Prudence sees also in the "head" "the One" (a symbol of unity) and a "cradle" (15,31), which she carries toward the well from whose depths she retrieves the history of her family.

Prudence's "act of memory"[1] proceeds from the very nature of her personality. Like most women in Harris's fiction, she is the muse who can both inspire and deceive though she shares this role with Rakka and in this respect is a further development of the modern/Amerindian muse in *Heartland* and *The Waiting Room*. She is also the psyche of the modern Guyanese, who draws from within herself and the world of Tumatumari resources indispensable to change. Both Prudence and, symbolically, the rock in the waterfall are a womb in which the "drama of conception" (41) takes place. Her own resources are memory, the mainspring of her re-creation of the past; imagination which, as her father says, is the only hope for the future (63); and foresight, as she shows in her capacity to envisage the future while reconstructing the past, notably when she recalls her visit to the abandoned native village and envisions the "TUMATUMARI OF TOMORROW" (66).[2] The interaction between past, present, and future is an essential feature of Prudence's perception of events and, consequently, structures the narrative. As in *The Eye,* history (personal and national) is freed from chronology and gradually pieced together by Prudence's associative memory. Thus remembering her recent past when she wondered whether her child would be black or white, she is naturally led to recall that her family (the Guyanese community and the family of man) is racially mixed: her mother and her sister Pamela passed for white, her father was dark with Indian features, and her brother, Hugh Skelton, black and forced by his mother to hide and play "skeleton in the cupboard" when distinguished visitors came. This was done with the tacit agreement of Henry Tenby who was torn, nevertheless, by the contradictory pressures of prejudice and conscience.

The remote past of Tumatumari is mainly that of the Amerindians, who since the Renaissance conquest have repeatedly vanished into the forest but reappeared from time to time to sell their labor, subsisting in this way "upon a dislocated scale of time" (80). When Prudence first lifts the lid of the well of history (31)—an abandoned stone well built by Roi five years before his death—she sees the symbolical lost tribe of the sun moving at the bottom of the falls. They are a constant reminder of her own, Guyana's, and humanity's origins. Yet through Tenby's youth and maturity, which evoke the colonial past as well as the more recent period of crucial choices for Guyana's future, the Indians have been remorselessly exploited as a people and as individuals. Rakka, who appears in Tenby's life as "the waif-of-the-street," is the cheap muse (and whore) of successive generations. Even Roi, himself half-Amerindian, declares that the Indians "are the conscience of our age" (35), yet admits that he too exploits them. For Prudence the retrieval of the Indians from the "bandage[3] of history" (49) becomes more than a question of economic justice. Though unaware of it, they are the remaining link with a primordial outer and inner landscape ("They sprang out of the ragged atmosphere within one's head"[31]) peopled with ancient gods (despite their fall) and animals, which man too often refuses to recognize as a part of himself. To retrieve the Indians from their eclipsed condition is thus to move toward a fuller conception of man.

In an extraordinary passage which re-creates the meeting between "huntsman and hunted" (37) Roi's hunt of a wild boar is superimposed on his descent into the waterfall (see 53). The rock toward which he falls looks like a boar. After the hunt Roi and the boar "sw[i]m towards each other" (apparently enacting the meeting between hunter and hunted). Then in Prudence's "dream of a loved one, drowning, decapitated" (54) it is as if the animal's head merged with Roi's: "the boar's lips . . . mingled now with hers as well as Roi's like the water of life" (55). Further, experiencing the "birth of conscience" (87) in both husband and father, Prudence sees that it involves the recognition of the animal in man and confesses that "deity wore chains after all—the chains of man's terrifying relationship to the mire of the depths as man wore chains—chains of primordial animal to which he was ironically indebted for his susceptibility to the 'openess' of nature" (87). Harris's rendering of the openness of nature and of the effect of man's response to it is most impressive. The following short extract will show that the growth of consciousness in Prudence goes together with her integration into nature and participation in its rhythms of life. In a moment of illumination the shock of revelation is so great that she begins to tremble:

At first she could not cease from trembling . . . but as she shook, vibrations were set up which rippled and fled across the basin of the world—Amazon to Orinoco—Atlantic to Pacific—a continent bedded in rivers and oceans. It was as if she gained some consolation from reciprocity, from reaction. (112)

The main theme of the novel is the conversion of Prudence in conjunction with Roi's and Tenby's as a result of the reconstruction of the collisions of history and its dismemberments of individuals and peoples, a conversion stimulated by a growing awareness that history and its dead actors are themselves subject to change. It develops through a remarkably coherent use of imagery. The "head" or first symbol in the narrative presents together the two entities Prudence must reconcile: nature, whether represented by the sun or the whole landscape ("a dense face reeking of vegetation"[67]), and society represented by the different masks which the head motif introduces. As already suggested, the head covers a whole spectrum of meanings, positive and negative, for it is not only the tragic emblem of all dismemberments—Roi's in the rapids, the tribes' which Roi's fall re-enacts, Prudence's (psychologically "trunkless and leg-less" [14], and Tenby's (92)—it is also the embryo of reconstruction. Ivan van Sertima rightly points out that "there are images of all parts of the human anatomy, which seems to be breaking up and reassembling itself in the restructuring of man."[4] He underlines the importance of the eye, and indeed its appearance on the rock-face (another "head' or "mask") of Tumatumari marks the beginning of Prudence's conversion. The eye is equivalent to "IT" (114) and, as in Harris's earlier novels, stands at once for the concrete instrument of exploration and vision and the metaphysical reality it discovers, the alien dimension Prudence discerns in the Amerindian and African victims of history. From the beginning, then, the "head" stimulates the reconstruction of its own severance and rebirth: "the vision of the 'head' in the water . . . was instrumental in invoking both the processes as well as the premises of recreation" (17).

The premises of re-creation are the falls of Tumatumari and the well Roi dug above them to measure their hydroelectric potential. The waterfall and the well are complementary and linked by a secret staircase, which to Prudence is "a passage to her own name" (31), which she has inscribed on the lid of the well, i.e., a passage to self-knowledge. In her eyes the upper part of the well has the configuration of her father's "chair of history" and to plumb its depths is to reconstruct Roi's fall in the rapids, which stands for all collisions due to the violation of men or cultures. The well enables Prudence to understand Roi's failure to harness the energy potential of the falls, a task he undertook in a technological attempt to conscript nature for the benefit of a firm on the coast. His first collision, when he fell into the well and knocked his head against its concrete framework, made him aware of nature's power to strike back, of the falls' "electric fiend" (also his own daemon behind his mask): "I was stricken . . . Electricity to last a lifetime. I saw everything lit up from within" (24−25). This incident is to be linked with the recollection of Tenby's deathbed scene when he struck Prudence a blow on the temple which "set everything ablaze and she saw his life illumined . . . the smallest cracks in an otherwise impeccable exterior became the gaping lighthouse of the past" (46).

The boiling waters of the rapids striking the rocks with fiery energy seem to correspond to the passions of men and exemplify a perilous but fertile duality in nature and man. The very name of the falls, Tumatumari, means *"sleeping rocks,"* and these are susceptible to "awakening," and "convertible" (26) like Susan Forrestal's waiting room. All the characters possess the falls' dual nature and can be *"ignited* by an element far older, though frailer, than uniformity or persuasion" (21, italics mine). Rakka's face, at first a dark mask, seems to Prudence "to wave and burn" (16). When Rakka's mother died, her "eyelids turned to stone: *lapis* of populations within which a sombre flame shone" (22). The eyes of Tenby's Rakka (the woman he visits in the "brothel of masks") are "made of stone" (94) but become "suddenly afire" (95). The Indians peer at Roi "like stones" (50) and appear to Prudence as "strange stony faces in the falls" (56), but they have merely retired after conquest into their "'death' or 'sleep' of fire" (32). Prudence's wish to balance the two proportions of loss and gain inherent in the past—a leitmotiv in the novel—rather than concentrate on its face of disaster alone shows her awareness of the possible discovery of "fire in stone" (17). In this her attitude differs from Roi's in his lifetime. His eyes too were "stone-dead" (23) and would suddenly be animated by a spark. But though aroused by the "sparks" (26) that flew through him when he was electrified in the well, he did not adopt the kind of behavior that would benefit the region and its early inhabitants. Instead, he took advantage of his recovery to impose his sovereignty over the Indians by way of "the Ceremony of the Rock" (36), in one sense the assumption of a monolithic persona that enabled him to parade a "mask of enlightenment" (35) as if he were the Indians' new god or Rock-Sun while actually subjecting them to his one aim of "upholding an economic establishment . . . by fair means or foul" (36), which he thought was the only means of survival.

Book II, entitled *The Ceremony of the Rock*, shows other characters involved in a similar process of hardening. There is Rakka, looking tragic, tender, and full of compassion but also "tempered as steel" (42). Like the rocks that her name evokes, she is both barren and fertile: barren owing to a fall for which Roi was partly responsible, yet pregnant "metaphysically speaking" (71) because involved in a relationship of reciprocity with him. This the Indians couldn't stand, wishing to preserve the tribe as a monolith for "fear of the stranger creeping in" (71). A similar fear kept Tenby's black and white children divided (45), as it was "the secret hardening of fear" (60) that made him agree to Pamela's marriage followed by the rejection of her black child and its adoption by strangers in America. In both the deathbed scene, when he cursed "god" and his progeny for their division, and in his paradoxical reproach to Pamela for acting according to "the pattern of conquest, of history as [he] had accepted it, lived it and written it" (60) Tenby revealed the stress and illness of which he seems to die, the result of his constant assumption of a "bogus historical mask" (62). So that in the last moments of his life he seemed to Prudence "a creature cloven in two, one face on top mask-like as before, the other face emerging from the old" (45). In the last section of Book II Prudence recalls a speech she heard in her childhood by one comrade Block (another monolith) at Port Mourant. His condemnation of the social and economic situation in Guyana was largely consistent with Tenby's awareness of its evils, though he would not acknowledge it when he heard the speech in 1952. But Block's accusing words were intended as "persuasion" only and offered no alternative for genuine change such as Roi intuits just before Block's speech is reported. Block's refusal to admit that the East Indian woman Tenby nearly ran over is alive—possibly a refusal to see the victim as other than a conventional flag to be branded for political purposes—throws an ironic light on Tenby's own self-deceptions, for in this instance it was Tenby who became the victim of misconception.

Both Roi and Tenby differ from the characters in Harris's earlier fiction, who had to discover in what way they erred in the past. The two men knew that their country's natural configuration and the social idiosyncrasies born of oppression demanded a complete revision of former policies. Yet out of self-interest and fear both steeled themselves against their deeper insights. Prudence states that her husband and father "shared . . . one vehicle of the imagination" (46), and, as her creation of "the epic of ancestors" (133) indicates, that vehicle or carriage is clearly herself (note that the alternative to her name on the lid of the well of history is "C-A-R-R-I-A-G-E O-F T-H-E S-U-N"[79]). That she *has* imagination is emphasized by her father, who was hoping she would marry an engineer in order to achieve the union between science and art that he saw as a prerequisite to the "treaty of sensibility" (104, 109) he secretly longed for. But hers is an imagination in great need of recovery. The re-creation of the brief period of her marriage to Roi shows that Prudence was already breaking down before the death of her child and of her husband, that she was ridden by fear since her arrival in Tumatumari: "'pregnant' fear of darkness" (28), fear of the content of the well (29), fear of "the seed of the future . . . brink of self-knowledge" (33), and above all fear of Rakka's power over her husband (68). These fears of what the interior represents are of the same kind as those that prompted her spiritual conception by her father. In Books III and IV (*The Chair of the Well* and *The Brothel of Masks*) we learn of Tenby's symbolical conception of his children in reverse order of their actual birth after his return from Europe to Guyana in 1921. The symbolical conception of each child corresponds to a crisis in his life and a catastrophe in the country, their real birth to his writing an essay or a play, in which his genuinely creative views were expressed, but which remained secret until Prudence reconstructed his subterranean life from them. Though the youngest of his five children (the first two were in his mind solely conceived by his wife), Prudence, born in 1940, was the first to be conceived as an ideal in 1922. Tenby was then "shopping in the womb of place [the brothel of masks] for the mask of a lifetime" (93). Finding himself face to face with the eternal Rakka, he was so horrified by "the stranglehold he detected upon [her] flesh and blood" (96) that he decided never to lift a hand to his unborn children and acquired the mask of gentility he would wear for the rest of his life. He was wholly deceived, however, since, as he bitterly acknowledged later, by refusing to recognize the "callous of history" (96) he was sacrificing whole populations to his illusion of rectitude. That it was an illusion was confirmed by his decision to match his outer mask with "a conception of . . . inner space" (130), i.e., the symbolically named Pamela, "virtue allied to beauty" (130), although as Roi explains to Prudence (71), virtue too can be the fruit of fear.[5] And fear was also at the heart of the conception of Hugh (130) as well as behind the impulse to "shove him underground" (101) when he was born black. Hugh was to be killed in the 1962 riots by a bullet fired by his *"father's rich kith and kin"* (120).

To come back to Prudence's role in her father's and husband's existence, it should be clear that whenever they acted in her name, they were moved by fear, the reverse side of Prudence. Even Roi's decision, prior to his death, to cross the river alone in the dark was motivated by a fear that his wife and his territory were in danger. The two men's self-deceptive notion of prudence explains why the young woman's reconstruction of the past is also a process of self-examination and renewed conception of herself.[6] It explains her vision of Roi's death in the falls "THROUGH HER" (28) and "IN HER NAME" (50), a death symbolizing, it must be recalled, the disasters incurred in the name of misconceived prudence. Her knowledge that Roi and Tenby exercised "an underground imagination . . . over a life-time of bitterness until from their own lips a heartrendering cry arose" (46), though at first a cause of resentment in Prudence left with the "burden of conception," is nevertheless a stimulus to her own and their conversion. Roi himself had told Prudence: "Must not my sceptical law as well as your sympathetic love . . . re-structure themselves through dislocation, poison, fissure, weakness . . . learn of themselves through alien proportions?" (35) His timeless fall is the loss that gives Prudence "a structure of metamorphosis . . . the medium out of which a new illumination of feeling would emerge" (17). Though he used to wear the brutal mask of reified technology, he was aware of "pockets of darkness, filth" (35), in the body of the community and knew that he was equally a "scapegoat" (36), who, like the "sick king"[7] in all mythologies, was responsible for the regeneration of his people. Like Carroll's death in *Palace of the Peacock,* Roi's is accidental and not intended as a sacrifice. Indeed, death in this as in all Harris's novels is too tragic a loss ever to be considered as in any way desirable. But because it does occur, the possibility of compensating the loss by unearthing its proportion of gain must not be overlooked. With Roi, who also represents the "dying god," die the ruling assumptions of an age, though the images of suffering and death evoked by his fall are the prelude to a creative rebirth. On the other hand, the abandoned Indian village of Tumatumari reminds Prudence of the sudden fall of ancient American civilizations, *"the head of ruler or rule severed in a flash"* (67), but she must resist the temptation to romanticize the past. Through the reconstruction of Roi's death in the rapids both she and Tenby, the "father of history" (124), can face and comprehend "the reality of sacrifice" (131).

Significantly, the long section entitled "THE DEATH AND FUNERAL PROCESSION OF THE KING OF THE SUN" (85) recalls Tenby's youth and its major options: first, his encounter in 1919 in Marseilles with Isabella, the "muse of the century," who reflected its contradictions of dazzling beauty and lust allied to inner misery and starvation. Each concealed from the other his/her material and spiritual poverty so that from the first there was an element of deceit in his relationship with the muse, who at this period vanished from his life as suddenly as the Indians were to vanish from Roi's. Back in Guyana he bought his mask of prudence, then in 1924 met "the waif-of-the street."[8] He treated her as a whore from the start and in retaliation she silenced him for the rest of his life with the effect that her prostitution meant the muzzling of his art. On each occasion of his encounter with the muse Tenby failed to realize that his real source of inspiration lay in visualizing the funeral processions of the past, whether of "the slaves of the sun" (90) or of African slaves, in whom he feared to recognize his ancestry, conceiving therefore his son "*in the* HEARSE OF THE WATERFALL" (97) (destined to be a victim); there was also the procession of the postwar starving millions, of those, in short, whose tragic fate Tenby did not have the courage to confront in his lifetime. That Rakka in her different guises represents them all appears clearly from Prudence's illuminations at the beginning of Books III and IV. These moments of vision give Prudence an intuitive perception of what recollected events substantiate, namely, that the arousal of imagination involves, to begin with, a reconciliation between the two faces of the muse, herself and Rakka, the one born of Tenby's (mankind's) attempt to reach an illusory perfection and draw "from the bottomless well of the sky," the other moving endlessly at "the bottom of the pool . . . the depths of history" (83,111). The reconciliation is conveyed by a symbolic vision of harmony between Prudence and Rakka (fire and water) who revolve and change places on the circumference of the whirlpool of death and rebirth. They draw toward them a "mountain of souls"—the "dead" of all funeral processions.

The reciprocity between Prudence and Rakka, a prelude to other "confrontation[s] of extremes" (135) and their symbolical harmonization into "a fantastic reprocity of elements" (114), foreshadows Tenby's resumption of the conversation with the muse or waif-of-the street since his own conversion partly depends on Prudence's and her capacity to contain imaginatively all latent, then gradually perceptible relationships. He must "descend into himself as into all men"

(104), "crawl back into the interior . . . into the womb" (134), but it is "through the eyes of Prudence" and "from within the seal of death" (144, 145) that he fully understands the role he played in life and its previously unsuspected effect.[9] Prudence's compassionate probing of her husband's life and Tenby's years of silence bring to light their hidden motives. She had been shocked by Roi's indifference to the death of Rakka's mother but realizes that his mask of harshness concealed a deep anguish; she also sees that he had no alternative but to act "in the name of rules he knew to be obsolete" (81). Similarly, she sees (and Tenby with her) that her father's silence *was* self-betrayal but that to be "non-party, non-vocal" was preferable to following the "new banners of serfdom" (132) under which he would have had to protest. She feels, moreover, that imprisoned as he was in his own fear, he shared the fearful silence of those who remained conscripted in the well of history. Just as Roi's contradictions (see 81) stimulate Prudence to an understanding of the "Metaphysics of the Alien,"[10] so her father's dichotomy becomes for her the catalyst of the treaty of sensibility they are both trying to achieve. As the past reveals its hidden face, Tenby's deathbed curse turns out to have been a blessing containing "the wisdom of conception" (131). Even Pamela and Diana, Tenby's seemingly self-possessed but neurotic wife, appear as pathetic figures, victims of their own unconfessed confusion and guilt.

It is thus through the characters' very limitations and an understanding of them that the birth of consciousness occurs. The Ceremony of the rock, now called "Ceremony of dreams," also involves the reverse process of hardening: "who could tell when . . . ROCK WOMB would part, until there emerged . . . ONE who had spent but a Night beneath the unequal burden of time?" (100) What would have been "premature" (81, 141) in Roi's and Tenby's lifetime remains, nevertheless, the seed of the future. Time plays a major role in the mutation that occurs in nature and in Prudence's inner world. The "womb of time" (67) secretes its own resistance against the conventions of each age, and history itself is like an egg whose frail shell (114) protects infinite resources. Not only does Prudence's vision change (like that of Harris's earlier characters) but the "pointed eye of time [comes] alive" (112). In other words, with the passing of time, the seemingly frozen past begins to move ("resumption of traffic into the psyche, into space, into the hinterland" [142]) and to return with a partly different complexion. Though Harris's earlier fiction implied as much,[11] it is only in Tumatumari that the resurrection of the past and the interrelatedness of past, present, and future *in the characters' consciousness* is so explicitly realized.

The unpublished work from which Prudence re-creates Tenby's life shows that the social and political monoliths hewed by the history of Guyana are liable to the same displacements as its soil (see the fissures in the rock of *Tumatumari*, the landslides in the Canje region); it lays bare "the unborn future in the heart of the dead" (99)—hence the title of Tenby's play "Funeral Cradle" (115). After immersing himself in his past with Prudence, he rises from "the bottom of the pool" with the muse (Prudence and the waif-of-the-street); because his former prejudices have melted, he himself turns into a "door of conceptions" (117). In this way he actualizes Prudence's earlier intuition that by entering the apparently empty settlement of Tumatumari (the seat of history) she was pushing open the "DOOR OF THE FUTURE" (69).[12] Equally important is the fact that while representing the diminished state of man ("primitive child, scarecrow" [142]), each character is also a child of the future. No progeny is born of Prudence's generation since her child, the offspring of her fear and Roi's anguish, dies at birth, Rakka is barren, and Pamela gives her child away. Tenby's imaginative return to the Canje (a region associated with the blackest features of Guyana's history where, significantly, he finally achieves consciousness) is punctuated by references to "children impaled upon the ramparts of inner space," at once the symbol of a sacrificed future and the price paid for the lifting of spiritual drought. But the representation of Roi as "CHILD OF THE SUN" (80) expresses both his doom and his rebirth through Prudence, and throughout the novel the symbol of the child and the cradle Prudence carries in her arms announce her own regeneration and the liberation of "the Child of Nature" (155) together with her participation in the "Game of the Conception" (156).

Roi's and Tenby's change in conjunction with Prudence brings to full maturity and blends three unique aspects of Harris's art: his conception of character, his view of a changing past, and the ambivalent function of imagination in his fiction. Increasingly since the Guiana Quartet Harris has tended to stretch the limits of his characters' personality and to present each central consciousness as a crucible in which all the elements of his/her country's and humanity's complex past merge and dissolve again to keep open man's infinite possibilities of renewal and progress. Whether consciously or not, each character carries an unlimited variety of experience at all levels and all stages of existence. Fulfillment consists in acknowledging it, in refusing to consider time and space as implacable and self-sufficient frames of life, and in transforming the separate monoliths of material selves into doorways opening onto the fluid mixture of instincts, emotions, high and low aspirations, that all men share and therefore should be sensitive to in each other. Out of this grows Harris's conception of character as a personality "cognizant of many existences through the fact that those existences are not sovereign devices."[13] Ivan van Sertima calls Harris's characters "microcosms or *foci* of community."[14] Prudence is indeed made to realize that the blend of races within her family and herself corresponds to the spiritual inheritance of her mixed ancestry. That is why she is the dynamic receptacle of her husband's and father's experience and becomes the seat of an interaction between the effect of time on the immaterial residue of men's lives (Roi's and Tenby's concealed emotions) and her own converting power of memory. She discovers that the past crumbles in time and discloses the disregarded or unsuspected feelings of individuals and peoples, the meaning also of their sacrifice. Once the barriers of time and space crumble, the recognition and assimilation of a changing past by an individual mediating consciousness can be seen as the fruit of reciprocity (note Tenby's realization that he must "transfer to Prudence the . . . equipment *she* needed to retrace *his* steps to [the] scene of liberation" [131, italics mine]). As Prudence's imagination reclaims and transmutes larger sections of her father's past, it is being healed by its very perception and digestion of the extreme and contradictory features of Guyana's history. This reciprocity between increasingly deeper (or further removed) elements in the landscape of history and in herself is most eloquently expressed in Prudence's illuminations:

she recognized that IT (the eye on the Face of the Wall) was itself but a ring or clasp in a chain of identity extrapolated into her fluid grasp and that in glancing at her, through her, with her (in binding her to itself in one light) it was being glanced at itself from another source through the window of its own disparity of perception and therefore unbinding her in another light. (114, 151)

It is only after Tenby's complete release from the shackles of his life that Prudence's final liberation takes place. This, it must be underlined, is as terrifying an experience as Roi's fall. The "treaty of sensibility" toward which she has been moving with her father in humility and compassion has entailed the breakdown of all former assumptions, "idols" or "models" (152), as Harris calls them, and the discovery of a tradition of sacrifice and endurance which she genuinely suffers with by yielding to the depths of the waterfall. Prudence wondered at the beginning of the novel whether she stood on the brink of self-destruction or self-creation (15). Through her actual and symbolical descent into the waterfall she achieves self-creation *through* self-destruction and participates in the endless dissolving and reshaping of the canvas of existence, a natural never-to-be-finished process that man (and society) must adhere to if he is to avoid petrification. Having formerly contributed to the arrest of that process (her jealousy of Rakka amounted in part to confining the "other," individual or group, to real or spiritual death) she experiences the remorse necessary to envisage a different future.[15] Her own Ceremony of the Rock is the *"Translation of a non-reciprocal establishment. Spatial womb . . . Translation of the Gorgon of History* (154–155).

Once again Harris finds in the individual consciousness alone and in its willingness to confront its own components, however terrifying, the term of a national consciousness (provided "national" is used in an unrestrictive sense). Indirectly, he has also exemplified in Prudence and, through her, in her father the role of the West Indian artist who, as he has written elsewhere, must "descend into [and] suffer creatively" the disorder of his people's alienation and so-called "historylessness."[16] In his re-creation of his characters' descent there is a striking correspondence between the use of symbols (particularly the waterfall, the well or chair of history, and the splitting rock) and the mutations of inner landscape they convey. On the whole, this novel combines a greater variety of styles than its predecessors. Primarily "social" characters like Diana and Pamela are portrayed in a few accurate strokes revelatory of their moral deficiency. The narrative alternates between the density of *The Eye* and the "refined" or quintessential texture of *The Waiting Room*. Discursory passages complement and clarify Prudence's moments of illumination without, however, replacing them. Each of the five parts begins with Prudence's visionary perception of truths she must realize painfully and digest so that the series of illuminations (there are brief partial ones within each part) is balanced by Prudence's conscious efforts to grasp the significance of the history she is piecing together. The juxtaposition of intuition with a more rational approach ("vision and idea," as Harris writes in *Palace)* is naturally reflected in the style, the high metaphorical concision of the opening section in each book alternating with dialogue or with the more explicit but still symbolical narration. Occasional authorial comments about Prudence throw light on her difficult progress without, I think, intruding into or impairing the unity of the narrative, a unity of content and form epitomized in Roi's fall and decapitation.

At the end of the novel Prudence's liberating vision culminates in the "conception of the game," the sum of the many partial conceptions she has formed during her exploration. What was merely a tentative game at the outset, possibly a reiteration of "the game of Tumatumari, sleeping rocks in her head" (23) that she used to play with her father as a child, has involved her in the great game of history or "terrifying Conception of the Game of the Rapids" (152). The pun on "game" suggests the hunted game, the boar or "human" game at last "conceived" and therefore susceptible to rebirth. It is also the game of death and life which, for Prudence, has been at once "the game of exploratory nature" and the *"game of inner space"* (152) that entailed the fall and splintering of all one-sided ideals as well as the opening of outer and inner rock-womb to give birth to the Eye of vision. By that time the severed head or "mask of phenomenon" Prudence beheld in the opening section of the novel has begun to live and move:

with each fluid bubble the Gorgon's head smiled, wreathed by the elements, translation of suns, subterranean as well as extra-stellar, across space, towards a reciprocal vacancy. An unprejudiced flesh and blood. (155—156)

Chapter Nine

A "Novel-Vision of History": *Ascent to Omai*

Ascent to Omai is the climax of Harris's second fictional cycle, his most daring experiment with the form of the novel, and it comes nearest to actualizing his concept of narrative as a dynamic structural design. It could be likened to an abstract painting whose components would have the capacity to move. This novel brings together the different perspectives from which Harris has approached his material since *Heartland* and initiates yet another line of development. The first part of the novel alone combines the inland expedition fundamental to *Heartland* and *The Eye* with the spiral-like progress of the lovers in *The Waiting Room* and the coincident movements of ascent and descent to be found in *Tumatumari*. The fragmentation that characterizes the earlier novels is still a necessary stage of discovery in *Ascent* but it goes together with a constant awareness of wholeness. It seems even that, to understand it rightly, the reader should be able to grasp the novel as a whole while discerning at the same time its interwoven elements and the correspondences between its several layers of meaning. He must also keep in mind that this novel is more clearly than any other about writing a novel and that it offers the most eloquent example in this cycle of Harris's conception of character as a vessel for other existences.

As in the earlier novels, events and actions can either imprison the characters in a deadlock of frustration or make them discover the light of compassion that explodes all self-made fortresses. The first conscious memory of Victor, the main character, is of a clout in his side his father, Adam, gave him when he was three years old because he was crying on the floor of their one-room lodging while his parent made love with a prostitute he had brought in from the street. At such moments of crisis a voluminous old petticoat of his mother would serve Victor as a refuge, a fortress of love. As an older child, he would wait for Adam, a welder by profession, to come out of the foundry. From the symbolic wound in his side inflicted by his father, he would flash the light of the sun reflected in a mirror on to Adam's brow and blind him. Victor had reached the age of puberty when his father started a six-month strike which ended with his burning down the factory and his own bed and board. On that same day Victor, by then an exhibition scholar in the best school in the country, burnt a hole in his exercise book and was caned. Adam served a seven-year sentence, then staked a claim as a pork-knocker on Omai, where he made and lost a fortune, while Victor was thought to have run away to sea after his father's trial. What became of him subsequently is uncertain.

The novel opens with Victor's search for Adam forty years after his trial and takes place in the six hours that separate Victor from his own death on Omai, a cloudy mountain covered with jungle in the Guyanese interior. Although the main facts relate to Caribbean history, Adam and Victor are representative of humanity, and their life-span even evokes the geological history of the earth. In the story of Victor the successive ages of mankind are eventually harmonized. Striking correspondences make clearer than ever Harris's view of the individual soul as an epitome of the world. There is, for example, an implicit parallel between the prehistoric Magdalene[1] period and a child's prenatal " 'trial or experience' " (123). There are signs of the civilizations that left an imprint on Adam and of the imprisoning as well as liberating agents they may have offered. In the first few pages alone Adam brings to mind the Christian church and its achievements ("*Patron saint of the watershed* . . . stained glass window" [15]), then its dual role ("saint and executioner of the watershed" [16]), as well as the Renaissance and the Russian revolution ("Donne to Mayakovsky" [17]). Later in the novel Osiris and Christ, who suffered a similar fate in separate eras, are both shown as possible objects of idolatry or, on the contrary, as omens of grace.

The power of the individual soul to fuse disparate areas of experience also applies to time apprehended subjectively and objectively. Forty years separate Adam's trial from its reconstruction which takes place in six hours. This specific frame of time is balanced by a timeless apprehension of events, appearing not as isolated occurrences but as foci of activity related to what has gone before and what will happen after. Similarly, the participants in events have a counterpart in "the disembodied ghost of time flying in anticipation and reality *before* and *after*, below and above the aircraft [the latest version of the courtroom of existence]" (56). Events in time are thus counterpointed or reversed in a timeless dimension in which chronology is meaningless. Harris even suggests that in the characters' vision the two dimensions are interchangeable: "It was also possible to reverse the material/immaterial function of the court" (57). It explains, for example, why Adam can stumble "upon the wreckage of his own past" (52) or why he can tell Victor "one must view the conqueror from the rear" (18). This is at the beginning of the novel when Adam is fleeing up the hill and dissolves into the elements until there only remains, in Mayakovsky's words, "a cloud in trousers" (17). The image fits Adam admirably, for he is a nebulous figure, a faceless and blind man ("holes for eyes"[2]) the eternal victim reduced to nothingness or *tabula rasa*. Victor's evanescent perception of his father is also in keeping with the "spectral" and "diffuse character of the environment" (15). The veil of cloud that separates him from Adam is a veil between life and death, and the territory he is treading, though unmistakably concrete, suggests both the mountainous jungle and a mysterious nowhere just above him, the unseen peopled land whose existence Stevenson had only suspected in *Heartland*. The narrative of *The Waiting Room* concentrated on a borderline between opposites that became reconciled through the metamorphosis of formerly static images. In this novel opposites are apprehended *together* from the start.

More than in any other novel the language of *Ascent* weaves a dense though extremely concise narrative which can best be unravelled by tracing essential metaphors and their meanings. To the superimposed structural patterns in *Omai Chasm* mentioned above correspond three complex metaphors. Victor's perception of the "chasm" opens the globe of his life. The chasm in the landscape is "the abyss of history" (17), containing the "psyche of history, stigmata of the void" (23) that Victor must understand. Its equivalent in his own life is the wound in his side inflicted by Adam's clout. His insatiable appetite as a boy made him want to fill his side with more than his father could give him. A pun on OMAI, "OH MY CHASM," expresses this solipsism. But facing now Omai chasm, he realizes that the symbolical spear that wounded him as a child could be a spear of renewal opening a "chasm of daring" (29). The second structural metaphor, linked to the chasm which opens the way to the inward journey, is the circle. When Victor follows the rim of the chasm he moves "within humid and arid cycles of memory. FORBIDDEN CYCLES OF THE HEARTLAND" (23). This form too offers contrasting possibilities since, from the beginning, Victor is aware that all imprisoning circles can open out and knows he is engaged in a "Reformation of the loop" (17 ff.). His mother's round petticoat, and his circular climb around his father's factory when he prevailed upon him to fill his side, created for Victor limiting horizons. But the liberating power of a moving circle is suggested in Victor's realization that the spear in his side created "its own revolving wheel of compassion" (34), which implies that the wound may be the origin of "reformation."

The third basic metaphor is the stone which unites outer and inner heights and depths, and at the end of the novel sends out the ripples and concentric rings that free both Adam and Victor from the enclosing horizons of Victor's childhood and adolescence. The stone too has a dual function from the start. The vanishing Adam dislodges a stone that strikes Victor on the brow and makes him temporarily unconscious but also helps him understand the *"Dialectic of the boot"* (17) and by association the *"Metaphysics of the axe"* (17),[3] the two methods by which people were ruled from the Renaissance to the Russian revolution. There is also the stone flung by the French founder of a plantation; it killed his young brother, as a result of which he went into self-imposed exile. Thanks to the money he left for orphans when he died, the stone of death initiated a "dance of the muse. Dance of evolution" (20) which clearly prefigures the "Dance of the Stone" at the end of the novel. And there is the stratified rock on Omai, seen as a "lantern of geological age" or as Adam's "Tombstone of light" (20—21). The rock on Omai is volcanic and can therefore rebound as Victor's past does in his consciousness. In this capacity to erupt and change the configuration of the landscape Victor reads an *Opus Contra Naturam*, i.e., the possibility to escape conscription by nature whether in the outer world or in oneself, to avoid being tricked by its images and the illusions it creates.

The dual function of all natural elements has a counterpart in Victor's experience. The juxtaposition OH MY/OMAI reminds us that for Harris it is the physical self (OH MY) that opens the way to the corresponding unseen reality that is being explored (OMAI). Omai is semantically related by Harris to "omen"; it is also associated with the lost or mythical worlds of Atlantis and Roraima and is clearly another version of El Dorado. Bringing together OH MY with OMAI amounts to balancing gains with losses. Adam is Victor's doppelgänger, his "secret agent" (18), and in a sense his "loss," though, from the beginning, he is also an agent of enlightenment. One of the difficulties in the novel is that in addition to the opposition between the living and the dead (Victor and Adam) each is presented with his own contradictions. In his ascent Victor shifts between a half-visual/half-intuitive perception of Adam in the landscape, spells of complete blackout, rationalizations of his intuitions, and finally a dreamlike reconstruction of his childhood and adolescence when the chasm parts the curtain of a stage on which his play, "SOUL," is enacted.

To sum up the four chapters in Book I: as Victor climbs toward Omai a myriad of contradictory impressions, all related to his and Adam's life, assail his senses and mind from the heights and depths of the landscape. Geology and history are united by the imagery. The stratified rock of Omai not only shows traces of the Magdalene period but its tin, copper, and gold deposits are so many witnesses of Victor's (man's) experience. To give one example, tin as a raw material corresponds to one stage in Victor's making ("Tin soldier of fortune" [32]) and to what Adam can afford to give him then; in Book II Victor first flies to Omai as Pilot Tin. Michael Gilkes has rightly suggested that Adam's Welding factory is the "melting pot"[4] of the Caribbean. It is also the welding shop of creation, at once a *locus* and a capacity given man to dissolve and weld again (as nature itself does) the multiform elements of his world. In this lies Adam's revolutionary power, though he does not seem to have known it. Victor's approach to the Omai watershed is sustained by his awareness of both the sacred and the profane (31) and of the convertibility of each into the other.

This is confirmed by what he sees as milestones on his way to Omai: the bump on his forehead made by Adam's stone and the scar on his neck where he (Caribbean man) was beheaded long before. There is also the "rain of many colours" (21), assailing his blinded (and therefore void) eyesight as a result of a meeting of opposites, enabling him afterwards to discern "a frail multiform conception of unity, terrestrial and transcendental" (22). The fourth milestone is the "spear of renewal" (29) which re-opens his side and makes possible the reconstuction of his past life and of Adam's trial.

This reconstruction, arising from the "chasm of memory" (24), is described in Book II, an enlargement of Book I, the medley of impressions and intuitions first received being now sifted out and clarified as Victor's understanding deepens. The exploration of Omai is a composite metaphor for Adam's (man's) trial, for Victor's gradual apprehension of the "fundaments of existence" (123), and for his writing a "novel-history" (52). In the Guiana Quartet Harris was preoccupied with a conception of genuine authority, and since the ending of *The Secret Ladder* he has built up his vision of the existential trial (both ordeal and judgment) through *Heartland*, *The Eye*, and *Tumatumari*, using it as a central metaphor in *Ascent*. Victor's re-enactment questions more than the judgment of Adam; it is a trial of the trial itself, of the court and its values, and of the role of the judge (Victor himself) in the sentence passed on Adam; it is also a re-examination of the identity and the essential "function" of man. Adam's trial, partly re-enacted in Chapter 6, comes as a revision of the sentence and its effects evoked in Chapter 5. Both Adam and Victor have been condemned for squandering taxpayer's money, and the effect of the sentence was similar on both. In appearance at least they became utterly insensitive, "robot prisoner[s]" moving in concert with "robot millions" (38). If I understand rightly, the sentence "passed in the very entrenched nature of things" (51), i.e., within the "fortress of the law" (54), was a negation of life, "extinction of species" (42). The "crucifixion of the robot" (41) is the martyr of man "desensitized" by an exploitation or a "sentence" which he accepts because he cannot conceive of a reality other than the "gross material idolatry" (42) of his judges. The sentence is a way of being as much as a form of punishment.

This is confirmed as the trial re-opens in a "courtroom of truth . . . as large and painful as the globe in Victor's head and as subjective as the mirror in his side" (42). Contrary to the one-sided court Adam rejects, this new courtroom is on the borderline territory Victor approaches. The essence of the revisionary trial is Victor's *conscious* apprehension (as opposed to intuitions and flashes of revelation in Book I) of a "sacramental union or balance" as well as "alternatives within history" (76) owing to his simultaneous perception of two existential dimensions. The mirror in which Victor used to reflect the light of the sun in order to blind his father becomes the instrument of his own reformation and vision. In order to understand its dual role, however, it is first necessary to see the link between Victor's "game" and Adam's destructive action since it was Victor who unconsciously pushed his father to set fire to the factory. As Adam realized after the death of his wife (whom he loved though he "never really *felt* for her" [94]), his desire for a son actually killed her; she died in a Caesarian operation. So that Victor's birth was due to a lack of genuine feeling allied to a wish for self-perpetuation, and it can therefore be said that Adam, a victim, fathered a "victor."[5] When his wife died, both Adam and Victor were cut off from the mother, the original source of life. Adam sought comfort in materialism, while Victor idealized—idolized even—his absent mother, turning her into a "madonna." As Victor grew up, he both hated his father for his poverty and idolized him as the one on whom he depended entirely for subsistence. It was then, out of love and hate for his father, that he started pouring on him the "light of attack" (46) from the "mirror of subsistence" (64) or "mirror of appetite" (126), planted in his side when he was born. Climbing higher and higher in a spiral of greed, he extracted from Adam first the equivalent of tin, then copper, and was dreaming of gold when Adam set fire to the factory or "claustrophobic Eden" (42).

The instrumental mirror could be Victor's soul, his consciousness or his imagination, entirely dominated in boyhood by conflicting emotions and only capable of reflecting the blinding light of a conquering sun, idol or ideal. Forty years later on Omai the sun reflected on the wing of an airplane blinds him but gives him the cue he needs, for he then experiences what his father had gone through and realizes that the mirror did not merely reflect the light but that somewhere there in space, over the years of subsistence, the energy he had stored as a child each time he flashed the light on his father's brow on his way to or from school possessed both psychic and technological features that were bound to return from the depths and heights of proliferate nature. It was as though each time he flashed the mirror he was relaying a series of ghosts that were born of his own unconscious reserves (past and future) within which lived a series of mirrors at various removes in time and eternity. (46)

The mirror is thus also a revealing instrument through which Victor discovers a series of inner selves and which now "translates" him, stimulates his perception of contraries, and in doing so liberates him from the limitations of space and time. Victor approaches Omai from below and, as we realize later, from above by plane. He sees that Adam first reached his claim after stumbling not only through the wreckage of his factory but also through the shattered aircraft in which he (Victor) would meet his death, a fact which he anticipates ("omen or warning . . . *before* and *after* the crash" [50]) just as he can visualize Adam stumbling on the wreckage a year or two later. Victor feels under "hypnotic compulsion" (56) to travel to Omai although in the words of the poet Donne which come to his mind the "currants yeeld returne to none." His capacity to look forward and backward as he nears the borderline between "West and East" unlocks the "tomb of space" which corresponds to the "fortress of limbo" in which he and his father have been living. He is now experiencing the ruined and vacant condition of the victims of catastrophe (his father's and that of the pilot of the aircraft), and he becomes aware of a rapport between Adam, the pilot, and his crew. They are all conjured up by Victor as he is "touched by his own holy/unholy lightning reserves" (49) and they appear as both witnesses of the past and the "serial ghosts" relayed by Victor's mirror. At first terrified by the "duality of function" (50) revealed to him on Omai, Victor becomes aware of its creative nature. It implies the "repudiation of the robot," which reveals itself as the "ruined instrument of an *unruined* consciousness . . . lighthouse within and beyond . . . fortress or wall" (50). Yet it is the ruined state he shares with Adam and the pilot, his incapacity even as judge to define either Adam or himself (a typically

West Indian predicament) that enables him to assume a multiplicity of roles and to proceed with the revision of the trial.

Victor's identification with the judge coincides with his attempt at self-definition, which demands that he define Adam first. The latter's origins are uncertain. He claims to belong to El Dorado, though the judge suspects him of being a communist agent and "the sick man of the world" (60). Adam himself reverses the procedure of the court and forces it to reconsider its own object by challenging its authority on the ground that it cannot *feel* his existence as a person. It is only when, prodded by Adam, Victor faces his responsibility as a judge that he admits the "lack of feeling, quasi-feeling" of the court and questions his own authority. Then for the first time he commits himself to a synthesis "beyond and beneath all crucifixions of the robot—into the lightning omen and revelation of true Christ as an organ of capacity for all men, dying Man. . . ." (62). This difficult sentence contrasts the callous condemnation of desensitized people ("crucifixion of the robot") "beyond and beneath" which the judge must travel to discover the "true Christ." In other words, the robot himself leads on to the true Christ, who is not necessarily the real Christ but any victim who, as a result of his undoing, becomes an "organ of vacancy" (63)[6] through which the lost balance between contraries can be restored. Adam is such an "organ" or "ruined instrument," who gives the court an unexpected version of his act of sabotage: "I sought to *unmake* myself to *make* something I had lost before I was born. The land that is nowhere. Manoa" (58).

Looked at in this light, Adam's sabotage of the factory was both a destructive and a creative act. Defense counsel's argumentation is less concerned with Adam's guilt, which he does not question, than with the need to demonstrate Adam's "evolution . . . from nothing into a source of revelation" (63). He first uses a passage from Darwin's *The Descent of Man* to show that in their evolution living creatures acquire features that may serve as mere ornaments, irrelevant "excess baggage," or, on the contrary, be instruments of survival. Similarly, the poem called "FETISH" (one of Harris's early poems), which defense counsel submits as a genuine expression of Adam's being, possesses an "ornamentation of features" distinct from "omen of grace." Yet it is again through its apparently lifeless elements, through ornament or fetish (as above through robot or ruined instrument) that the court (humanity) is urged to discover the light of omen. FETISH, defense counsel argues, "is a poem about disintegration . . . but you are unable to see you are being *assisted* . . . to break the callous you deplore" (72). Fetish (the poem and the condition it expresses) may appear to be "unfeeling raw material." It is, as everyone agrees, "the rubbish heap of civilizations" (72). But this untidiness and the process of disintegration it implies (as opposed to tidy "callouses of conceit we plaster upon everything") precisely lay bare the "flesh and blood within the masks of history" (74), the real man rather than an abstraction, and so can become a source of compassion, the "new experimental source of wealth" that defense counsel advocates. In this first part of the reconstruction Victor has successively discovered in Adam a desensitized robot, the ruined instrument of an unruined consciousness, and finally a possibly fertile fetish. There is in this no exaltation of "base idolatry" but an attempt to uncover a "sacramental vacancy" (73) or void suffered by the victims of history.

Chapter 7 shows the judge (Victor) approaching Omai in an airplane and makes clear the role of one witness, Dr. Wall, who, the judge now realizes, was often quoted at the trial though he never appeared. The revisionary process by which the narrator ceaselessly approaches and presents the same material in renewed guise illustrates in the very form of the narrative the nature of the trial as defined by the judge:

"It's a question of the uncomfortable region one must approach time after time, again and again, down the ages shrouded by death in order to learn to bear by degrees what would otherwise be quite clearly . . . unbearable." (55)

The judge is now elaborating on sketches he made forty years before: it is a reconstruction within the reconstruction, which therefore juxtaposes two time periods too: the first (in chapters 5 and 6) when Victor (the judge) is shown mainly ascending the hill of Omai and relives the actual trial; the second (in chapters 7 and 8) when the judge (Victor) approaches Omai from a plane which he knows is going to crash and the forty years that have elapsed provide him with a new

perspective. His instrument of revision, like the novelist's, is "imagination" (78). He now discerns in his sketches of the original trial the
invisible presence or essence of Wall "whose voice sprang from
nothingness like an archetype of silence . . . ruined personality within
whose rubbish shone nevertheless an illumination of function" (80).
This associates Wall with Adam and Fetish, though a new element is
brought in with the description of time as "the spectre of humanity"
responsible for the breach in the wall and consequently the appearance
of "*one* frail thread . . . unity [or] love" (80). Harris is suggesting here
that the invisible but very real wall embedded in most human
attitudes crumbles in time, provided time itself is not an absolute or a
material prison. To be aware of the possible dislocation and spectral
function of time is to be able to see a nontemporal dimension through
linear or cyclic time[7] and so allow, as the judge does, "a qualitative
illumination" to emerge. In fact, the judge has been engaged in
transforming the rigid frames of existence into transparent vessels
allowing the coincidence of contraries. He has liberated first space,
then time, from their exclusively "material base" (84). The last stage
of the trial is the realization of his intuition that "the ruined fortress of
personality could subsist . . . as *blank* cheque of compassion . . . As a
consciousness without content which nonetheless permitted all alien
contents to exist" (85). This is the object of his art.

Enough has been said so far about Harris's purpose as a novelist to
understand the identification of the exploration of Omai and the
reconstitution of Adam's trial with fiction writing. In Chapter 7 the
judge probes further into the possibilities of his art when he shuffles
like a pack of cards the sketches he had made at the trial. These elicit
now

the other *silent* voices he felt beneath everyone and everything: *mute* sensa-
tions . . . that returned to address him as if he, himself, were on trial, and
what had *not* been said then was endeavouring to be heard now.

. . . .

Those pencils [of the imagination] *spoke* by illumining the curious disintegration of the past and invoking through the granular sensation of images—the dust of memory, the rubbish heap of landscape—a sequence of

words allied not simply to pictures but to the very brokenness of all fabric
inherent in vision. *Language for him, therefore, was a vision of consciousness as if
what one dreams of in the past is there with a new reality never so expressive before
because nothing stands now to block the essential intercourse of its parts, however mute,
however irrelevant.* (78)

I have quoted this passage at some length because it sums up what
Harris and, at a further remove, the judge are doing and because it
adumbrates Harris's conception of the "novel as painting."[8] "Painting" for Harris implies a vision of the reality within and beyond
appearances. It is process rather than a finished picture, an exploratory metaphor expressing his attempt to render the ineffable through
an accumulation and transformation of images which are necessarily
partial expressions of a wholeness that can never be represented in its
totality. In the "novel as painting" the writer is engaged in constantly
revising his limited and therefore prejudiced view of the past, as the
judge does when he elaborates on his sketches in order to approach the
unbearable. In this respect there is no distinction between the judge
and the novelist. Earlier in the trial the judge thought it possible "to
reverse the sentence of the court" (67) (change the insensitive spirit of
the age). Discovering what had not been expressed forty years before
and illumining "the dust of memory" with "pencils of the imagination" (thus meeting the unexpressed in its attempt to make itself
heard) he is breaking down the earlier tyranny of the law and as a
novelist breaking down a one-sided, conventional version of events—
so that what the narrator calls "the very brokenness of all fabric
inherent in vision" now makes possible the reversal of the sentence.

The judge repeatedly approaches the same material from different
space and time perspectives. While shuffling his cards (the partial
images of the reality he judges), he is envisaging alternatives to the
accepted interpretation of Victor's and Adam's history and the roles
they may have played. In Chapter 8 the judge rereads his early version
of the catastrophe and the court's sentence as he reaches and flies over
the lost city of Manoa. Immediately, a reversal of this early version is
set in motion as he sees Manoa "like a pool in the clouds into which a
stone . . . had fallen, and concentric rings representing frontiers of
memory spread across the sea of the atmosphere" (89). The stone,

which at the beginning of his quest made Victor unconscious, is now "lapis of ambivalences," the catalyst which enables him to see at once the density and transparency of the inner territory or past experience he is exploring. The material of that experience can be either "a fortress of illusion" or a source of revelation. As the stone falls into the pool of Manoa which contains the material of Victor's past, this material becomes "the dark mirror of judgement seat" (89). And the mirror (Victor's childhood reflector) is seen to contain "an inner lighthouse whose store of energy re-activated horizons of conquest as subsistence of grace or memory" (89).

The horizons of conquest are drawn in a diagram representing the falling stone and the ripples it sends out. It is inspired by a game Victor used to play as a child. First he threw into a canal the stone on which he fell when nearly run over by a car at the age of three-and-a-half; then he went on throwing other pebbles in order to feel, as the ripples expanded and each horizon died, the numbness *and* sense of being born into a new self he experienced when he fell under the car. Each ripple on the diagram is the reversal of an "epitaph" named after the successive shelters or masks which have protected and imprisoned Victor in his life. The legend of the diagram points at once to the double function of the stone and the horizons and sums up man's history down the ages (FACTORY OF THE GILDED MAN). In the subsequent revision it is as if the stone became the element through which Victor's consciousness frees itself from the burden of the past since it reverses the horizons of conquest of his youth (the landmarks of his solipsism) into living, expanding ripples and links together the self that began to live in his mother's womb with the many selves into which he grew or may have grown.

The new feature manifest in this last version of the reconstruction is feeling. The very stone on which Victor fell as a child had bled for him. As the incidents of his childhood are recalled, Adam's deep concern for his son becomes obvious as well as the terrible anguish that made Victor seek refuge in one overarching shelter after another. At this stage the judge interrupts his narrative and uses a blank card to offer an alternative to conventional novel writing, reminding his reader that genuine art, if it is to illumine man's predicament, cannot shirk the difficult task of confronting the origin of man's suffering, the mystery of "inequality, repression, oppression" (96), however obscure it may be. Similarly, when the moment of illumination becomes possible, its meaning asserts itself through Dr. Wall (the personification of disintegrating material life) addressing posterity on a blank card too. More precisely, it is the significance of Victor's experience after the catastrophe that speaks through Dr. Wall.

Child Three represents the crucial age of puberty when Victor used to make concentric rings around his father's foundry. In the light of the present revision Victor appears to have been at once terrified of his father's workplace (of the unendurable blaze of its furnaces) and relieved by his father's reappearance at night and the shield he provided against fire. The paradoxical image "dawn of night" epitomizes Victor's contradictory reactions of fear and relief arising from one identical source, the basic feelings men experience in the face of incomprehensible forces. His present insight into his own contradictoriness and into his father's role in exposing him to, yet shielding him from, fire frees him from his earlier idolatrous fixations, his mother's petticoat or womb to begin with. And the feeling by which he is moved as he looks on the ruined state of such fortresses (a mixture of despair and tenderness for man who needs to build them) prompts him again to the essential stage of the exploration, the negative state in which opposites coincide. He himself is by then a vessel or "vicar of lighthouse" in which fetish or ornament and omen or vision exist through one another. As "Sailor" he reads out a letter from Rose, a prostitute and one of the horizons in his globe, which testifies to the fertilization of the living by the dead as if there was always an "absent" Christ-like or Osiris-like victim to make us feel "the weight of our non-feeling" (106).

As in the earlier novels and in spite of the three letters by the judge, Dr. Wall, and Rose, this final section of the reconstruction is highly symbolical, not only of Victor's state but also of the kind of fiction the judge is writing about him, the "equation in art or language to the fundaments of existence" he is groping for "*through* history or the void which was native to history" (123). There is, for example, Victor's immersion into the "uncharted seas" (of his unconscious, of his past and the past of the limbo populations whose history went unrecorded) and the evocation of the different personalities he may have become (writer, judge, explorer, sailor). Although he reappeared forty years after the original trial, we never know with certainty what he really did: the judge's novel about him remains unfinished, which may be a way of suggesting that he never reaches one condition finally. On the other hand, his alternative existences seem to imply that life, whether in reality or in fiction, need not be imprisoned within one possibility. The sailor at the bottom of the sea counterpoints Victor who had "sketched in charcoal on the housecoat of stars" (109). Charcoal is only one of several metaphors for a ruined dark state that is yet susceptible of light. All this time, as we are frequently reminded, the dualistic stone sinks into the pool or sea. The fixed horizons and shelters of Victor's known life expand while Sailor and Rose begin to dance at the bottom of the sea and "restructure" the formerly frustrating scenes of Victor's youth. The dance, Sailor says, "celebrates the alternatives that lie before you, within you" (111). The end of the reconstruction is a dramatized exchange between prosecuting and defense counsels, between Victor and Sailor, and between Sailor, Parrot, and Raven, all of which illustrates what the judge has defined as *"the essential intercourse of {the} parts {of consciousness}, however mute, however irrelevant"* (78).

In the last chapter this free intercourse is represented by the *"Dance of the Stone,"* which reverses the stunning action of the stone at the beginning of Victor's quest and initiates the true "reformation of the loop." Throughout the novel the dance metaphor has conveyed the possibility of movement (usually the sign of a progress in consciousness in Harris's fiction) and harmony. It was linked with imagination ("dance of the muse" [20]) or feeling ("dance of mercy, dance of compassion" [31]) and evoked limbo which "spatializes" the West Indian predicament as well as the capacity for rebirth it offers. The dance of the stone is a dynamic metaphor which harmonizes slices of Victor's life as well as their "equation," i.e., extracts of the narrative reproduced as movements of the dance; it finally frees him from the fixations of puberty when his father burnt the factory. The last two movements in particular free him from his most constricting fortresses: the baboon (possibly the consenting scapegoat) and its very opposite, the madonna; these movements issue into the moment of vision above Manoa or El Dorado, similar in essence to the vision in

Palace though more far-reaching and complex. The judge remains to
the end the chief medium of narration. He is "a creative struggler"
involved in the "task of being born through words" (123), who
therefore sees his art as an instrument of rebirth. His (Victor's)
vision coincides with the moment of death and metamorphosis. He is
one and many, Sailor/Adam counterpointing Victor/Adam on the
"ground of alternatives," the negative ground on which all possibilities exist and all opposites meet, which can yet set up its own activity
"*beyond*" (126, italics mine) these opposites. From this "beyond"
Victor feels pushed for the last time out of the madonna fortress and
the different forms it has taken. He had run away after the original
trial because the catastrophe and its consequences were unendurable
to him. But at the climax of vision he stares at the fire ("the last
flickering beams of El Dorado" [127]) and sees that "his father had
been engaged in fighting . . . the very blaze he had started. Originator
of the fire" (127−8). This confirms the dual role of man and god as
both creators and destroyers. We are back where we started for Victor
sees his father once more in rags. His own breath, like the wind,
dissolves his main refuge, the petticoat of the idolized madonna:

His faint breath lifted it, expunged it of fear, of loss, of degradation, of
extinction of species, so that—in conformity with the very ruin of catastrophe—it retained a living spark, a frail star, star of the Madonna. (128)

In the light of the whole novel this dissolution of material life into a
living spark becomes the seed of the future. The madonna figure is
also at the center of Harris's preoccupations in his next fictional cycle.

The novel ends with an implicit affirmation of the resurgence of life
in which catastrophe (burning factory or plane crash) can issue. The
whole catastrophic spirit of an age has been reversed into a living
spark of creation. Instead of leading to imprisonment, the reconstructed trial has broken the rigidity of the law and enabled the prisoner to
reach "freedom *through* knowing unfreedom" (111). The multiplicity
of forms that convey the attainment of a spiritual reality (Omai)
through its opposite or its material counterpart (Oh My) is, to say the
least, astounding. Sections of the trial read as a dramatization of ideas
and these also assume various concrete forms[9] in other parts of the

novel. The trial as a whole combines different styles (narrative, metaphorical, and expository) and different literary forms (prose, poetry,
drama). Such variety is clearly part of the novelist's view of language
as "a vision of consciousness," which has required many ways of
approaching the source of vision (the ruined Adam).

It has been objected that the judge's address to the reader to explain
his conception of the novel smells of the lecture hall and that the page
numbers which locate the extracts equated with movements of the
dance are an authorial intrusion. This second objection carries little
weight, for Harris would have obtained the same effect if he had
omitted the page numbers as he does at the end of *The Eye*. It would be
more relevant to wonder whether the juxtaposed extracts or slices of
narrative are convincing components of the dynamic design the dance
of the stone is intended to create. I can only answer this question
tentatively by saying that, as far as I can see, Harris's experiment
makes sense when viewed in the light of his equation of language with
vision or the "fundaments of existence" and if one keeps in mind the
structural function of the extracts quoted. Nevertheless, it remains an
experiment which does not seem to have led to new developments in
his narrative technique although it has contributed to the makeup of
characters in such novels as *Companions* and *The Tree of the Sun*. The
first objection is a more serious one for the judge's letter does read as a
declaration of his intention as a novelist, which is the more striking
for contrasting with the metaphorical texture of, say, Book I. But can
one confuse Harris with his character even if their approach to fiction
is similar? The judge's voice is only one among many in Harris's
"serial" character, and he meditates on a subject-matter that Victor,
his alter ego, has approached through a series of illuminations. The
judge's letter on a blank card is both structurally fitting and in
keeping with the role he is playing.[10] It must also be pointed out that
criticism of the novel in English has often looked askance at the
nondramatic presentation of ideas in fiction, whereas in France the
novel within the novel, and the reflections it leads to in the hero, has
been acclaimed in Andre Gide's *The Counterfeiters* and overexploited
since then. This is a far-reaching issue that should be discussed at
greater length than is possible here. *Ascent to Omai* no doubt pursues
the effort of earlier twentieth-century writers to render the totality of

experience. It is perhaps too early to say whether the result is flawless unless we are absolutely certain we understand the real function of each part in this complex composition. I would not make this claim but suspect that, like Dr. Wall's theory, this novel may be "in advance of its time" (82).

Chapter Ten

"The Novel as Painting": From *The Sleepers of Roraima* to *The Tree of the Sun*

Between *Ascent to Omai* and his next novel, *Black Marsden,* Harris wrote two volumes of short stories based on Amerindian myths and rituals and historical anecdotes. There are seven novellas[1] in all, which, together, form a unique experiment in fiction, an essential link or, to use a Harrisian term, a gateway between the second and third cycles of novels. I hope to have shown clearly so far that the so-called "historylessness" and cultural void of the Caribbean were for Harris an essential source of originality which, to him, does not lie in dominant cultural or behavioral models but in frail hidden resources. Such resources are to be found in remnants of African myths, in limbo and voodoo, and in Amerindian vestiges of myth and legend. Harris dealt with the first in his earlier fiction, while in his volumes of short stories native Amerindian myths and history are his only source of inspiration. This is important if one keeps in mind the fact that the novels Harris wrote subsequently all stage a confrontation between conquering and suppressed civilizations not only in the Caribbean but on a global scale. Before moving on to this wider subject, he explored the creative potentialities of what appears today as a neglected cultural inheritance. Yet as Yurokon exclaims in the story that bears his name: "here am I . . . no one and nothing, yet here I stand. . . . Whose spirit is it that will not—*cannot*—die?" (69) We know that tradition as a living though often unacknowledged reality underlying conventional and unquestioned orders of existence is central to Harris's work. Related to it is the distinction he illustrates in the novellas between history as given authoritarian consensus of opinion and fables or myths as carriers of a seed of renewal, the germ of a "native host consciousness."[2] In "The Mind of Awakaipu," for example, Harris starts from an anecdote[3] according to which Awakaipu, a nineteenth-century Arekuna Indian, behaved heroically but unfeelingly when bitten by a *perai,* and he indirectly suggests that this interpretation was probably plastered over the stoic behavior of the Indian. Actually, the wound he received (not only from a *perai* but from the conqueror) had aroused a "seminal tear," the expression of a deep anguish that remained hidden from his masters but is seen by the artist as a "phenomenon of sensibility" capable of dispelling the drought of history and of eliciting a new consciousness, "rain of nativity" (57).

The theme of resurrection, so important in Harris's third fictional cycle, is present in all the stories, not as an achievement but as an open possibility through the retrieval of what Harris has called the "phenomenal legacy" or "alternative realities."[4] In this way history is redeemed by myth provided the mythical imagination is viewed both as individual (and therefore susceptible of breaking given historical molds through feeling) and universal. Closely related to the theme of resurrection is the archetypal child, the central consciousness in each story of *The Sleepers of Roraima,* who learns to understand and transform the myth in which he himself is involved. All the myths and fables are presented from the inside through the consciousness of individuals, the sleepers and rainmakers of the titles, who are both Amerindian mythical or historical characters and present-day "artists." Indeed, each becomes an artist through his own regenerated vision and the transformation of the myth which takes place through him. Harris makes the most of the poetic or metaphorical and transformational nature of myths as defined by Lévi-Strauss, the French anthropologist, specialist of Amerindian myths and one of the pioneers of structuralism.[5] More important still, both for the form of the stories and the developments it leads to in his third cycle of novels, is Harris's equation of language with music and painting, using all three as living "texts."[6] In order to illustrate this, I shall briefly discuss "Yurokon," often referred to by Harris himself as a good example of the kind of analogies he was exploring.[7]

The main theme in this story is cannibalism, surely the most misunderstood ritual of primitive peoples. It appears here as in all Harris's fiction as a metaphor for an unbounded lust for possession of material riches or of people, a way of gaining strength at the expense of another. "Conquest," writes Harris, "is cannibal realism."[8] The Caribs, whose name was distorted into "cannibal," were themselves fierce conquerors before being conquered by Spain. The basic data of the story are mythical elements and a few know facts about the Caribs. The myth of Yurokon, the Bush Baby specter arising from their pots, appeared among them in pre-Columbian times just before their decline, which they seem to have sensed coming (partly because they saw their intermarriage with Arawak women as an encroachment on their hegemony and strength). The myth was linked with a strong sense of guilt among the Caribs, for it told how a woman threw the Baby Yurokon (who had appeared among them as mother and child) into her pot, as a result of which its mother brought pain, misery, and death into the world.[9] It is interesting to note that cannibalism (throwing the baby into the cooking pot) is the source of guilt in this version of the original sin. In the various spatial forms he took (not only mother and child but also tree or dog) it can be said that Yurokon was similar in nature to the Arawak Zemi.[10] The pot or vessel in which the specter appeared is itself significant, for the Caribs were known for their beautiful pottery. Harris merges these elements with the fact that, after eating a ritual morsel of the flesh of their enemies, the Caribs used to fashion flutes out of their bones, thus transforming dead human bone into music, a process called in the story "transubstantiation of species" (67).

From the beginning Harris juxtaposes in "Yurokon" twentieth-century with mythical or "dream" time, the imaginative dimension in all his works. Yurokon is at the outset a twentieth-century Amerindian boy who questions his uncle about the Caribs' reputation as "huntsmen of bone" (66), i.e., cannibals; he identifies in dream with a sixteenth-century Yurokon and with his mythological namesake. The experience of conquest he relives explains why he is the last Carib and "the first native" (68), this expression suggesting the state of nothingness to which the Caribs were reduced together with the spiritual renascence and "original" identity inherent in this state. Yurokon has been given a kite by Father Gabriel, a missionary, and has fallen asleep at the foot of the tree to which his kite is attached; his sleep is at once real and representative of the Caribs' unconscious state immediately before and after conquest. While awake, he sails "through the book of space" with his kite but in his dream he sails "in pages of psyche" (66). There is thus the usual equation between space and psyche, and the ensuing re-enactment of history takes place within Yurokon's psychological landscape. The musical analogy has a deeper meaning than obvious formal elements would suggest. These, however, can also be taken into account. The story has four movements like a symphony. The tension between two different tones and the resolution of this tension at the end, typical of a symphonic structure, find a correspondence in the confrontation between Caribs and Spaniards resolved in the denouement. And the orchestral component is there in the guise of ancestral participants but above all in the interplay of natural elements which, in Yurokon's inner landscape, take part in an "unwritten symphony."

One essential feature in the story is that the encounter between Caribs and Spaniards is rendered wholly through images, some of which evoke sounds, and one is reminded of Lévi-Strauss's assertion that there exists "a logic of sensory qualities."[11] Among the key images introduced in the initial movement or exposition is the cross, in the name of which the Spaniards fought but which they also had to bear when they fell into Carib hands. In this sense the cross is interchangeable with the bird (an emblem on the Spanish flag) whose wings were transformed by the Caribs into a musical instrument. There is also the image of the octopus and of the sponge suggesting alternately the voraciousness and spirit of absorption of Caribs and Spaniards, who both behaved as godlike conquerors. The central metaphor is the kite which takes on innumerable forms such as sea-kite (Spanish) and land-kite (Carib) but also stands for "a timeless element in all places and things" (81). It is throughout Yurokon's instrument of exploration and gradually becomes an instrument of vision, thus reconciling, as in all Harris's fiction, the means with the end of exploration. All through there is a juxtaposition of contraries but also two ways of looking at the same phenomenon. For example, when Yurokon first hears an unwritten symphony, he perceives "a strange huddle of ancestral faces attuned to quivering wings [of the Spanish bird] which they plucked with their fingers like teeth" (67), an image which combines the eating of a Spanish morsel with the

Spaniards' transformation into music. But he also hears for the first time the fear of the strings (the Spaniards'), and this helps him understand his ancestors' own feelings, the fact that they resorted to cannibalism partly in self-defense, to persuade the Spaniards that the Caribs too were conquerors, *"Make them think they had been eaten"* (67).

In the second movement Yurokon, a manifestation of the spirit, arises from his uncle's pot as a spiralling twine of smoke, a breach in the proud homogeneous psychological landscape of the Caribs. The twine of his kite, at first a chain, is the instrument of rupture that entails the disintegration of the Caribs' outer and inner landscape or psyche ("Break the land. Break the sea. Break the savannah. . . ." [69]). This enables Yurokon to hear the "unwritten symphony of the wind" (69), which is both a "music of ignominy," the "song of silence" that follows the Caribs' defeat, and "the music of origin" (70). The encounter of the "wild warring elements" shows that these play a dual role. For example, fire (the sun, which stands for the former gods or Caribs) is, contrary to all expectations, cooked by water (the mist, but also the Spaniards who came from the sea), and this suggests a complete reversal of situation for the formerly godlike Caribs now conquered and "cooked" by the new gods of Spain. The Caribs' arrogance and the guilt of their spirits ("Yurokon bowed his head to conceal the ash of many a war feast, sculpture of blood" [68]) subside as they become victims, and their "victorious shroud" becomes the "cauldron of heaven" (71), a holocaust which is not devoid of re-creative possibilities since the confining leash becomes "the easter twine of endless participation" (71). The possibility of resurrection ("birth-in-death" [72]) is conveyed through an extraordinary complex of images and puns developing from one nucleus, a metaphorical piano with black keys and white bones to which the Caribs dance their retreat "within the music of the century" (72).

The third and fourth movements re-create in different sets of images the encounters between Caribs and Spaniards and the final retreat of the Caribs into the continent, so that Yurokon's kite becomes an underworld one, which flies "in the broken sky of conquest" (74) and represents the burning out, smoldering imagination of the vanquished. This is no one-sided reconstruction. Though in the Caribs' eyes evil has "a stomach of mail which drank tin" (73) (an allusion to the mailed Spaniards' cannibalistic greed for mineral riches), Yurokon nevertheless sees that the Spaniards must have been struck by the "savage character of the land" (74) and that the music of the flute to which the Caribs dance is in fact "a music of silence" (74), a way for the Caribs to absorb their defeat and the invading element. The encounter had already given rise to the creation of a "native organ" in which "innocent evil" (the Caribs') and "maleficent good" (the Spaniards', destroying in the name of an ideal) met as "living morsels of divinity" (73) (a meeting between equally cannibalistic gods?). As a result of the Caribs' defeat, the daytime (Spanish) octopus is still "a morsel of divinity" but the nighttime (Carib) octopus has become "the very antithesis of the gods" (74). Yurokon is a link between the two, a "victor-in-victim" (75), at first born of the Caribs' premonition of their fall and fatalistic acceptance of it (see the uncle's "we, too, will succumb" [69]), then "the new organ of capacity," the potential interpreter of the "native symphony" (76) or consciousness of which Father Gabriel dreams. Harris sees even the extinction of the Caribs in dual terms:

They ceased to fret about names since namelessness was a sea of names. They ceased, too, to care about dwindling numbers since numberlessness was native to heaven, stars beyond reckoning. (75)

The very loss of the natives is the source of their universality ("sea of names . . . stars beyond reckoning"), and "numberlessness" clearly means both without numbers and innumerable. The natives becoming stars shows that Harris also visualizes the denouement in metaphorical terms while possibly recalling the myth of the Amerindians transformed into the Pleiads after running away from their enemies into a tree which was set on fire.[12]

Of particular interest is the way in which the Caribs' loss is being transmuted into the "annunciation of the native of the globe" (77), though Harris does not envisage an actual rebirth of the Caribs but the rebirth of a native consciousness. After a day of battle the music of the flute was "a music of silence." In the shell of the sea (another image for the conqueror's hard carapace) Yurokon hears a music that is also rain (a reminder of the notes breaking into a fountain in *Palace*), a symbol of fertility. After Yurokon's awakening, while his vision takes shape, that "music of silence" becomes a "music of colour" on Carib vases which

embroiled the savannah in the sea, the mountain in the valley, forest in scrub: bowl of earth, pottery of earth, toast of the valley by the huntsmen of bone who had drunk before from the bowl of the sea. (80)

It is first necessary to recall that painting is the metaphorical device used to express the Caribs' visualization of the underworld to which they withdraw after their defeat (see 72,73). We are familiar from earlier novels with the transformation of sound into sight. In the passage just quoted Harris brings together music and painting to convey a reconciliation of elements in a landscape of consciousness, a reconciliation which makes sense only as the transformed vision of formerly polarized attitudes within each person. Moreover, in "music of colour" music is at a further remove than color since it suggests the subtle alterations of boundaries of perception in variations and harmonizations of sensation on Carib *painted* pottery that *sings*. When Father Gabriel says to himself "Eastertide again . . . annunciation of music" (81), he equates the means with the end, music with the "painted" consciousness it expresses, as language was equated with visions of consciousness in *The Eye* and *Ascent to Omai*.

In Wilson Harris' third phase the painting metaphor becomes so important that it is woven in the very structure of the narrative in order to convey the protagonist's "double vision." The cycle begins with *Black Marsden*, a novel which initiates a new manner in that it creates an impression of realism while also foreshadowing a sensuousness more fully developed in the following novels. This realism, however, is largely illusory since the sense of immediacy it conveys is counterpointed by what might be called an inverse realism, best illustrated in the characters who have sprung into being as a result of the protagonist's sensitiveness to a theater of consciousness within himself.

Clive Goodrich has won a fortune on the pools and been around the world but he now lives in Edinburgh, conscripted into his role as patron of the arts. On a winter afternoon he comes across the "half-

frozen spectre" (11) of Doctor Black Marsden in the ruined Dunferm-
line Abbey and invites him to stay in his house as long as he likes. It is
not the least achievement in the novel that Marsden and his agents,
the beautiful Jennifer Gorgon, Knife, and Harp exist in their own
right as well as being existences that are part of Goodrich's personality, his community of being, or, to use the novel's terminology, the
tabula rasa theater within himself. The link with the *tabula rasa*
personality of Adam in *Ascent* is obvious. The doppelgänger of Harris's
earlier novels has developed into a whole cast, "naked apparitions in
search of density and cover" (36), or, to put it differently, personaliza-
tions of "the human or cosmic desert" (54).

The structure of the novel and the narrative remain essentially
dualistic, not in any clear-cut way, but as a precarious balance
constantly endangered and restored between a self-sufficient reality
and the "fabric of invisibles" (33) Marsden brings to Goodrich's
awareness. Of Marsden himself Goodrich says:

It was this aspect of strange immunity to the elements and strange immersion in the elements—half-pathetic and sorrowful, half-ecstatic and joyful—
that became now a kind of vivid black humour. (12)

Black here as in "Black Marsden" is used in the sense explained by
Harris in *History, Fable and Myth* (20) suggesting an "undiscovered
realm" or "eclipse" which, as we know, is a dynamic state that
precedes rebirth. Marsden plays a dual role as "clown or conjurer" and
a Hypnotist Extraordinary" (12). As clown or conjurer, he makes
Goodrich alive to the theater of the uninitiate, as already suggested,
as well as to the contrast between memory and nonmemory. Memory,
however necessary, is "a storehouse of initiations" (30) which may
confine man to partial and deterministic attitudes. It is in a way what
gives rise to a one-sided view of history. "Non-memory," as Marsden
puts it, is "our most fallible identity kit"; it corresponds to "areas of
the human sphynx in which millions are eclipsed . . . at starvation
point; or vanished . . . in Hiroshima, for example" (30). The distinction is an important one and is illustrated in various ways by
Marsden and his agents, by Goodrich when twice he becomes invisible to Jennifer Gorgon, but most characteristically in Namless,

Goodrich's country of origin in South America, which he revisits in imagination.

Marsden stimulates or "fire[s] in some degree" (52) everyone with whom he comes in contact. But as hypnotist he exerts a dangerous fascination, for he does not refrain from snapping his fingers at Goodrich. Although the latter is indebted to Marsden for his growing insight, he must resist the temptation to yield his face to Marsden or to acquire the coat of uniformity that Marsden's depleted agents tend to wear. In this respect *Black Marsden* is a signal advance on *The Eye of the Scarecrow* which it complements (Goodrich is said to have a "scarecrow eye" in his moments of vision). We saw, indeed, that Hebra, one of the uninitiate, could become possessive in turn. A major theme in *Black Marsden* lies in the fact that the uninitiate can offer "a dangerous hypnotic legacy at times as well as a revitalized caveat of originality and community" (55). Ironically, though Marsden is an agent of fascination, he himself provides Goodrich with the instrument that will help him resist fascination. For example, Goodrich sees Marsden dressed as a camera (twentieth-century man's instrument for reproducing his own view of reality) acting out his role as a featureless beggar and using Jennifer as "currency of beauty" to fascinate Goodrich. "At the very edge of fascination" (21) Marsden's camera dress is slashed by Knife, his own agent, and Marsden is revealed in his vulnerability, nakedness, and self-parody. This leaves Goodrich uncomfortably aware of the necessity for faith in a living creation, of the need to see through the "featureless" mirroring of people in an authoritarian mass media, a process which Harris equates with the death of the imagination.

Marsden's agents present a similar duality. The beautiful Jennifer Gorgon is like a fascinating fashion plate and represents the temptations or pressures for the sake of which twentieth-century man so often relinquishes his individuality: love, sex, freedom (she is "the resurgent Gorgon . . . twentieth-century fascination with freedom" [44]). With her beauty pack, she even represents "the hideousness of all charm, the hideousness of all compulsion" (59). But there is a fissure or crack in that "bandaged head of stillness" (60), and from their first meeting Goodrich knows that if he unscrewed the head of the Gorgon he would "be seized by the open-ended mystery of beauty which revealed and concealed all its parts *ad infinitum*" (14). As to Knife, who serves Goodrich as a guide to Namless, he may wear the face of the collectivity since he looks the same whether he is white, black, or brown, but his very existence (particularly as Black Jamaican Knife) makes Goodrich aware of the polarizations in the world, the gap which separates the saved from the damned, just as in Namless it is he who confronts Goodrich with the pitfalls of collectivity and uniformity. Involuntarily, it seems, he is the persona through which Goodrich "re-senses" the premises of an extreme or "deep-seated" but genuine community.

Before commenting on the Namless section in which this takes place, it is first necessary to point out that all the aspects of the novel are marked by a subtle interplay of contrasts which concur to a repeatedly re-created awareness of otherness in Goodrich. There are the contrasts in the landscaspe around Edinburgh and between the old and the modern city. These are beautifully rendered, and one feels Harris's extreme sensitiveness to the atmosphere of the place as well as to the contradictions in the Scottish personality which serve to introduce Goodrich's interest in the submerged or buried side of Marsden. Goodrich discovers a contrast between cultures in Namless too. An alternation between the third-person narrator and Goodrich as I-narrator gives outer and inner perspectives to the narrative as well as rendering the interplay of existences within Goodrich. There is also an alternation between Goodrich's moments of exaltation and his occasional sense of oppression when Marsden becomes too assertive, although the latter too oscillates between self-assertion and depletion, an indication of the dynamic character of his personality. Finally, the narrative progresses through alternative forms of expression, for this is partly a novel of ideas but one in which ideas are also concretized into characters or incidents.

The *tabula rasa* comedy stages Goodrich's participation in the lives of normally eclipsed personae who have suddenly impressed themselves upon his consciousness and *their* participation in his life. It implies the kind of self-distancing that has been explained *à propos The Eye*. "What is freedom without the blackest self-mockery" (23), writes Goodrich. When he "dreams" or loses himself in the intuitive dimension that made him respond to Marsden in the first place, he

puts down his thoughts and sketches in his diary or "book of infinity."[13] It does not necessarily involve writing or sketching except in a
metaphorical sense for vision as, for example, when on Dean Bridge
Goodrich "re-sensitize[s] our biased globe into moveable squares
within and beyond every avalanche of greed or despair" (66). The
moveable squares or "chessboard of visibles and invisibles" (64) can be
the conscious and unconscious elements or existences within oneself
that tend to be frozen and therefore paralyzing. They correspond to
those sheltering and imprisoning horizons or circles in *Ascent* from
which Victor liberated himself through the dance of the stone.
Goodrich recalls the "avalanche" of despair in his mother after the
death of his father and the disappearance of his step-father into the
Brazilian jungle when he was five. It is thus "square five" that he
wants to resense when, stimulated by his vision on Dean Bridge and
after being "invisible" to (cut dead by) Jennifer for the second time, he
takes his visionary trip to Namless as a way of re-assessing the
"blocked perspectives" (54) in his existence.

Apart from being his country of origin, Namless is also his inner
landscape, the *tabula rasa* theater, and the prevailing condition in the
twentieth-century world. Namless offers contrasts of snowy mountains and tropical valleys but it has been turned into a desert and the
population is hidden or eclipsed. The people sleepwalked themselves
from one strike into another and were unknowingly pushed further
than they thought. When the authorities decided to agree to all their
demands it was too late; the claim mechanism had been deified and
the revolution turned Namless into a desert. Things were no better
under the "American dinosaur" (82) where rulers had made friends of
their former victims in order to preserve their economic bastions. The
idea seems to be that, whether in totalitarian or capitalist areas,
uniformity prevails; it is represented by the robot Goodrich discerns
on a rock. Significantly, as Goodrich's guide and as an agent of the
Director General of Namless Theatre, Brown Knife merely repeats
what he has heard or read in the newspaper, *Dark Rumour.* Yet
apparently without realizing the implications of what he says, he also
explains to Goodrich the "emergent philosophy of [genuine] revolution bound up with a re-sensing, re-sensitizing of dead monsters"
(82). As Goodrich's understanding deepens, the landscape awakens

and "a curious subtle *fleshing* [appears] upon the rocks" (82). Thus Namless, which at the outset was both an "archeological phenome-non" and the "cradle of exiled men and gods" (73), becomes a place where "the very stillness still *moved* endlessly" (85)[14], and therefore lived. From "re-sensing" these contrasts, Goodrich is deeply upset by the fate of the eclipsed (he cannot remain indifferent to the robot) but feels the need to *move* and retreat from Namless. It is this simultaneous sympathy and need for retreat (or refusal to be engulfed in nameless-ness) that *Black Masrsden* illustrates more specifically than Harris's earlier fiction. Knife illustrates in his person the transformation of a susceptibility to namelessness into a totalitarian extinction of indi-viduals, the stage before what Goodrich calls "self-execution into infinity" (90).

Knife's guiding role comes to an end when his terror at another agent's assassination makes him adopt an authoritarian attitude to Goodrich and so reinforces the totalitarian trend in Namless. Good-rich resists this, and when he hears a piping music associated with a nameless piper who had played to warn his master of an ambush, he reads in the song a warning to himself in spite of Knife's assertion that the song now means the contrary, i.e., an encouragement to go forward. Goodrich's rejection of Knife prefigures his resistance to Marsden and his other agents, who have taken increasing advantage of his hospitality. Jennifer has become pregnant by one of her depleted lovers, whom she doesn't want to marry because she is merely con-cerned with perpetuating herself while remaining faithful to Marsden. She asks Goodrich whether she may use his house as a refuge and he mistakenly believes that she wants to be free of Marsden too. A few days later he buys a flamboyant shirt "made of fire" (106) (an echo of the "shirt of flame" in "Little Gidding"?) to match the "intuitive fire music" (94) which had warned him out of death in Namless and to celebrate his relationship of trust with Jennifer. But she does not even notice the shirt and is only eager to tell him that she has confessed all to Marsden and that he agrees with their plan. Goodrich, who had not yet given his consent, is furious to have been taken for granted and throws them both out, thus freeing himself from his conscripted role not merely as patron of the arts but as another face Marsden wears. To those who, like Goodrich, can read appearances, *Black Marsden* shows that there is a complex distinction between enslaved patronage and the patronage of innovation and hard-won freedom in the arts. Goodrich's trip to Namless has meant a necessary wrestling with "other buried traumatic existences" (94); it ended with a newfound compassion for his mother, who had given in to despair when he was a child, but also with a necessary retreat from Namless:

How close can one come to [oblivion], learn from it without succumbing to it, without being swallowed up in it? (96)

Goodrich has stopped short of succumbing, of having his personality swamped by Marsden's hypnotic power. He remains "alone, utterly alone, as upon a post-hypnotic threshold" (111). This "aloneness" beyond all conscripting roles is the condition of genuine freedom.

In *Companions of the Day and Night*, a sequel to *Black Marsden*, Goodrich travels further into namelessness together with Idiot Nameless, the main "character," whose papers, paintings, and sculptures Marsden has asked him to edit. As I have explained in the chapter on *The Eye*, Idiot Nameless or "the Fool" personifies a free and fluid condition, a kind of intermediary state between what is solidly established and entrenched, on one hand, and the mystery of what is eclipsed but contains a seed of rebirth, on the other. He represents at once a state of "negative identity" as well as the mobile medium of consciousness through which it is possible to reach that state ("Descent *by* a spark. . . . Descent *into* a spark" [66]). His character is thus in keeping with the role he plays in *Companions*, that of falling into and breaking down old established orders one after another. The novel takes place in Mexico where layers of vestiges of such orders abound, which testify to the domineering presence of Aztec gods, driven underground by the Spanish conquering Christ, himself ridden by the bullets of twentieth-century revolutionaries. The role of Goodrich is to translate into a "novel-gospel" Nameless's discovery of "unsuspected proportions" (36) in these vestiges, "unsuspected corridors, underseas, underskies, of creation" (32).

The diary, paintings, and sculptures Goodrich edits "were doorways through which Nameless moved" (13), which suggests that the very people he came across and the vestiges he visited while in Mexico opened the way to their own unacknowledged side. An example of this is when the "majestic self-portrait" (24) of the sovereign Mexican Christ sculpted by a fire-eater becomes the very torch that illumines (or a door that leads into) the "rejected abysses" (25) into which Nameless descends under a Christian church. This transformation of Christ from a dominating, and therefore oppressive, figure into an illuminating torch points to the fluid role of Christ in the novel, indeed in Harris's fiction as a whole. He presented an Arawak Christ in *Palace,* and in *Companions* he creates a Mexican Christ in whom merge the layers of sacrifice imposed on the Mexican people in successive ages. So Christ becomes filled with what Harris has called elsewhere "complexities of nakedness,[15] which Nameless "falls" into and experiences, thus becoming in turn a Christ figure:

The strange humour of Christ lay in this, in susceptible spaces, susceptible executions, susceptible carvings, susceptible resurrections and descent into apparent oblivion, apparent nakedness woven into the intuitive chasm of his world. . . . And it was this combination of levels . . . that gave him the magic of universality. (31)

The paintings and sculptures or the visions they represent merge with the time-structure of Nameless's visit to Mexico to give the novel its form. Nameless is said to have come to Mexico just under a fortnight before Easter. But his days in Mexico are also counted according to the pattern of the Mexican calendar stone which comprised a nine-day cycle (companions of the night) and a thirteen-day cycle (companions of the day). Days eight and nine were called Dateless Days, as they are in the novel, in order to absorb the remaining four days into the nine-day cycle. Significantly, it is the nine-day cycle (companions of the night) that punctuates Nameless's experience in Mexico and merges with the period just under a fortnight (thirteen days) of the Christian calendar. The dateless days which come at the end of the novel re-create the Fool's visit to sisters Rose and Maria in New York in Mrs. Black Marsden's house, an event which took place *before* his visit to Mexico. The structure of the novel is thus circular since the end touches the beginning and juxtaposes as in earlier novels (*Palace*, *The Far Journey*, *Tumatumari*, and *Ascent*) conventional time structures (here pre-Columbian and Christian) with timelessness. It is also specifically "vertical" in its emphasis on gravity and its various renderings of a falling body unravelling "historical investitures" to provide a glimpse of indestructible and uncapturable inner reality.

The time and timeless dimensions are both conveyed through Nameless's "fall" into legendary characters and into the remains of eclipsed cultures. In his introduction Goodrich compares the pre-Columbian's fear that the sun might fall and never rise again (a fear which led to the institutionalization of human sacrifices to the sun) with modern man's fear that his world might fall into a "black hole of gravity."[16] What Nameless relives intensely in his falling sickness and in his descent into the past is at once modern man's anguish of sudden total extinction and the anguish (as well as the blindness, deafness, dumbness) that the fallen victims of the past have experienced: those who were sacrificed to the sun, then the Aztecs who fell victim to the Spaniards, the Christian conquerors who later became themselves victims of the revolution, and even the post-revolutionary workers who are the unconscious victims of the uniformity, false unity, they seek to impose. In the face of this range of oppressors-turned-oppressed (and vice versa) the ambivalent figure of the fire-eater whom Nameless first meets is all-important *since he re-enacts the fall of the sun (fire) into his devouring mouth but brings it out again and thus points to the possibility of rebirth*. He is an artist whose ambivalence is illustrated in the fact that he is the creator of both the statue of the majestic Christ and the *unfinished* statue of the Absent Virgin, a point I shall comment on presently. A close reading of the novel will show that he is related to all the other male figures, the old fire-god Huehueteotl, who appears at the center of the calendar stone, Christ, and the guide Hosé.

It is the fire-eater who stimulates Nameless's many descents as a spark, first, into a canal under an avenue where Montezuma sails (can be perceived as a "living" presence), then into the church of the Absent Virgin, where he meets the fire-eater's model for his statue of the Virgin. After this first meeting Nameless sleeps with the model, and as a whore she is a concrete presence, a commodity of love. But she is also the madonna, the Absent Virgin whom Nameless once sees and follows from afar in the vicinity of the pyramid of the sun, though he never comes upon her again. It seems that in the fullness of her being as *both* virgin and whore she is unreachable. She is a "spark within ghost" (61) and also the lost and never-to-be-found mother of origins. "How close does one come to the madonna as rejected commission of an age?" (28), Nameless wonders. Her statue has indeed been commissioned by the Church, then rejected probably because the whore served as a model for her. Similarly, when searching for her, Nameless visits a former convent turned into a church outside Mexico City; he discovers that a procession has been instituted in honor of her raped grandmother, Sister Beatrice, but that she, *"the child of a child born from rape"* (41), is rejected as a whore. Her role is a pendant to that of Christ and, if I understand rightly, the four nuns of the vanished religious order, Sister Beatrice, Sister Joanna, Sister Rose, and Sister Maria, whom Nameless seeks out but never actually meets, are different versions of the Madonna. Sister Beatrice was raped by revolutionaries while dressed up as a bullet-ridden Christ in a procession. After that she used to seduce a Fool each year to play the part. But Hosé, the guide, and most people prefer to ignore the interchangeability of roles between the raped virgin and the Fool although Nameless during his visit *is* the seduced Fool who relives the genuine role of the sacrificed Christ. They monumentalize Sister Beatrice as a martyr of the revolution. It is Sister Joanna who, from her convent in an old European city, explains to Nameless in a dream the real meaning of Beatrice's martyrdom and association with a Christ-like figure, that what she really wanted was, like Nameless himself, an "equation between revolution and religion" (47). Until the revolution it was Christ the conqueror who prevailed in Mexico. By suffering His martyrdom in her person or through the Fool (in modern times Christ is not crucified but shot) she gives Him back his original religious role as a redeemer. Hosé himself suggests this unconsciously when he tells Nameless that her portrait offers "the seed of a place" (43).

Don Hosé is not the only one who monumentalizes people into a static role. Sister Maria, who appears to be Sister Beatrice's counterpart (like her, she died "last autumn" [40,75]), monumentalizes herself as a "prince of the church" (77) and, though killed accidentally by gunfire from a passing police car, she asserts her so-called heroic role through her sister Rose. Even Nameless must resist the temptation to monumentalize the Absent Virgin into a "sacrificed angel pinned to the sky" (35), as he realizes in his first dream: "the art of murder . . . is the art of love of heaven too through winged premises."[17] Most of the time, however, the Fool breaks down the shell into which mythical and historical figures are conscripted and uncovers the sacrifice they suffered in its nakedness (hence, the expression "unfrocked spaces"). The accumulated layers of vestiges he explores are so many "wagons of subsistence" (67) into which one former victim after another fell and lay "at the bottom of the world" (68). That is why the "dreams of subsistence" arising from the "unwritten reserves planted in the death of obscure men and women" (67) are interchangeable, as are the "absence and presence" (26) of those whom Nameless encounters. Thus contrasting states are here clearly presented as interchangeable. "Interchangeability" is also illustrated in another sense when a "transaction of vision" (59) takes place between "Idiot spark" or Nameless and the Emperor Stone Rain or pre-Columbian emperor. In his descent into "accumulated levels of sacrifice" (36) Nameless does not identify completely with victims but stands halfway between *vision,* when he glimpses the inner proportions of the figures he encounters, and *reflection,* i.e., a state of passivity.[18] When he falls into Emperor Stone Rain, the precarious balance between vision and reflection occurs but also a "movement of being glimpsed by each other across ages" (60). This visionary exchange is linked to the process of mutation illustrated in several places in the novel when "the shape of each body, each vision is made already subtly *different* to what one thought it was" (23, italics mine). Mutation goes together with rediscovery and is ironically brought forward to Nameless's attention when he realizes that

There were post-revolution convents that seemed to sink when their end came into excavations that had recently commenced, after centuries of eclipse, into pre-Conquest Toltec shrines concealed in mounds and hills. (31)

The duality between the concrete and the "apparitional," the sensory and the abstract or "structural," which is so distinctive a feature of Harris's second phase and of the novellas, is perhaps even more beautifully rendered in this novel than in the earlier fiction. Each character is at once solidly there and evanescent. The whore/madonna, for example, is both a flesh-and-blood woman and an elusive, never-to-be-wholly-possessed muse. That is why her statue by the fire-eater remains unfinished: she is not an absolute but seems to represent an ever-changing source of inspiration and is, like Christ, "susceptible to all rejected visions" (26). Nameless's interview with Sister Joanna, one of the preparations for his visit to Mexico, takes place both in an actual convent in Europe and as a visionary re-creation in a mid-Atlantic cabin (a middle ground between European and American civilizations). During the interview Sister Joanna's voice comes and fades as if to suggest that the confrontation with the "other" can only be discontinuous. This recalls the woman in Nameless in *Black Marsden* who "comes and goes" or the passage in which Goodrich sees that "something moved, reappeared, flashed again, darkened."[19] Similarly, when Nameless visits Mrs. Black Marsden in New York he finds that hers is a "contagious theatre of absences and presences" (74). Sister Rose is one of Mrs. Black Marsden's roles and comes alive from a "heap of wigs and costumes" (76) in her room. Mrs. Black Marsden explains that

There is a technicality to Rose. . . . But also there is a ghost to Rose which may become visible within that technicality. . . . And . . . it is only when the ghost is partially visible through the dress of technicality that the past really connects with the present. (75)

Nameless's perception of the ghost in the technicality or of the ghost-like residues of experience in Mexico corresponds to his partial visions of the living element in them. In this respect his progress in consciousness takes the form of a discontinuous dialogue with the dead. There is an element of continuity, however, in his progression toward the pyramid of the sun which he ascends and from which he falls. As suggested above, and as Harris himself has recently pointed out,[20] his fall from the pyramid is also timeless and in that sense it is ceaseless. It is as if his many descents into others and into various Mexican *loci* were facets (partial re-creations) of his great and continuous fall. This fall is indirectly conveyed through a superposition of truncated pyramid images: one is formed by the landscape ("A truncated pyramid of landscape man Popocatapetl was. Deprived of a skull" [29]), another is alive on the billowing curtain as Nameless keeps falling although he is also in Mrs. Black Marsden's room, and another yet is composed of "Rose's face animated and alive [but severed?] at the base of the pyramid" and "Maria's head elongated like bone, upright reflection" (77). At one stage it seems to Nameless that "for centuries . . . he had been ascending, descending . . . falling into rain . . . into shelters of paint . . . sacrificed paint" (58). If I am not mistaken, the Fool's ceaseless fall amounts to his dynamic (because never final) identification with the uninitiate.[21] It is what Marsden calls in his letter to Goodrich an "advance of 'dying structure' into 'living present' " (81) or what Harris was to call "immortal dying tradition" in *Da Silva da Silva's Cultivated Wilderness*. Admittedly, on the realistic level Nameless dies at the base of the pyramid. Also Mrs. Black Marsden, whom he had asked whether he could spend a day and a night with her, has rejected him (though recognizing Christ in him) as it seems Christ in his sacrificial capacity is always rejected. But, to quote again from *Black Marsden,* Nameless "endure[s] a state of crisis beyond infection by despair," and in the timeless dimension he dies into life and seems in fact to be reborn as the child Sister Joanna took in before she died: "It was the beginning of the child of humanity" (52). That his dying coincides with rebirth is the last thing the Fool understands:

to be born was to be *unmade* in the legendary heart of Rose in compensation for Maria's bone and death, to be born was to be *broken* in the dream-play of history in compensation for unfulfilled models of sovereign subsistence, to be born was to *descend* into a depth of frustrated appetite and need arching back across centuries. (78, italics mine)

Does the "child of humanity" announce the rebirth of a genuine community in conquest-ridden Mexico?

If, as has been suggested, Harris's opus is a continuous canvas on which he and the exploring consciousness in his novels advance and retreat between two poles of life and light on one hand, death and nothingness, on the other, then *Da Silva da Silva's Cultivated Wilderness* is a leap forward toward what is called in the novel the "genie of space" (50) or "forgotten genie in oneself" (26). Da Silva himself is "resurrected" from Harris's earlier fiction (*Palace* and *Heartland*) as a "deep-seated painter" (10), one who apprehends together the material and immaterial dimensions inherent in all beings, objects, and experience. Whereas Idiot Nameless in *Companions* was part of the explored reality, his own experience becoming accessible through Goodrich only, da Silva and the characters he "paints" impose themselves with an immediacy and a sensuousness undiminished by the nonmaterial element elicited from each. The protagonist's very name, "Da Silva da Silva "(6), expresses his own duality as well as his "double vision." This is also conveyed through the time structure of the narrative, which once more juxtaposes a conventional time unit, one winter day, with the thirty-odd years of da Silva's experience since, as a five-year-old orphan, he was adopted by the British ambassador in Brazil, Sir Giles Marsden-Prince.[22] These reconstructed years blend into the one day with shifts backward and forward. Da Silva is a painter who spends the winter day getting his pictures ready for an exhibition. But the canvases he gathers together are as much as real paintings, slices of life which present themselves differently to him from what they were originally and through which he hopes "to discover . . . the origins of change" (10). Painting here is synonymous with experience and therefore with fiction, and as da Silva "paints" his way through existence, he re-envisions the past, his own and that of figures at once individual and representative of the dominating or the sacrificed element in society or both. Although it is also true of earlier novels, *Da Silva da Silva* is more specifically about the nature of creativity which, for Harris, is connected with a double movement from and toward the suppressed or violated element in the individual or humanity:

. . . as he returned to each painting again and again as varieties of transparent eclipse, he began to observe an implicit bank there in that a deep-seated mutation of tone rose into each canvas and one saw a spirit there as one *sees* a never-to-be-painted, never-to-be-trapped, light or element on earth. (38)

This sentence sums up da Silva's visionary journey and its outcome. The first set of his paintings is the "madonna pool" series which accumulates pool images with their dual possibility of mirror-like immobility and moving densities. Actually, they are areas in both elegant and destitute London;[23] the pool is the seat of experience and therefore "sea of redress, undress, unravelling elements" (13). Da Silva is married to one of the madonnas or muses, Jenine Gold, who is of mixed Celtic and Peruvian descent, as he is of mixed Portuguese and Arawak ancestry so that together they span civilizations. She is omnipresent in the novel because she and da Silva live in and through each other ("you are in me I in you forever" [5]) and because she is at once his main source of inspiration and the globe he tries to bring to life through his painting, "Jenine Gold where masked populations reside" (5). A major skeletal theme in the novel is that their union engenders a potential rebirth of humanity, of men's sensibility and imagination. Because Jen means so much to him and is in addition his material support, da Silva instinctively resists her self-sufficiency, "the halo of a stern goddess" (8) she sometimes wears and to which he could become subservient. She is in any case only one version, if eventually the most fruitful one, of the madonna; her portrait is complemented by that of Manya, da Silva's model, like him from Brazil, and Kate Robinson, a teacher who wants to take Manya's son, Paul, from her because she thinks Manya doesn't take proper care of him. Manya wears a black coat of uniformity and her house is littered with the paraphernalia of "economic deity, industry, fashion"; da Silva loathes "imprints of changelessness" (18) in her. But he is aware of her essential nakedness, of the suffering person beneath the changeless coat, which she leaves behind at their last meeting, later to be interpreted by da Silva as the "trailing coat of the madonna" (75) which eventually may be one of the sources of his "flying," moving inspiration. Manya has come to seek his help to be able to keep her son, and her intense love for her child *heals* her back to life.

Just as Manya's unlighted coat is the seed of the madonna paintings, so da Silva's unlighted T.V. set is the vacant frame in which the "paradise paintings" take shape. Each setting, incidentally, is a vacant frame for da Silva's paintings while he at the beginning is "void of identities" (13). He had once seen Kate Robinson, the third madonna figure, in a T.V. program on abortion during which she had been provoked into confessing that she had an abortion herself and thus killed the need for Adam in herself. But da Silva discovers that her self-sufficiency is scarred, and her self-inflicted wound is for him a source of compassion: "at the heart of box [T.V.] or body [Kate's] unlit by the senses lay signal lit by the non-senses as seed of paradise" (25). In other words, a negative condition lies once more at the very source of creation. Besides, Kate's intense concern for Manya's child is an indication that she too is susceptible of a "new arousal of blood" (38). Although the three madonna figures seem on the surface to have nothing in common, they are linked by their feeling or desire (in Jen's case) for a child.

Apart from the madonna figures, another link between the "madonna pool" and the "paradise" paintings is the sixteenth-century print that comes alive through da Silva's identification of the presences that "swim" on it with his own antecedents. It represents a meeting between civilizations: Portuguese courtiers march toward Amerindian beauties up to the waist in a Brazilian pool. The callousness of its first legend, *Sex and the Portuguese in Brazil*, evokes the suppression of the weaker culture by the stronger. Its other legend, *Paradise,* is largely ironical, for if it suggests the creation of a new world, it also represents an illusory perfection, as the individual lives of da Silva's antecedents show. On his paintings these assume the personality of Magellan, the limping Portuguese circumnavigator of the globe who has a modern namesake in the father of Manya's child, and Legba Cuffey, a composite figure in whom merge the eighteenth-century slave rebel Cuffey, the West Indian god Legba (also limping), and their modern namesake, a barman and model of da Silva. Magellan was glorified by history while his crew was ignored but he got little reward for his daring feats. Legba Cuffey was a mere footnote in history books but he now tends to compensate the losses of the past by denying the former exploiter the right to exist, whereas da Silva wants "to join the *fact* of broken power long long ago . . . into netted Legba, as threshold to the game of universal . . . cross-cultural divinity" (10). And indeed by "painting" the two limping men into himself, he elicits a "whispered dialogue" (11) between them. Da Silva also paints into himself the earl of Holland, a member of the ruling class victimized by Cromwell. These men's lives show the reversibility of situation that makes Harris find life in death or light in darkness. They also illustrate the polarizations that inevitably result from the attempt to create ever-new Edens at the expense of others; hence the illusoriness of perfection in the "paradise" they try to create. The "principle of healing" (32) (at work in the modern Magellan unexpectedly healed of leukemia) is a frequent rationale behind such an attempt. It is the need "to *prove* survival" (37)—after expectations of death—by accomplishing ever greater deeds. Whereas Manya was healed psychologically by her love for her son, Magellan's physical healing contains a warning against the need to die heroically on the beaches of conquest and to incur or impose sacrifice again and again.

The male figures in the novel represent the contrasting faces or complex levels of "immortal dying tradition" (61) into which da Silva travels (26). Indeed the contradictions in the lives of Magellan and the earl of Holland (domination followed by victimization) and the recurring victimization of Cuffey (despite expectations of sovereignty when a reversal of history occurs) show that beyond the oppressive and oppressed but equally mortal (dying) faces of tradition, another immaterial, undying tradition secretes itself out of the accumulated sufferings of men. It is in forms of this immaterial tradition that da Silva discovers the "varieties of transparent eclipse" mentioned above. In it too is to be found the light that has been "pushed under . . . suppressed, even violated" (38) and never to be wholly retrieved just as the "unfathomable coherence" that runs through each "trackless wilderness" (38) can never be attained. However, da Silva realizes as he "re-lives" each canvas that mutations occur, bringing with them partial illuminations such as he discovers through the "spiritual corpses" (17) in Manya's room or through the black coat she leaves behind when she runs away to save her child. The "prodigal" return of life or of light is illustrated in many concrete and symbolical ways in the novel. Da Silva was saved from a flood in Brazil by Sir Giles, who saved a child in London at the cost of his own life. When Jen returns from Peru and they make love in the middle of the day, da Silva becomes aware of their "mutual prodigality or resurrected body" (47); da Silva's many self-portraits through the resurrected lives of his models amount to their return to life. But, above all, there is the re-enactment of Cuffey's death in the "wildernesse'" area of Holland Park followed by the regeneration of his vision ("the eyes in his head were aflame" [59]). This re-enactment brings about the reconciliation between Cuffey, the victim of the middle passage, and Magellan, the restless seeker after paradise, so that in the "prodigal" paintings the "wildernesse" becomes the "middle ground of paradise" (48). Whereas, before, each was conscripted in his role as victim and conqueror, they have become "conscripted into an elaborate plot to heal each other's wounds in the conception of a child" (60).

Before commenting on the child as product of a prodigal return to life, it is necessary to point out that the immaterial dimension in tradition also manifests itself in a "drama of savage art" (5). Da Silva cultivates (re-creates or envisions) endless varieties of "wildernesse," all man-made, some beautiful, some hideous. But beyond man's obvious achievements there is a demonic force, a wildness (it flashes through in various images), which to da Silva is a "source of terror" (3) and of fascination and which, as much as beauty, is part of the hidden genie of man. Multifarious illustrations of that genie appear in da Silva's last visions, the "exhibition" series he paints on the "wildernesse" of the London Commonwealth Institute and in which the experience of individuals he has so far visualized is transposed to a universal scale. Here a dying tradition (the Empire) has been replaced by the new Commonwealth but for the optimistic motto that accompanies the exhibition of new technological achievement da Silva substitutes what underlies the birth of the Commonwealth: *"Self-survival, self-interest, self-sacrifice"* (67). In the very architecture of the Commonwealth Institute he reads a contrast between the uniform cloak that runs through the three exhibition decks and the line of *"non-tone"* they contain. This refers to what he calls "zero conditions," the extreme poles of experience of the "violated bodies of history" (Cuffey and Magellan), poles of "unbearable hell" and "unattainable beauty or heaven" which nevertheless bring forth the "middle-ground regenerated eyes of . . . compassion as original vision" (70). The question remains, however, whether "new superstition" or "new mutation" will prevail in the Commonwealth.

"Compassion as original vision" is the equation between feeling and regenerated vision which is always the purpose of the quest in Harris's novels. Here it is pursued through canvas after canvas as an ever-present but only partly discernible light. That light is the genie of man, the park which lies in his greatest as in his poorest achievements. The following passage is a good example of the way in which the narrative blends throughout the reality of the physical world with the transparency of its "immaterial constitution":

Da Silva would paint his way past [a demolished area] on a summer evening long ago it seemed (though perhaps it was only yesterday) with his brush dipped into the sky. He felt a tightened grip in his flesh, a sense of deprivation in those rotting beams or walls that belonged to a past economic code or day, and yet he was utterly amazed as the paint seeped out of the sky—transparent densities of blues and greens, white fire, edges of orchestrated delicacy touched by unfathomable peace, consensus of open-hearted privacy in a dying sky—as if to alert him to the reality of the radiant city within every city, the reality of the genie's gift, the genie's potential reconstruction. (63)

The "genie's potential reconstruction" epitomizes the process of survival, mutation, resurrection at work in the novel. The genie assumes many different shapes but is mostly associated with a child. For example, Manya's son is a spark on Manya's canvas. There is also the "abused child, eclipsed child" to which one comes near as to a "prodigal daemon of heaven" (41) when the genie of man awakens. This awakening is best rendered through the relationship between da Silva and Jen (the artist and the muse), a marriage of both senses and minds; they have "ceaselessly conceived [an immortal presence] through each other" (48). Jen's homecoming at the end of the winter day and her announcement that she is pregnant brings together several strands in the novel. Her pregnancy fulfills a marriage that has so far remained barren but it is also a token of da Silva's "birth . . . as a painter" (65), for his own creativeness is revitalized, and together they are on the point of "resurrecting" the genie of man. This is the main significance of the "genie's return" or "homecoming of spirit" which sets the light circulating again:

He caught her to him. . . . He encircled the globe then, a global light
whose circulation lay through and beyond fear into unfathomable security.
(77)

The end of *Da Silva da Silva* adequately prefaces *Genesis of the Clowns*
published in a single volume with it and subtitled "A Comedy of
Light." Like the "drama of consciousness" and the "*tabula rasa*
comedy" in which Harris's earlier characters were involved, it stages
eclipsed personae moving in the protagonist's consciousness. Frank
Wellington is a white Creole who used to work for the colonial
government in British Guiana. When the novel opens, he has been
living in London for twenty years. He receives an anonymous letter
announcing the death of Hope, foreman of a crew he led into the
Guyanese interior in 1948, and this urges him into a one-day journey
into the past. As each member of the crew is resurrected from the
marginal sketches he used to make in his field book and again
approaches his paytable, he sees they were steeped in a "dying light"
which nevertheless "store[d] itself as the germinating seed of the
future" (110). The novel grows out of that seed as Wellington's
original suspicion of their emotions of fear and love turns into a deeper
awareness of the real debt he owes them.

We know from earlier novels that the Fool or Clown stands for
naked, eclipsed man whom Harris associates with the divine (his
characters are also involved in a "comedy of divinity" [102]). The
clowns here are the exploited crew, men who have either lost all
expectations or, on the contrary, turn their deprivations and frustra-
tions (emotional, political, economic) into capital investments to be
used later. They are plagued by the imprints of various legacies of the
past of which they cannot free themselves although conditions have
changed. Hope, for example, a kind of Black Marsden who stimulates
Wellington's understanding of the crew, still acts as if women were
"at a high and cruel premium" (137) as when there was one woman to
fifty or a hundred men in Guyana. He eventually succumbs to a
"tyranny of affections" (147) similar to the political tyranny of the
men of deed he admires; the letter Wellington receives explains that
Hope has killed a rival lover (Wellington's black namesake) and
committed suicide. The crew are also ridden with terrors for which

the scant "currency" they receive while serving an alien power can in no way compensate them. The Amerindian Reddy, for whom water falling from the "pole of the sun" was a guarantee of light, sees with dread Atlantic tidal currents carrying logs upriver but conceals his disorientation and fears behind a mask of laughter. Wellington now sees his misinterpretation of Reddy's behavior and his former blindness to the Amerindian's terror as typical of the misunderstanding that has endured for centuries between sovereign employer and exploited men, a "misconception" responsible for the "frozen genesis" (112) not only in the relation between the crew and their leader but "in the encounter between alien cultures" (122). The novel, however, is not a one-sided indictment of imperialist and capitalist powers although Wellington represents both. Like the crew, he is beset by unavowed lusts and fears. He too has "undressed " Ada, the "Fertility Goddess," and desired Lucille, Chung's wife and Hope's mistress. He senses the crew's malaise as menacing, though unconscious energy, an anonymous gun pointed at himself and threatening to kill him as he is nearly killed by the released energy of the storm that brings down his tent. Yet even in 1948 the storm and the "spatial gun imprinted" (85) in it set in motion a mutation only fully realized in 1974 when he receives the anonymous letter, an unravelling of "frozen" premises "As though the wheel of Empire began to turn anew . . . began to return to me as a moving threshold of consciousness" (86).

As in *Companions of the Day and Night*, Harris draws his chief metaphor from a cosmic phenomenon. While Frank Wellington re-creates the experiences of the crew, he is involved in a "Copernican revolution of sentiment" (92), a displacement in his consciousness, and a recognition, of men (and the cultures they represent) he once took for granted. The crew who in colonial times revolved around the central authority or sun of Empire (Wellington) had begun in 1948 to secrete their own "buried suns" toward which Wellington turns as to a "shadowplay of a genesis of suns—the shadowplay of interior suns around which I now turned whereas before they had turned around me in processional sentiment" (86). This revolution illustrates in the individual consciousness the theme of the mutation of buried cultures developed in *Companions* and in da Silva's Commonwealth paintings. It implies a relativization of cultures: "Not one earth turns but many imprints relate to the sun. Not one sun but many buried suns relate to imprinted landscapes, peoples" (92). Significantly, there is no question of merely reversing the old dominating order, of replacing one center (earth or sun) by another, but rather of taking into account "revolving and counter-revolving potentials to which we begin to relate" (108). Harris does not stop at a Copernican revolution, for this is accompanied by a counterrevolution: "revolving and counter-revolving imprints of earth turn around the eye of the sun" (92); it even finds a parallel in the contrary tidal flows that so frighten the Amerindian Reddy, "revolutions turning in opposite and contrary directions" (87).

A diagram on page 91 shows revolving and counter-revolving currents drawing nearer to each other while turning around the "stilled eye of the sun." It seems to epitomize the view of existence that Harris gradually builds up as his contrary figures (Wellington and the crew) learn to move toward each other while also moving "around a central darkness of buried sun" (92). For, if I understand rightly, the "stilled eye of the sun" is an illusion. Wellington thinks at one stage that "implicit in the Copernican wilderness is an unfathomable (rather than static) centre around which cultures revolve. I glimpse this as the complex theme of objective and subjective freedom" (117). This unfathomable center seems to be the fluid, nameless dimension which Harris's earlier protagonists have approached and to which both the crew and Wellington relate although the latter alone is aware of it. It also implies what Harris calls the "mediation of uncapturable light" between partial frames or cultures, a mediating "force" that cannot be tamed and is therefore a source of infinite potentiality. It is a force that may inspire terror but also contains, as Harris suggests, a "therapeutic capacity."

Retrospectively, after he has faced the "terrifying otherness" (126) of his crew, as they once faced the terror of the strange world he was imposing on them, Wellington transforms his encounter with the crew into one of reciprocity and perceives "a capacity still beneath the pole of the sun to give, to receive . . . as the pain of unfrozen genesis" (127). This reciprocity is further illustrated at the end of the novel when Wellington reads the letter that started the "comedy" in which he took part all day. He sees his "own clown's shadow welling up on the page" (143) and realizes that as the crew have been moving to him, so he has been moving to the nameless stranger who was addressing him. The comedy has been a "shadow-play of genesis. Light-play of genesis" (143), opposites playing against each other through which Wellington receives "the gift of life without strings" (148). While reliving the past, he had several intuitions that the crew's unconsciously ambivalent attitude might equally release gifts of death or life: "ammunition, animation" (140). On first receiving the letter, he felt that "Perhaps fate and freedom are mixed . . . twins one meets afresh, sees afresh in the womb of self-knowledge of selves other than oneself" (81). The letter which tells of Hope's crime and suicide is subtitled *"Counter-Revolving Currencies Of Fate and Freedom On The Paytable Of The Sky"* (142). It is as if the real wages Wellington had not paid Hope in the past were now returning (counter-revolving) because Hope could not resist the climax of "antecedent emotions" (147) built up in him. The suggestion is that because his (and the crew's) emotions were at one time ignored, these are now striking back in a totalitarian spirit, "a jealous right to possess properties of flesh-and-blood" (148). Hope's gesture, however, offers dual possibilities of blind submission to fate and of freedom: "I say 'humour of fate'. . . . But why not . . . 'mystery of freedom'?" (146). Wellington understands that freedom can be reached through recognition of a previously unconscious subscription to fate as he rereads the letter ironically signed "F.W." The anonymous stranger is himself or rather an inner self toward which he has turned, thus distancing himself from the sovereign sun of his personality. It is therefore Wellington who realizes that on the brink of death Hope may have seen "another head among the clowns . . . another shadow" (148). By killing the black Wellington, he sent him into the nameless dimension into which he himself dies, the source of compassion and freedom white Wellington glimpses:

Perhaps as apparently hopeless as one's time is, there is a new movement, a new genesis of the clowns, a new subsistence upon the biases of Hope . . . that runs . . . far deeper than deliberate consciousness towards compassion. (102)

Aspects of Harris's fiction developed in the second and third cycles of novels come to a head in *The Tree of the Sun*. The joint process of interiorization and expedition into "otherness" that began with *The Eye of the Scarecrow* is still linked with a probing into the working of a creative mind as into the very nature and mystery of creativity. The novel is a sequence to *Da Silva da Silva's Cultivated Wilderness* and takes up the narrative where Jen announces that she is pregnant. Da Silva recalls that on the very morning when they conceived a child, he also conceived a mural called "The Tree of the Sun" on which he now starts to work anew. The two main figures in his mural, and on the canvas of his imagination, are Francis and Julia Cortez, the former tenants of his flat who died twenty-five years before. While remodelling the flat, the da Silvas came across an unfinished book and letters that the Cortezes secretly wrote for each other. Da Silva's editorship of Francis's book and Julia's letters is both the material of the novel and the subject of his "painting." Secondary characters emerge from the Cortezes' life and writings and these too da Silva "paints" into himself in a serial way. Nowhere better than here is it possible to apply to Harris Yeats's belief that "the borders of our mind are ever shifting, and that many minds can flow into one another, as it were, and create or reveal a single mind, a single energy."[24] Da Silva's inner self provides the framework for the narrative. The reader sometimes tends to forget this, however, so vivid is the intercourse between Francis and Julia, the "living" dead whose relationship is posthumously modified by da Silva's "painting," and between da Silva and the Cortezes. Not only does da Silva bring the dead to life, *they* bring *him* to life in their writing and envisage the role he will play in their future "existence." It seems that in this dialogue between the dead and the living and their awareness of each other across time and space lies the way to what Harris calls "the resurrection of the self," that is the return to life of buried antecedents or the surfacing and assimilation of unconscious elements into the consciousness. The characters in this novel partake of one another's existences, enter one another's skin (Jen conceives the child Julia always wanted but repeatedly miscarried); similarly, different times and spaces merge and each event is seen with its ramifications in the past and in the future from a specific point in a character's consciousness. Harris stretches further than ever the limits of the human personality as if the creative imagination could defy all categories of being, run through all levels of existence and nonexistence. He is also clearly engaged in revising and extending his characters' (and the reader's) limits of perception, a process which started with *Palace of the Peacock* but has become increasingly more complex. I have had occasion before to draw attention to the complexity and unifying quality of his language, particularly his metaphors. In this novel they once more convey several layers of meaning like "the tree of the sun," basically a metaphor for the process of creation, which combines several modes of achieving vision. The combination of levels in the narrative texture, its fusion of immediacy and "otherness," are particularly striking in the following passage, in which the Cortezes' lovemaking suggests at once their participation in a cosmic movement in which opposites meet and the coming to life of the inanimate world around them, while also evoking the process of resurrection in which they and other unseen beings are involved:

Francis drew her into bed. The sound of a faint call in the distance, a telephone beak in the shell of the sea, a telegram, rather than a letter, drew them into each other's arms. Perhaps they were attuned to living ink as the surf ascended once again, to charcoal voices of birds in foodbearing tree at the heart of fire, to midnight eyes in the middle of broad daylight.

"I spent the morning writing letters," she confessed inwardly. Their bodies clung together into the language of a living tool, cultivated living bed, carpentered living tables and chairs in the room around them like attendant yet invisible courtiers, flesh-and-blood wood, grassgrown parks and ponds, carven benches, milestones of penetrative flesh in the theatre of a bed that secreted the memories of lives lived or unlived a generation and more ago, a generation and more to come. (26)

As usual in Harris's fiction, there is a symbiosis between "vision and idea," between imagined worlds and people and the philosophical substance extracted from the vision. There is also a close correspondence between form and content. Da Silva attempts to grasp the "inimitable," "the unfathomable centre" or wholeness that can never be totally apprehended but will assume various shapes in the "resurrection of the self." Francis and Julia (and the characters they create) are so many agents arousing that resurrection, "approximations" to it, or, as da Silva thinks, "wedded apparitions . . . within a quest for the resurrection of the self" (27). Da Silva's self-distancing and penetration of these *partial* selves thus entails a multiplicity of approaches to the unfathomable wholeness. So do the sculptures, paintings, and dramas he envisions as if only a variety of coincidental forms of art could provide a suitable approximation to the elusive otherness. This otherness and the ways to it have assumed innumerable shapes in Harris's fiction. What emerges in this novel is the correspondence between the search for otherness and for wholeness, the arousal of sensibility, the partial achievement of community, and the process of creation itself. I have shown before that catastrophe can issue into rebirth, and here the wound received by historical antecedents (Montezuma and Atahualpa) is seen as a "blow" of creation. Julia's miscarriage becomes converted into "profound sensibility of apparitions of community" (50), and in re-creating the conversion Harris attempts to approach through imagery the mysterious essence of the creative process. As in earlier novels, the renascence of imagination and the arts goes together with a retrieval of buried or "unborn" antecedents from the apparent void of Caribbean or new world history (the Cortezes are West Indian). Indeed, "painting" is clearly a gateway into being or toward resurrection. But the retrieved one is not to be idealized. As already suggested about *Da Silva da Silva*, creation seems to arise unpredictably from a double movement between the born and the negative condition of the unborn:

Each intimate womb painting, or experience of naked enterprise in a body of elements, possessed intertwining forces that had crossed from one bank of cosmos to another to confront each other *in a sudden breath or seizure of flesh*. (60, italics mine)

In this double movement too lies the achievement of community, the "treaty of sensibility between the born and the unborn" (50). Thus community *is* creation, unfinished creation as "unfinished community" (86) since no state is ever reached finally, no absolute ever institutionalized; on the contrary, whether "on this bank of heaven or that bank of earth" (30), god or man, dead or living being must efface himself and move toward an otherness that can be glimpsed but finally eludes him. *The Tree of the Sun* also evokes "parallel expeditions" (64), i.e., separate areas of experience which do not meet directly yet relate to each other through the spark that resides in each. To retrieve that spark is to open the way to dialogue.

The reciprocal movement between the living and the dead, the conception of characters who are at once themselves and other than themselves in another dimension, the fluidity of the narrative form, and the rich complexity of a language which presents together and in their constant movement the antinomies of existence, are the fundamental aspects of an opus as much concerned with the spiritual salvation of man as with the renewal of the art of fiction. It is an open-ended opus since, like each novel, it finds no resolution but rather presents life in the making with its self-deceptions and revelations, "a hand dissolving the elements, constructing the elements" (72) in the hope of running into the moment of vision:

To accept incompatible visions, to accept what is like and unlike oneself, to accept the tricks of nature as a versatile warning that truth exists but stands on unfathomable foundations, and still to believe in the unity of the self, is to run fleetingly (but sometimes securely) *in* a presence of glory. . . . (17)

Notes and References

Preface

1. Wilson Harris, *Explorations*, A Selection of Talks and Articles, edited with an introduction by Hena Maes-Jelinek (Aarhus, 1981).

Chapter One

1. Wilson Harris, *The Eye of the Scarecrow* (London, 1965), p. 25.
2. See Harris's much quoted essay "Tradition and the West Indian Novel," *Tradition, the Writer and Society* (London, 1967), p. 28.
3. Ibid., p. 32.
4. "A Talk on the Subjective Imagination," *New Letters* 40 (October, 1973):30.
5. Wilson Harris, *Tradition, the Writer and Society*, p.51.
6. The concept of namelessness was to give rise in *The Eye of the Scarecrow* to the creation of a character called Idiot Nameless.
7. Wilson Harris, *The Eye of the Scarecrow*, paperback ed. (London, 1974), Author's Note, p. 9.
8. The episode recalls the myth of Ulysses' approach to, and flight from, the sirens, which Harris discusses in *Tradition, the Writer and Society* (pp. 52−53) and treats more fully in *The Waiting Room*.
9. In *Tumatumari* also the fall down a high escarpment stands for the collapse of the Amerindians.
10. " . . . all threads of light and fabric from the thinnest strongest source of all beginning and undying end" (*Palace of the Peacock* [London, 1968], pp. 138−39). See also "All else was dream borrowing its light from a dark invisible source" (Ibid., p. 141).
11. " . . . curious hands and feet, neck, shoulder, forehead, material twin shutter and eye. They drifted, half-finished sketches in the air, until they were filled suddenly from within to become living and alive" (Ibid., p. 146). Connect the tree's transformation into the peacock with "they alone were left to frame Christ's tree and home" (p. 137).

Chapter Two

1. See Wilson Harris, *The Far Journey of Oudin* (London, 1961), p. 69:

"In truth it was like an olden mystery to know the real hour and time. It might have been morning, and yet again evening. . . ."

2. Harris, *Tradition, the Writer and Society*, pp. 44–45.

3. The flight into the forest is for Oudin "a flying journey . . . a crucial rehearsal . . . that would be repeated once again over thirteen dreaming years of his marriage to Beti" (*Far Journey*, p. 100).

4. The severed head is a recurring symbol in Harris's fiction and illustrates the dislocation of personality suffered by the slaves. Oudin "experiences" this trial to redeem the community.

5. In Harris's later novels the dead seldom revive in so concrete a shape but rather haunt the characters' consciousness as "ghosts."

6. In *Heartland* Kaiser at last achieves fulfillment and helps those who reach the heartland to achieve it too. Compare "Time will teach us to undermine every obstacle . . . in a kingdom he had a long way to go *to begin to learn* to build" (*Far Journey*, p. 75, italics mine), with "I was a rich landowner and a teacher some years ago but I lose everything in a fire . . . and I finding since then that I got *to begin to learn* to live and help others live on next to nothing" (*Heartland*, [London, 1964], p. 15, italics mine).

7. See, among others, *Far Journey*, pp. 55, 58 and 116.

8. See ibid., pp. 56, 58, 84 and 105.

9. Quoting alchemists, C.G. Jung explains that the shadow is emitted by the sun since without it there is no shadow. The sun contains the light and the dark, the conscious and the unconscious. *Mysterium Coniunctionis* (London: Routledge & Kegan Paul, 1970), pp. 97–98.

10. *The Secret of the Golden Flower*, a Chinese Book of Life, translated and explained by Richard Wilhelm with a Foreword and Commentary by C.G. Jung (London: Routledge & Kegan Paul, 1969), pp. 24–25. The "square inch between the eyes" is the site of the "third eye," i.e., the means of paranormal vision.

11. Ibid., p. 53.

12. Ibid., p. 26.

13. See John Hearne, "The Fugitive in the Forest," *The Journal of Commonwealth Literature* 4 (December, 1957):99–112.

14. See also the transformation of "seed-water" into "spirit-fire" (*Far Journey*, p. 54) and note the generally illuminating role of the two elements in the novel.

15. The Baptist is a recurring figure in Harris's fiction (see, e.g., *Black Marsden*); he is also evoked in the epigraph to Book III: "the dayspring from on high hath visited us," Luke, 1:78.

16. Wilson Harris, "The Reality of Trespass, " *Kyk-Over-Al* 2 (December, 1949):21.

17. See *Far Journey*, p. 15: "[Ram] trembled, unable to discern . . . the shadow of the sun he wished to corner and possess with . . . every acre of land he acquired from his tenants who had mortgaged their labour and their world to him."

18. Harris, *Tradition, the Writer and Society*, p. 45.

Chapter Three

1. Magda looks like an idol: "Her brow and cheeks were a black fantastic mood of mahogany, her eyes narrow and unbelieving slits . . . her . . . limbs [were] strong like the most ancient sculpture" (*The Whole Armour* [London, 1973], pp. 25,29).

2. Ibid., p. 48: "Her part . . . was the hidden salvation of Cristo's life out of hopeless loyalty and brutal maternal instinct."

3. To the crowd the wake is a "collective roll-call" (Ibid., p. 49).

4. "Serial" suggests a line of ancestors.

5. Harris obviously uses "wake" in two interdependent meanings: the mourning for the dead and the process of illumination it can engender.

6. See in particular when Peet tells Mattias: "the tiger is none other but you" and the accusation brings out the tigerish instinct of the crowd: "the voice of the crowd *roared* in Mattias's ear as if the ancient tiger had truly entered the wake out of chaos and eternal nightmare. . . . He felt the desolating uprush of panic and rape and death reflected in every snarling face" (*Whole Armour*, p. 76, italics mine).

7. Wilson Harris's use of the tiger symbol seems to fit in with the Arawak "counsel of prudence" mentioned by Michael Swan in *The Marches of El Dorado*: "Everything has jaguar." Mr. Swan further explains that "Jaguars are the most common first ancestor for the many tribes who claim an animal pedigree—and the original name of the Carib tribe—*Carinye*—means 'arising from a jaguar.' " *The Marches of El Dorado* (London: Jonathan Cape, 1958), p. 97.

8. "He was of medium height, slenderly built, poise of a dancer. High questioning cheek-bones, penetrating eyes, a restless way of shaking hands and wrists, the sensitive nervous shuddering joints and limbs of a sprinter at the start of a race" (*Whole Armour*, p. 22).

9. The ancient belief that the moon receives the souls of the dead before their second death and rebirth is mentioned, among others, by Plutarch. C.G. Jung also quotes a Manichaean text which explains that the moon takes

in the souls of the dead. *Psychologie et Alchimie* (Paris: Buchet/Chastel, 1970), p. 484n.

10. Kenneth Ramchand, Introduction to *Palace of the Peacock* (London, 1968), unpaginated, or *The West Indian Novel and its Background* (London: Faber & Faber, 1970), p. 10.

Chapter Four

1. In Greek mythology the hero Perseus slew the Gorgon's head and out of her neck emerged the winged horse Pegasus (whose name means "source"), the son of Medusa and Poseidon. Perseus then crossed Ethiopia and fell in love with Andromeda who had been tied to a rock to free the country from a monster sent by Poseidon. In *The Secret Ladder* (London, 1973) the role of Perseus (p. 171) seems to be divided between Fenwick (who slays the Gorgon in himself) and Bryant, who first opens Fenwick's eyes to what Poseidon represents. Both men come to the rescue of Catalena (who has come to the Canje region on the *Andromeda*), though Fenwick does so indirectly, when she has been tied down by Poseidon's followers. Bryant is naturally the Perseus who marries her.

2. See, for instance, ibid., pp. 165, 195 and 225, where "parody" suggests the existence of both an apparent and an authentic reality.

Chapter Five

1. See interview by Ian Munro and Reinhard Sander, *Kas-Kas* (Austin: University of Texas at Austin, 1972): "I view the novel as a kind of infinite canvas, an infinity" (p. 52).

2. *Palace of the Peacock*, p. 123.

3. A pork-knocker is a gold or diamond digger in the Guyanese interior.

4. DaSilva seems to be "addressing" someone in the depth of the bush (*Heartland* [London, 1964], p. 39) and to be "addressed" by his other self (p. 44). There are many other instances of "address" in the novel. Note the first appearance of "address" to describe an attempt at a dialogue with the unseen in *Palace of the Peacock* (pp. 55, 59).

5. Note the frequent use of words relating to food in the novel as well as Petra's role as a taker (she has stolen daSilva's rations) and a giver of food (see *Heartland* pp. 65, 68, 70).

6. Like the muse in *Palace of the Peacock*, Petra contains both conqueror and conquered (see *Heartland*, p. 65), an indication that rebirth and incentive to consciousness and imagination depend on a marriage between the two.

7. See *Heartland*, p. 84: "Who could say how dangerously arrogant one might become if one followed one's purest instinct of absolute rage for good?"

8. Book III contains other images of release particularly related to the muse. See ibid., p. 73: "The fortress of the past was yielding to a timeless rent and sacrifice in the mother of the present."

9. The postscript consists in half-obliterated poems which prefigure the broken narrative fabric of *The Eye of the Scarecrow* and the disjointed diary of *The Waiting Room*. The blanks seem to stand for the void that Harris will explore in the subsequent novels, an exploration that culminates in his conception of the *tabula rasa*. Stevenson's poems are in fact extracts from *Eternity to Season* (Georgetown, 1954), which confirms Harris's use of Stevenson as an "agent of personality." See *Kas-Kas*, p. 52.

Chapter Six

1. Wilson Harris, *Ascent to Omai* (London, 1970), p. 123.

2. Harris, *Tradition, the Writer and Society*, p. 32.

3. The narrator draws attention to the many shapes his source of inspiration can take by quoting John 14:2: *"In my Father's house are many mansions."* See *Eye of the Scarecrow* (London, 1965), pp. 21, 31, 82.

4. See "Author's Note," paperback edition, p. 10.

5. Ibid., p. 9.

6. In alchemy Raven's Head is at once the initial stage of the process of exploration and the state of blackness that precedes the *cauda pavonis* or resurrection. For a parallel between alchemy and the process of individuation in Harris's novels, see Michael Gilkes, *Wilson Harris and the Caribbean Novel* (London: Trinidad & Jamaica, 1975).

7. Cf. the I-narrator's intuitions of these contraries within himself in *Palace of the Peacock*.

8. The explorer is now discovering the "flock of reflections" (*Eye of the Scarecrow*, p. 25) N. and L. were trying to detect in East Street canal as children. The shepherds themselves are part of the explorer's "flock of himself" (p. 70).

9. See ibid., p. 77: "the crash is . . . architecturally unclear and unsound to me—unpredictable vacancy of ascent or block of descent?"

10. Although both forms refer to the nameless dimension, it seems that a distinction can be drawn between *it* (italicized) and IT, which refers more specifically to the relation between TWO (one and the other). See ibid., p. 76: "IT was engaged—even as it supported and bore the company of TWO—in preparing a new map of the fluid role of instinct."

11. Several passages have prepared the reader for this birth. See, among others, "the ghostly idiot stranger . . . in one's own breast" (ibid., p. 20). The Idiot or Fool in Harris's novels seems to have developed from the West Indian trickster, who identifies with the victim (see *The Far Journey*). He is nameless because associated with the nameless "uninitiate" and because he represents the deep inner reality shared by all men and discovered by breaking down the imprisoning self.

12. In *Companions of the Day and Night* (London, 1975) Idiot Nameless says: "The art of murder . . . is the art of love of heaven too" p. 35.

13. Nameless reaches that state, equivalent to freedom, when he becomes "hollow artist" (*Eye of the Scarecrow*, p. 95). Harris's notion of "negative identity" is related to Keats's "negative capability," with which he expresses an affinity in "The Phenomenal Legacy," *The Literary Half-Yearly* (July, 1970):2.

14. The distinction has been drawn between Harris's "narrative" and "reconstructive" styles. See Eva Searl's review of *Companions of the Day and Night*, *Commonwealth Newsletter* 9 (January, 1976):52. In *Palace of the Peacock* Harris had created a style that conveys *together* the surface reality of life and its underlying flow, and he used it episodically in the other three novels of the Guiana Quartet. In *Heartland* he adumbrates an exclusively "reconstructive" style, i.e., one which refines outer-world experiences into an inner-world, largely symbolical, action. He has perfected this style in *The Eye of the Scarecrow*.

15. See *Eye of the Scarecrow*, p. 107: "from the ghost of my beginning to the spirit of my end."

16. In the three parts of the novel there are as many references to silence as to the void, and the two must be linked. Like the void, silence becomes creative.

17. There are many examples in the novel of "the other" in its various forms enlightening N.'s consciousness in a flash. See, for instance, "the dazzling sleeper of spirit . . . slid in a flash" (*Eye of the Scarecrow*, p. 49); "The dusty answer flashed through and through hollow artist" (p. 95); "the 'flash' of explosive freedom you [L. as the other] possess" (p. 101); "You flashed your 'dead' thought like the beam of a torch" (p. 103).

Chapter Seven

1. Harris, *Tradition, the Writer and Society*, p. 55.
2. Ibid., p. 48, italics mine.

3. Interview by Ian Munro and Reinhard Sander, *Kas-Kas*, p. 53.

4. Harris, *Tradition, the Writer and Society*, p. 48.

5. Wallace Stevens, *The Necessary Angel* (New York: Alfred A. Knopf, 1951), p. 174.

6. "A cerebral and sensual novel," quoted in Paul Valéry, *La Jeune Parque* (Paris: Gallimard, 1974), p. 142. Note also the parallel between Harris's conception of the novelist as agent and Valéry's remark "Il se fait des contes en moi," tales write themselves in me" (translation mine).

7. The second "Thief" is no mere repetition. It counterpoints the first and evokes an invisible presence in the heart of the nameless dimension. See also "DaSilva. DaSilva . . . Stevenson. Stevenson" in *Heartland* (p. 44) and compare the "nameless person" in *The Waiting Room* with the mysterious thief of daSilva's rations in *Heartland*.

8. The now-dark waiting room represents a state of weakness and negation of the self which leads on to a recognition of the "other."

9. The paradox is understandable. She gratifies his pride and therefore "serves" him.

10. "The sea and the sky became his spectacles as well as hers within which a new intercourse of the gods began, involving and dismantling every blockade of vision" (*The Waiting Room* [London, 1967], p. 38). Note that the natural elements are, like human beings, the material reality *through* which vision is achieved.

11. Harris, *Tradition, the Writer and Society*, p. 55.

12. This sentence brings together a series of images that have so far been associated with the lover: fire (blaze); instrument (he is the instrument of Susan's blindness and of her insight); day. Even "abstract" evokes "he," phenomenon of sensibility to which Susan is allied.

13. Harris's phrasing in *Tradition, the Writer and Society*, p. 52. In *The Odyssey* Ulysses leaves Circe with her consent, and she warns him against the sirens' song, although at an earlier stage she has herself turned his crew into swine. In Harris's recreation of the myth Circe and the sirens become one, probably because both exert a fascination conducing to states associated in Harris's fiction: animal-like unconsciousness and death.

14. Harris, *Tradition, the Writer and Society*, p. 51.

15. See, among others, "he was . . . in process of being informed by her about himself" (*The Waiting Room*, p. 39).

16. The reader will recall that in *The Eye* the nameless energy or "it" is called "dazzling sleeper of spirit." In this novel it is "wildcat of earthen fury" (p. 49) or "swift runner of life" (p. 67) and recalls the tiger in *The Whole*

Armour. In my opinion, the bushmaster which kills Amerindian Susan's husband is a destructive form of "it" (see p. 79).

17. "The seal of the sun [see *'ancient seal,'* p. 15] was upheld and splintered again and again" (p. 77). This corresponds to "in that instant of recall her eyes splintered" (*The Waiting Room*, p. 70).

Chapter Eight

1. Harris's phrasing in "The Unresolved Constitution," *Caribbean Quarterly* 14 (March-June, 1968):45.

2. It is interesting to note that memory, imagination, and foresight correspond to the attributes of the virtue of prudence as described by Frances Yates in *The Art of Memory* (Harmondsworth: Penguin Books, 1969). In *Tradition, the Writer and Society* Harris emphasizes the relevance of "the art of memory" as described by Dr. Yates to the "drama of consciousness" he creates in his fiction.

3. This refers to the fact that the Indians are "blindfolded creatures" (*Tumatumari* [London, 1968], p. 48). The mountains too are blindfolded ("bandage of the elements" [p. 48]) and Prudence's head is bandaged by Rakka (pp. 43,154).

4. Ivan van Sertima, "The Sleeping Rocks: Wilson Harris's *Tumatumari*," in *Enigma of Values*, ed. Kirsten H. Petersen and Anna Rutherford (Aarhus, 1975), p. 121.

5. In Tenby's conception of Pamela, Harris criticizes mainly the "perfectionist assumptions" or ideal "models," (*Tumatumari*, p. 153) for the sake of which men are prepared to sacrifice their fellow-beings. That the perfection Pamela is supposed to represent does not exist (her name is, of course, ironical) is suggested by her hypocritical behavior even as a child (p. 145).

6. Note that Prudence has to wrestle *in* and *with* her own name (Ibid., pp. 41,61).

7. Roi's name is symbolical. The "sick king" is not only a mythological figure, he had an important role to play in the alchemical process. A close reading of *Tumatumari* will show that, of all Harris's novels, it provides the most explicit illustration of the creation of the "alchemical imagination." There are obvious examples of alchemical symbolism, like the marriage of fire and water through Prudence and Rakka, and the role of the *Petra Genetrix* (stone "maturing" and giving birth) already mentioned in *Heartland*, in which the muse named Petra becomes a "numinous boulder" (p. 71).

8. Isabella is really the first version of the "waif-of-the-street." She too is

first treated as a whore and when Tenby first makes love to her "it was as if she lay naked at the heart of the street" (*Tumatumari*, p. 89).

9. In a sense Prudence becomes the mother of a new Tenby.

10. As in *Palace of the Peacock*, the Amerindians represent the "alien" enduring reality in the heart of the landscape and the elements. The short section entitled "METAPHYSICS OF THE ALIEN" describes Prudence's recognition that, however repulsive and upsetting their way of life, the Amerindians are an essential link in mankind's chain of being. Her vision ("IT") arises from the confrontation between the "archangel of sewers," the humble representative of Rakka's world, and the compassionate "archangel of God" (Ibid., p. 83).

11. The "free construction of events" in *The Eye* and the fact that the logbook in *The Waiting Room* is a "medium of invocation in its own right" imply the changeability of the past. Note also Harris's reference to the "sexuality of time" in *Fossil and Psyche* (Austin, 1974), p. 2.

12. See Prudence's awareness that the inhabitants of Tumatumari, who, like her brother, have been "swept underground," are "LAMP-POSTS OF THE FUTURE" (*Tumatumari*, p. 66).

13. Interview by Ian Munro and Reinhard Sander, *Kas-Kas*, p. 53.

14. Van Sertima, in *Enigma of Values*, p. 123.

15. Prudence also sees Roi as an "Outrider of the future . . . Outrider of remorse" (*Tumatumari*, p. 83).

16. Harris, "The Unresolved Constitution," p. 44.

Chapter Nine

1. "Magdalene" is a river and a province in Columbia, the possible seat of the legendary El Dorado, from where Adam came to Albuoystown; it is also mother earth idolized by Victor and the "Magdalene of Compassion" who protects him.

2. The phrase "holes for eyes," first used in *The Waiting Room*, also suggests a mask.

3. In this passage Harris suggests that Victor's (modern man's) conscience is "half-metaphysical, half-dialectical" (*Ascent to Omai*, [London, 1970], p. 17) influenced still by Renaissance (Donne) and modern revolutionary thought (Mayakovsky).

4. Gilkes, *Wilson Harris*, p. 135.

5. This substantiates a statement made by Harris two years after the publication of this novel: "the victim is projecting out of himself that reinforcement which makes the monster/victor possible. . . . The victor on

the other hand projects his monstrous victim" (Interview by Ian Munro and Reinhard Sander, *Kas-Kas*, p. 46).

6. Later in the novel this organ is called *"vacancy or corridor of Christ"* (*Ascent to Omai*, p. 104).

7. The judge contrasts his dual apprehension of time with the Mexicans' obsession with cyclic time and their fear that their fifty-two-year cycle would not be renewed if they did not offer human sacrifices to the sun. In Harris's *Companions*, however, even the Mexican calendar offers an opening into timelessness.

8. Harris, *Fossil and Psyche*, p. 12.

9. Cf. Kenneth Ramchand's comment: *"Ascent to Omai* is Harris's most concentrated attempt so far to give sensuous reality to a number of ideas we can infer from the work," in Introduction to Bibliography on the West Indies, *Journal of Commonwealth Literature* 6 (December, 1971):105.

10. Certainly, the judge's comment on his own novel is substantiated by the reconstruction of Victor's experience. In this respect, *Ascent to Omai* can be favorably contrasted with Aldous Huxley's *Point Counter Point*, in which the theories of the novelist within the novel are never actualized. Compare also the judge/narrator's comments on the art of fiction with the narrator's in John Fowles' *The French Lieutenant's Woman*.

Chapter Ten

1. *The Sleepers of Roraima* or "Carib Trilogy" contains "Couvade." "I, Quiyumucon," and "Yurokon." *The Age of the Rainmakers* contains "The Age of Kaie," "The Mind of Awakaipu," "The Laughter of the Wapishanas," and "Arawak Horizon."

2. Wilson Harris, *History, Fable and Myth* (Georgetown, 1970), p. 26.

3. Reported by the explorer Richard Schomburgk and told by Michael Swan in *The Marches of El Dorado*, p. 243. See Ch. 3, note 7.

4. Harris, "The Phenomenal Legacy," p. 3.

5. Although I would not call Harris's fiction "structuralist" because many of its aspects cannot be covered by that label, I find a strong affinity between the Lévi-Strauss of *Mythologiques* (Paris: Plon, 1964, 1967, 1968, 1971) and Harris's second cycle of novels and the stories.

6. James Boon uses this term in *From Symbolism to Structuralism, Lévi-Strauss in a Literary Tradition* (Oxford: Oxford University Press, 1972), p. 11. However, he defines "texts" as "derived sensory systems," and one can certainly not speak of systems where Harris's narratives are concerned.

7. The best example of a structural analogy with the visual arts is probably to be found in "Arawak Horizon." For a full-length discussion of that story, see Jean-Pierre Durix's remarkable article "Crossing the Arawak Horizon," *Literary Half-Yearly* 20 (January, 1979):83–92.

8. Wilson Harris, "The Native Phenomenon," in *COMMONWEALTH*, ed. Anna Rutherford (Aarhus, 1971), p. 148.

9. See Walter Roth, *An Inquiry into the Animism and Folk-Lore of the Guiana Indians* (Washington, D.C.: Government Printing Office, 1915), p. 179.

10. For a discussion of these, see *History, Fable and Myth*, p. 23.

11. Claude Lévi-Strauss, *Mythologique I, Le Cru et le Cuit* (Paris: Plon, 1964), p. 9 (my translation).

12. This myth inspired the chief metaphor in *The Tree of the Sun*. For different versions of it, see ibid., pp. 246–252.

13. For Harris's concept of infinity see interview by Ian Munro and Reinhard Sander, *Kas-Kas*, (p. 52).

14. This recalls the phrase "nothing moved" in *The Waiting Room*, (p. 65).

15. Wilson Harris, "The Making of Tradition," in *The Commonwealth Writer Overseas*, ed. Alastair Niven (Brussels, 1976), p. 35 ff.

16. The "black hole," a fairly recent scientific discovery, has been described as "formed by the collapse of a heavy star to such a condensed state that nothing, not even light, can escape from its surface," in John Taylor, *Black Holes, the End of a Universe?* (Glasgow: Fontana/Collins, 1976), p. 9. It is scientifically uncertain whether the matter inside the black hole is annihilated or transformed and, as it were, reborn.

17. As mentioned above, this is a further development of the "art of murder" illustrated in *The Eye of the Scarecrow*. Making people into "commodities of love" is a way of killing them. But one can also "kill" (make static) by idealizing inordinately. For Harris's view of the dangers inherent in the idealization of the Virgin, see *Enigma of Values*, Petersen and Rutherford, eds., p. 32.

18. For the distinction between reflection and vision, see *Companions*, p. 59, as well as Harris's essay "Reflection and Vision," in *Commonwealth Literature and the Modern World*, ed. Hena Maes-Jelinek (Brussels, 1975), pp. 15–19.

19. Harris, *Black Marsden*, pp. 78, 64.

20. See Harris's postscript to "The Making of Tradition" in *Explorations*.

21. See also what Idiot Nameless explains to the workers: "If we are to move [the highest canvases], transform them in the slightest real way, we

need to regress into them as sacrificed bodies into which a spark fell and still falls" (*Companions*, p. 65).

22. As his name suggests, Sir Giles Marsden-Prince represents the two faces of tradition, the serving (Marsden) and the ruling (Prince) one.

23. The novel contains a beautiful evocation of London with its variations of light at all times of the day. Not only are the contrasts in the city presented, but Harris manages to intimate an immaterial reality as a counterpoint to its solidity. With remarkable use and control of the imagery he re-creates the world, and the growth and death of empires, in the limited space of Holland Park and the Commonwealth Institute.

24. W.B. Yeats, *Essays and Introductions* (London: MacMillan, 1961), p. 28.

Selected Bibliography

PRIMARY SOURCES

1. Novels and Short Fiction

The Age of the Rainmakers. London: Faber & Faber, 1971. Contains "The Age of Kaie," "The Mind of Awakaipu," "The Laughter of the Wapishanas," "Arawak Horizon."

Ascent to Omai. London: Faber & Faber, 1970.

Black Marsden. London: Faber & Faber, 1972.

Companions of the Day and Night. London: Faber & Faber, 1975.

Da Silva da Silva's Cultivated Wilderness and *Genesis of the Clowns*. London: Faber & Faber, 1977.

The Eye of the Scarecrow. London: Faber & Faber, 1965. Reprinted with an Author's Note. London: Faber & Faber, 1974.

The Far Journey of Oudin. London: Faber & Faber, 1961.

Heartland. London: Faber & Faber, 1964.

"Kanaima." *West Indian Narrative*, an Introductory Anthology edited by Kenneth Ramchand. London: Nelson, 1966, pp. 196–205. Reprinted in *Commonwealth Short Stories*, edited by Anna Rutherford and Donald Hannah. London: Arnold, 1971, pp. 109–115.

Palace of the Peacock. London: Faber & Faber, 1960. Reprinted with an Introduction by Kenneth Ramchand. London: Faber & Faber, 1968, 1973, 1977.

The Secret Ladder. London: Faber & Faber, 1963.

The Sleepers of Roraima. A Carib Trilogy. London: Faber & Faber, 1970. Contains "Couvade," "I, Quiyumucon," "Yurokon."

The Tree of the Sun. London: Faber & Faber, 1978.

Tumatumari. London: Faber & Faber, 1968.

The Waiting Room. London: Faber & Faber, 1967.

The Whole Armour. London: Faber & Faber, 1962.

The Whole Armour and *The Secret Ladder*. London: Faber & Faber, 1973. Page references in the text are to this edition.

2. Poems

Fetish. Guyana: Miniature Poets Series, 1951.

Eternity to Season. Georgetown: published privately, 1954. London: New Beacon Books, 1978. These poems were originally published under the pseudonym "Kona Waruk."

3. Early Writing. Contributions to *Kyk-Over-Al*: 1945 — 1961. This bibliography was compiled by Reinhard W. Sander and first published in *Commonwealth Literature and the Modern World*, edited by Hena Maes-Jelinek. Brussels: Didier, 1975, pp. 175 — 76.

"Art and Criticism" (Nonfiction), 13 (Year-end, 1951):202 — 5.

"Banim Creek" (Extract from an unpublished novel), 18 (Mid-year, 1974): 36 — 42.

"The Beggar Is King" (Poems), 16 (Mid-year, 1953):148 — 51.

"Bim n° 17 (Vol. 5, n. 17, Dec., 1952)" (Review), 16 (Mid-year, 1953): 195 — 98.

"Bouquet for Burrowes: II" (Nonfiction), 18 (Mid-year, 1954):8 — 9.

"Charcoal" (Poem), 22 (1957):25.

"The Chorus" (Poem), 19 (Year-end, 1954):128 — 29.

"The Death of Hector, Tamer of Horses" (Poem), 22 (1957):23 — 24.

"The Fabulous Well" (Poems), 15 (Year-end, 1952):48 — 55.

"Fences Upon the Earth" (Fiction), 4 (June, 1947):20 — 21.

"Greatness and Bitterness" (Letter to A.J. Seymour), 23 (May, 1958):23.

"Green Is the Colour of the World" (Poem), 6 (June, 1948):7 — 8.

"The Guiana Book by A.J. Seymour" (Review), 7 (Dec., 1948):37 — 40.

"In Memoriam 1948" (Poem), 7 (Dec., 1948):6.

"Orpheus" (Poem), 14 (Mid-Year, 1952):38.

"Other Dimensions" (Poem), 14 (Mid-Year, 1952):39.

"Palace of the Stillborn" (Poem), 9 (Dec., 1949):19.

"Poems by Leo I. Austin" (Review), 20 (Mid-year, 1955):205 — 6.

"The Question of Form and Realism in the West Indian Artist" (Nonfiction), 15 (Year-end, 1952):23 — 27.

"Quiet's Event" (Poem), 5 (Dec., 1947):8.

"The Reality of Trespass" (Non-fiction), 9 (Dec., 1949):21 — 22.

"Review" (On Denis Williams's Paintings), 9 (Dec., 1949):32.

"Savannah Lands" (Poem), 2 (June, 1946):8. Also 19 (Year-end, 1954): 76.

"The Spirit of Place" (Poems), 17 (Year-end, 1953):228 — 34.

"Spirit of the Sea Wall" (Fiction), 28 (Dec., 1961):181 — 83.

"Spring Equinox" (Poem), 8 (June, 1949):5 — 6.

"The Stone of the Sea" (Poem), 22 (1957):24—25.

"Studies in Realism" (Poems), 4 (June, 1947):7—8.

"The sun (Fourteen Poems in a Cycle)," 20 (Mid-year, 1955):175—82.

"Sun Poem XV" (Poem), 23 (May, 1958):7.

"Tell Me Trees: What Are You Whispering?" (Poem), 1 (Dec., 1945): 10. Also 19 (Year-end, 1954):91—92.

"These Are the Words of an Old Man" (Poem), 19 (Year-end, 1954): 117.

"Tomorrow" (Fiction), 1 (Dec., 1945):30—34.

"Troy" (Poem), 22 (1957):26—27.

"Two Periods in the Work of a West Indian Artist" (On Denis Williams's Paintings), 20 (Mid-year, 1955):183—87.

"Words Written Before Sunset" (Poem), 3 (Dec., 1946):9.

4. Critical Essays, Extracts from Novels, Interviews

"*Benito Cereno.*" In *Enigma of Values*, edited by Kirsten H. Petersen and Anna Rutherford. Aarhus: Dangaroo Press, 1975, pp. 43—58.

"Carnival of Psyche: Jean Rhys's *Wide Sargasso Sea.*" *Kunapipi* 2, 2 (1980): 142—50. Reprinted in *Explorations*.

"A Comment on *A Passage to India.*" *Literary Half-Yearly* 10 (July, 1969): 35—40.

"The Complexity of Freedom," In *The Art of Wole Soyinka*, edited by Henry Louis Gates. New York: Oxford University Press, 1982. Also published in *Explorations*.

"Da Silva da Silva's Cultivated Wilderness." From a Novel in Progress. Carifesta Forum. Jamaica: Institute of Jamaica, 1976, pp. 169—76.

"The Enigma of Values." *New Letters* 40 (October, 1973):141—49.

Explorations, A Selection of Talks and Articles. Edited with an Introduction by Hena Maes-Jelinek. Aarhus: Dangaroo Press, 1981.

Fossil and Psyche. Austin: University of Texas at Austin, 1974, pp. 12. Reprinted in *Explorations*.

"The Frontier on which *Heart of Darkness* stands." *Research in African Literatures* 12, no. 1 (spring 1981):86—93. Reprinted in *Explorations*.

"Genesis of the Clowns." Excerpt from a Novel in Progress. In *Commonwealth*, edited by Victor Dupont. Rodez: Subervie, 1974—1975, pp. 57—61.

"Genesis of the Clowns." *Review* 75, pp. 69—74.

History, Fable and Myth in the Caribbean and Guianas. Georgetown: National History and Arts Council, 1970. Reprinted in *Explorations*.

"Impressions after Seven Years." *New World*, 1 (July, 1966):17—20.

"Interior of the Novel: Amerindian/European/African Relations." In

National Identity, edited by K.L. Goodwin. London/Melbourne: Heine-
    mann, 1970, pp. 138—47. Reprinted in *Explorations*.

Interview by Anna Rutherford and Kirsten H. Petersen. *Commonwealth
    Newsletter* 9 (January, 1976):22—25.

Interview by Helen Tiffin. *New Literature Review* 7 (1979):18—29.

Interview by Ian Munro and Reinhard Sander. *Kas-Kas*. Austin: University
    of Texas at Austin, 1972, pp. 43—55.

Interview by John Thieme. *Caribbean Contact* (March, 1980), pp. 17—18.

Interview by Michel Fabre. *Kunapipi* 2, no. 1 (1980):100—106.

"Journey into the Canje." In *Neo-African Literature and Culture*, Essays
    in Memory of Janheinz Jahn, edited by Bernth Lindfors and Ulla
    Schild. Wiesbaden: Heymann, 1976, pp. 346—52.

"Kith and Kin." *Journal of Commonwealth Literature* 7 (June, 1972):
    1—5

"The Making of Tradition." In *The Commonwealth Writer Overseas*, edited
    by Alastair Niven. Brussels: Didier, 1976, pp. 33—39. Reprinted
    in *Explorations*.

"Metaphor and Myth." In *Myth and Metaphor*, edited by Robert Sellick
    (Essays and Monographs Series), Centre for Research in the New Litera-
    tures in English. Flinders University of South Australia, 1982.

"The Native Phenomenon." In COMMON WEALTH, edited by Anna
    Rutherford Aarhus: Akademisk Boghandel, 1971, pp. 144—50. Re-
    printed in *Explorations*.

"The Phenomenal Legacy." *Literary Half-Yearly* 11 (July, 1970):1—6.
    Reprinted in *Explorations*.

"The Place of the Poet in Modern Society: a Glance at Two Guyanese
    Poets." *The Graphic* (May, 1966). Reprinted in *Explorations*.

"Reflection and Vision." In *Commonwealth Literature and the Modern World*,
    edited by Hena Maes-Jelinek. Brussels: Didier, 1975, pp.15—19.
    Reprinted in *Explorations*.

"Scented Gardens for the Blind." In *Bird, Hawk, Bogie*, edited by Jeanne
    Delbaere. Aarhus: Dangaroo Press, 1978, pp. 63—67. Reprinted
    in *Explorations*.

"Some Aspects of Myth and the Intuitive Imagination." Lecture given at
    the University of Guyana in March 1978. Printed in *Explorations*.

"A Talk on the Subjective Imagination." *New Letters* 40 (October, 1973):
    37—48. Reprinted in *Explorations*.

Tradition, the Writer and Society, Critical Essays. London: New Beacon
    Books, 1967. Reprinted London: New Beacon Books, 1973.

"The Unresolved Constitution." *Caribbean Quarterly* 14 (March-June, 1968):43–47.

The Womb of Space. To be published by Greenwood Press, Wesport, Conn., in 1983.

SECONDARY SOURCES

1. Books

Gilkes, Michael. *Wilson Harris and the Caribbean Novel.* London: Long-man; Trinidad and Jamaica: Longman Caribbean, 1975. Very good introduction to Harris's novels up to *Black Marsden.* Places Harris's work in its Caribbean context and gives special emphasis to theme of psychic reintegration.

James, C.L.R. *Wilson Harris—A Philosophical Approach.* Trinidad & Tobago: University of the West Indies (General Public Lecture Series), 1965. Relates Harris's thought to existentialism, particularly Heidegger's.

Lacovia, R.M. *Landscapes, Maps and Parangles.* Toronto: Black Images, 1975. Presents numerous extracts from Harris's work to demonstrate that he creates a "reticulum of resonance" by superimposing images.

Maes-Jelinek, Hena. *The Naked Design,* A reading of *Palace of the Peacock.* Aarhus: Dangaroo Press, 1976. General introduction to Harris's fiction and reprint of "The Poetry of Space in *Palace of the Peacock*"; detailed study of the language and imagery in that novel.

2. Articles

Adams, Rolstan. "Wilson Harris: the Pre-novel Poet." *Journal of Commonwealth Literature* 13 (April, 1979):71–85. Traces back to Harris's poetry the major themes, characters, and images in his fiction.

Adler, Joyce. "The Art of Wilson Harris." *New Beacon Reviews,* Collection One (1968), pp. 22–30. Analyzes *The Waiting Room* in connection with *Tradition, the Writer and Society.*

——"Attitudes Towards 'Race' in Guyanese Literature." *Caribbean Studies* 8 (July, 1968):23–63. Helpful presentation of Guyanese novelists. Deals with Harris's novels up to *The Eye of the Scarecrow.*

——"*Tumatumari* and the Imagination of Wilson Harris." *Journal of Commonwealth Literature* 7 (July, 1969):20–31. Perceptive analysis of *Tumatumari.* Raises fundamental questions implicit in Harris's fiction.

————"Wilson Harris and Twentieth-Century Man." *New Letters* 40 (October, 1973):49—61. Points to Harris's response to our age in several novels. Draws parallel between scientific imagination and Harris's creative imagination.

————"Melville and Harris: Poetic Imaginations Related in their Response to the Modern World." In *Commonwealth Literature and the Modern World*, edited by Hena Maes-Jelinek. Brussels: Didier, 1975, pp. 33—41. Compares Melville's and Harris's approach to the possible regeneration of man and the forms it takes in their novels.

Boxill, Anthony. "Wilson Harris's *Palace of the Peacock*: a New Dimension in West Indian Fiction." *College Language Association Journal* 14 (June, 1971):380—86. Emphasizes poetic quality and philosophical meaning of the novel.

Brahms, Flemming. "A Reading of Wilson Harris's *Palace of the Peacock*." *Commonwealth Newsletter* 3 (January, 1973):30—44. Largely descriptive; emphasis on Jung's influence. Criticizes lack of realism in the novel.

Crew, Gary. "Wilson Harris's Da Silva Quartet." *New Literature Review* 7 (1979):43—52. Traces the development of a major character (da Silva) through the novels in which he appears. Particularly good on *The Tree of the Sun*.

————"The Eternal Present in Wilson Harris' *The Sleepers of Roraima* and *The Age of the Rainmakers*. *World Literature Written in English* 19 (Autumn, 1980):218—27. Analyzes "the original and timeless quality of the imagination" in Harris's stories.

Durix, Jean-Pierre. "A Reading of 'Paling of Ancestors.'" *Commonwealth Newsletter* 9 (January, 1976):32—41. On imagery of the last section of *Palace of the Peacock*.

————"Crossing the Arawak Horizon." *Literary Half-Yearly* 20 (January, 1979):83—92. An excellent study of the formal aspects of "Arawak Horizon."

———— "Along Jigsaw Trail: An Interpretation of *Heartland*." *The Commonwealth Novel in English* 2 (July 1982). Thorough and perceptive analysis of *Heartland*.

————editor of a special number of *World Literature Written in English* on Wilson Harris to come out in spring 1983.

Fletcher, John. "The 'Intimacy of a Horror': The Tradition of Wilson Harris's *Palace of the Peacock*." In *Commonwealth Literature and the Modern World*, edited by Hena Maes-Jelinek. Brussels: Didier, 1975, pp. 43–50. Compares *Palace of the Peacock* to symbolist novels, particularly Conrad's *Heart of Darkness*.

Gilkes, Michael. "The Art of Extremity, a Reading of Wilson Harris's *Ascent to Omai*." *Caribbean Quarterly* 17 (Sept.-Dec., 1971): 83–90. Review article.

————"*Da Silva da Silva's Cultivated Wilderness* and *Genesis of the Clowns*." *World Literature Written in English* 16 (November, 1977):462–70. Review article.

Griffiths, Gareth. *A Double Exile*, African and West Indian Writing between two Cultures. London: Marion Boyars, 1978, pp. 171–92. Offers a perceptive study of *Palace of the Peacock* and *Ascent to Omai*.

Hearne, John. "The Fugitive in the Forest: a Study of Four Novels by Wilson Harris." *Journal of Commonwealth Literature* 4 (December, 1967):99–112. Shorter version in *The Islands in Between*. edited by Louis James. London: Oxford University Press, 1968, pp. 140–53. Brings out original and specifically West-Indian aspects of Guiana Quartet.

Hench, Michael. "The Fearful Symmetry of *The Whole Armour*." *Revista Interamericana* 4 (Fall, 1974):446–51. Discusses tiger imagery in *Whole Armour*. Associates symmetry with Harris's conception of community.

Howard, W.J. "Wilson Harris's *Guiana Quartet:* from Personal Myth to National Identity." *ARIEL* 1 (January, 1970):46–60. Also in *Readings in Commonwealth Literature*, edited by William Walsh. London: Oxford University Press, 1973, pp. 314–28. Places Guiana Quartet in symbolist tradition and points to affinity with Blake and Yeats. Harris transforms history into myth.

————"Wilson Harris and the 'Alchemichal Imagination.'"*Literary Half-Yearly* 11 (July, 1970):17–26. Discusses *Eye of the Scarecrow*.

————"Shaping a New Voice: the Poetry of Wilson Harris." *Commonwealth Newsletter* 9 (January, 1976):26–31. On early poems and their relation to historical events in Guyana.

James, Louis. "Wilson Harris and the 'Guyanese Quartet.'" In *A Celebration of Black and African Writing*, edited by Bruce King and Kolawole Ogungbesan. Zaria: Ahmadu Bello University Press and Oxford University Press, 1975, pp. 164–74. Places Guiana Quartet in the context of emerging black literature.

Mackey, Nathaniel. "The Unruly Pivot: Wilson Harris's *The Eye of the Scarecrow*." *Texas Studies in Literature and Language* 20 (Winter, 1978):

633—59. Perceptive study of the form of *The Eye*. Insists on the increasingly self-reflexive nature of Harris's fiction.

————"Limbo, Dislocation, Phantom Limb: Wilson Harris and the Caribbean Occasion." *Criticism* 22 (Winter, 1980):57—76. Discusses the specifically Caribbean sources of Harris's art.

Maes-Jelinek, Hena. "The Myth of El Dorado in the Caribbean Novel." *Journal of Commonwealth Literature* 6 (June, 1971):113—27. Compares Harris's treatment of myth of El Dorado with Naipaul's and Carpentier's.

————"The True Substance of Life: Wilson Harris's *Palace of the Peacock*." In *COMMON WEALTH*, edited by Anna Rutherford. Aarhus: Akademisk Boghandel, 1971, pp. 151—59. Presents regeneration of imagination as a major theme in *Palace of the Peacock*.

————"The Writer as Alchemist: the Unifying Role of Imagination in the Novels of Wilson Harris." *Language and Literature* 1 (Autumn, 1971):25—34.

————"*Ascent to Omai*." *Literary Half Yearly* 13 (January, 1972):1—8. Review article.

————"The Poetry of Space in *Palace of the Peacock*." In *Enigma of Values*, an Introduction, edited by Kirsten H. Petersen and Anna Rutherford. Aarhus: Dangaroo Press, 1975, pp. 59—108. See *Naked Design* by Maes-Jelinek under "Secondary Sources."

————"The 'Unborn State of Exile' in Wilson Harris's Novels." In *Commonwealth Writer Overseas*, edited by Alastair Niven. Brussels: Didier, 1976, pp. 195—205. Mainly on *The Eye of the Scarecrow*. Presents exile from the self as a rewarding spiritual pursuit.

————"'Inimitable Painting': New Developments in Wilson Harris's Latest Fiction." *ARIEL* 8 (July, 1977):63—80. Concentrates on painting as an exploratory metaphor and on notion of tradition in *Da Silva da Silva's Cultivated Wilderness* and *Genesis of the Clowns*.

————"Wilson Harris." *West Indian Literature*, edited by Bruce King. London: MacMillan, 1979, pp. 179—95. General introduction to Harris's work. Traces major developments through three phases.

Moore, Gerald. *The Chosen Tongue*, English Writing in the Tropical World. London: Longman, 1969, pp. 63—73, 76—82. Concentrates on landscape and characters in Guiana Quartet.

Moss, John, G. "William Blake and Wilson Harris: the Objective Vision." *Journal of Commonwealth Literature* 9 (April, 1975):29—40. Traces similar development in Blake's and Harris's conception of character. Sees in both writers a fusion of various dimensions of reality.

Petersen, Kirsten H., and Rutherford, Anna, eds. *Enigma of Values*, an Introduction. Aarhus: Dangaroo Press, 1975, pp. 9—41. A very useful exposition of major critical Harrisian concepts.

Ramchand, Kenneth. "The Dislocated Image." *New World* (Guyana Independence Issue, 1966), pp. 107—10. Discusses development of vision of consciousness in Guiana Quartet.

————Preface to *Palace of the Peacock*. Paperback edition. London: Faber & Faber, 1968, unpaginated. Good, concise introduction to Harris's fiction.

————"The Significance of the Aborigine in Wilson Harris's Fiction." *Literary Half Yearly* 11 (July, 1970):7—16. Reprinted in *The West Indian Novel and its Background*. London: Faber & Faber, 1970, pp. 164—74. Shows relevance of Amerindian characters to Harris's basic themes.

Russell, D.W. "The Dislocating Art of Memory: an Analysis of Wilson Harris' *Tumatumari*." *World Literature Written in English* 13 (November, 1974):234—49. A good explication of *Tumatumari*.

Searl, Eva, and Maes-Jelinek, Hena. "Comedy of Intensity: Wilson Harris's *Black Marsden*." *Commonwealth Newsletter* 4 (July, 1973): 21—29. Review article.

Searl, Eva. "T.S. Eliot's *Four Quartets* and Wilson Harris's *The Waiting Room*." In *Commonwealth Literature and the Modern World*, edited by Hena Maes-Jelinek. Brussels: Didier, 1975, pp. 51—59. A sensitive comparison of the thought that informs Eliot's poem and Harris's novel.

————"Companions of the Day and Night." *Commonwealth Newsletter* 9 (January, 1976):46—58. A thorough and perceptive review article.

Sharrad, Paul. "*Palace of the Peacock* and the Tragic Muse." *The Literary Criterion* XVI(1981):44—58. Compares *Palace of the Peacock* with classical tragedy.

Van Sertima, Ivan. "The Sleeping Rocks: Wilson Harris's *Tumatumari*." In *Enigma of Values*, edited by Kirsten H. Petersen and Anna Rutherford. Aarhus: Dangaroo Press, 1975, pp. 109—24. Answers basic questions about form and content in Harris's fiction. Relates *Tumatumari* to Guyanese background and discusses imagery.

————"Into the Black Hole: a Study of Wilson Harris's *Companions of the Day and Night*." *ACLALS Bulletin*, 4th ser., no. 4 (1976), pp. 65—77. An illuminating analysis of the novel. Also makes clear recurring concepts in Harris's fiction.

Williams, Denis. *Image and Idea in the Arts of Guyana*. Georgetown: Edgar Mittelholzer Memorial Lectures, 1969. Discusses concept of "the complex womb" and *The Eye of the Scarecrow*. Emphasizes Guyanese source of Harris's art.

Index